SUCCESS READING PROGRAM
FOR OLDER STUDENTS

Learn To Read English
Textbook

Color Edition

ISBN 978-1-945738-44-9
©2022 – Wendy A. Charles & Alexander J. Charles
All Rights Reserved
Baldwin, New York
www.intellastic.com

All rights reserved. No portion of this book may be reproduced, stored in a retrieval system, or transmitted in any form or by any means – electronic, mechanical, photocopy, recording, video presentation, private instruction, scanning, or other – except for brief quotations in critical reviews or articles, without the prior written permission of the writers.

All Rights Reserved. Printed in the USA.

Table of Contents

Unit A

Lesson 1.0	Introduction of the Letter A/a	1
Lesson 1.1	Reading Words with the Letter A/a	1
Lesson 1.2	Reading Words with the Short Vowel "a" Sound	2
Lesson 1.3	Reading Words with the Long Vowel "a" Sound	6
Lesson 1.4	Reading Words with the "age" Letter Combination	10
Lesson 1.5	Reading Words with the "ai" Vowel Pair	11
Lesson 1.6	Reading Letter "a" Words with the Schwa Vowel Sound	12
Lesson 1.7	Reading Words with the "ar" Letter Combination	13
Bonus Lesson	Reading Words with the Vowel "a"	15
Lesson 1.8	Reading Words with a Silent Letter "a"	16
Lesson 1.9	Reading Multisyllable Words	17
Lesson 1.10	Proper and Common Nouns and Adjectives	18

Unit B

Lesson 2.0	Introduction of the Letter B/b	21
Lesson 2.1	Reading Words with the Letter B/b	21
Lesson 2.2	Reading Words with the "br" Letter Combination	23
Lesson 2.3	Reading Words with the "bl" and "ble" Letter Combinations	24
Lesson 2.4	Reading Words with the "mb" and "bt" Letter Combinations	25
Lesson 2.5	Reading Words with a Silent Letter "b"	26
Lesson 2.6	Reading Multisyllable Words	27
Lesson 2.7	Proper and Common Nouns and Adjectives	28

Unit C

Lesson 3.0	Introduction of the Letter C/c	31
Lesson 3.1	Reading Words with the Hard Letter "c"	31
Lesson 3.2	Reading Words with the Soft Letter "c"	33

Copyrighted Material

Lesson 3.3	Reading Words with the "cr" Letter Combination	34
Lesson 3.4	Reading Words with the "cl" and "cle" Letter Combinations	35
Lesson 3.5	Reading Words with the "ct" Letter Combination	36
Lesson 3.6	Reading Soft Letter "c" Words	37
Lesson 3.7	Reading Words with the "ch" Letter Combination	38
Lesson 3.8	Reading Words with the "cc" Letter Combination	39
Lesson 3.9	Reading Words with a Silent Letter "c"	40
Lesson 3.10	Reading Multisyllable Words	41
Lesson 3.11	Proper and Common Nouns and Adjectives	42

Unit D

Lesson 4.0	Introduction of the Letter D/d	45
Lesson 4.1	Reading Words with the Letter D/d	45
Lesson 4.2	Reading Letter "d" Words with the /d/ Sound and /j/ Sound	47
Lesson 4.3	Reading Words with the "ed" Suffix/ Past Tense Verbs	48
Lesson 4.4	Reading Words with a Silent Letter "d"	49
Lesson 4.5	Reading Multisyllable Words	50
Lesson 4.6	Proper and Common Nouns and Adjectives	51

Unit E

Lesson 5.0	Introduction of the Letter E/e	53
Lesson 5.1	Reading Words with the Letter E/e	53
Lesson 5.2	Reading Words with the Short Vowel "e" Sound	54
Lesson 5.3	Reading Words with the Long Vowel "e" Sound	59
Bonus Lesson	Reading Words with the "age" Letter Combination	60
Lesson 5.4	Reading Words with Letter "e" Vowel Pairs	61
Lesson 5.5	Reading Words with the Final Letter "e"	63
Lesson 5.6	Reading Letter "e" Words with the Schwa Vowel Sound	64
Lesson 5.7	Reading Words with the "er" Letter Combination	65
Lesson 5.8	Reading Words with the "eu" and "ew" Letter Combinations	66
Lesson 5.9	Reading Words with the "ey" Letter Combination	67
Bonus Lesson	Reading Words with the Vowel "e"	67
Lesson 5.10	Reading Words with a Silent Letter "e"	68

| Lesson 5.11 | Reading Multisyllable Words | 69 |
| Lesson 5.12 | Proper and Common Nouns and Adjectives | 70 |

Unit F

Lesson 6.0	Introduction of the Letter F/f	73
Lesson 6.1	Reading Words with the Letter F/f	73
Lesson 6.2	Reading Words with the "fr" Letter Combination	75
Lesson 6.3	Reading Words with the "fl" and "fle" Letter Combinations	76
Lesson 6.4	Reading Words with the "ft," "lf" and "ff" Letter Combinations	77
Lesson 6.5	Reading Words with a Silent Letter "f"	77
Lesson 6.6	Reading Singular and Plural Forms of Words Ending in "f" and "fe"	78
Bonus Lesson	Exploring an Exception to the Letter "f"	78
Lesson 6.7	Reading Multisyllable Words	79
Lesson 6.8	Proper and Common Nouns and Adjectives	80

Unit G

Lesson 7.0	Introduction of the Letter G/g	83
Lesson 7.1	Reading Words with the Hard Letter "g"	83
Lesson 7.2	Reading Words with the Soft Letter "g"	85
Lesson 7.3	Reading Words with the "gr" Letter Combination	87
Lesson 7.4	Reading Words with the "gl" and "gle" Letter Combinations	88
Lesson 7.5	Reading Words with the "gh" Letter Combination	89
Lesson 7.6	Reading Words with the "gn" Letter Combination	90
Lesson 7.7	Reading Words with a Silent Letter "g"	91
Lesson 7.8	Reading Multisyllable Words	92
Lesson 7.9	Proper and Common Nouns and Adjectives	93

Unit H

Lesson 8.0	Introduction of the Letter H/h	95
Lesson 8.1	Reading Words with the Letter H/h	95
Lesson 8.2	Reading Words with the Letter "h" Combinations: "ch," "gh," "ph," "rh," "sch," "sh," "th" and "wh"	97

Bonus Lesson	The Position of the Letter "h"	98
Lesson 8.3	Reading Words with a Silent Letter "h"	99
Lesson 8.4	Reading Multisyllable Words	100
Lesson 8.5	Proper and Common Nouns and Adjectives	101

Unit I

Lesson 9.0	Introduction of the Letter I/i	103
Lesson 9.1	Reading Words with the Letter I/i	103
Lesson 9.2	Reading Words with the Short Vowel "i" Sound	104
Lesson 9.3	Reading Words with the Long Vowel "i" Sound	107
Lesson 9.4	Reading Words with Letter "i" Vowel Pairs	111
Lesson 9.5	Reading Words with the Final Letter "i"	113
Lesson 9.6	Reading Letter "i" Words with the Schwa Vowel Sound	114
Lesson 9.7	Reading Words with the "ir" Letter Combination	115
Lesson 9.8	Reading Letter "i" Words with the Long Vowel /ē/ Sound	116
Lesson 9.9	Reading Words with a Silent Letter "i"	117
Lesson 9.10	Reading Multisyllable Words	118
Lesson 9.11	Proper and Common Nouns and Adjectives	119

Unit J

Lesson 10.0	Introduction of the Letter J/j	121
Lesson 10.1	Reading Words with the Letter J/j	121
Lesson 10.2	Reading Multisyllable Words	123
Lesson 10.3	Proper and Common Nouns and Adjectives	124

Unit K

Lesson 11.0	Introduction of the Letter K/k	127
Lesson 11.1	Reading Words with the Letter K/k	127
Lesson 11.2	Reading Words with the Letter "k" and "ck" Letter Combination	129
Lesson 11.3	Reading Words with the "kle" Letter Combination	130
Lesson 11.4	Reading Words with a Silent Letter "k"	131
Lesson 11.5	Reading Multisyllable Words	132
Lesson 11.6	Proper and Common Nouns and Adjectives	133

Unit L

Lesson 12.0	Introduction of the Letter L/l	135
Lesson 12.1	Reading Words with the Letter L/l	135
Lesson 12.2	Reading Words with the Letter "l" Combinations: "bl," "cl," "fl," "gl," "pl" and "sl"	137
Lesson 12.3	Reading Words with a Silent Letter "l"	138
Lesson 12.4	Reading Multisyllable Words	139
Lesson 12.5	Proper and Common Nouns and Adjectives	140

Unit M

Lesson 13.0	Introduction of the Letter M/m	143
Lesson 13.1	Reading Words with the Letter M/m	143
Lesson 13.2	Reading Words with a Silent Letter "m"	145
Lesson 13.3	Reading Multisyllable Words	146
Lesson 13.4	Proper and Common Nouns and Adjectives	147

Unit N

Lesson 14.0	Introduction of the Letter N/n	149
Lesson 14.1	Reading Words with the Letter N/n	149
Lesson 14.2	Reading Words with the "ng" Letter Combination	151
Lesson 14.3	Reading Words with a Silent Letter "n"	152
Bonus Lesson	Reading Words with the Letter "n" Blends	152
Lesson 14.4	Reading Multisyllable Words	153
Lesson 14.5	Proper and Common Nouns and Adjectives	154

Unit O

Lesson 15.0	Introduction of the Letter O/o	157
Lesson 15.1	Reading Words with the Letter O/o	157
Lesson 15.2	Reading Words with the Short Vowel "o" Sound	158
Lesson 15.3	Reading Words with the Long Vowel "o" Sound	160
Lesson 15.4	Reading Words with Letter "o" Vowel Pairs	162
Lesson 15.5	Reading Words with the Final Letter "o"	164
Bonus Lesson	Reading Words with the "oll" and "ost" Letter Combinations	164

Lesson 15.6	Reading Letter "o" Words with the Schwa Vowel Sound	165
Bonus Lesson	Reading Words with the "ow" Letter Combination	165
Lesson 15.7	Reading Words with Vowel "o" Sounds: /ŏ/, /ō/ and /o͞o/	166
Bonus Lesson	Reading Letter "o" Words with the Short Vowel /ŭ/ Sound	166
Lesson 15.8	Reading Words with the "or" and "ore" Letter Combinations	167
Lesson 15.9	Reading Words with a Silent Letter "o"	168
Lesson 15.10	Reading Multisyllable Words	169
Lesson 15.11	Proper and Common Nouns and Adjectives	170

Unit P

Lesson 16.0	Introduction of the Letter P/p	173
Lesson 16.1	Reading Words with the Letter P/p	173
Lesson 16.2	Reading Words with the "ph" Letter Combination	175
Lesson 16.3	Reading Words with the "pr" Letter Combination	176
Lesson 16.4	Reading Words with the "pl" and "ple" Letter Combinations	177
Lesson 16.5	Reading Words with a Silent Letter "p"	178
Lesson 16.6	Reading Multisyllable Words	179
Lesson 16.7	Proper and Common Nouns and Adjectives	180

Unit Q

Lesson 17.0	Introduction of the Letter Q/q	183
Lesson 17.1	Reading Words with the Letter Q/q	183
Lesson 17.2	Reading Words with the Letter "q" and "qu" Letter Combination	185
Lesson 17.3	Reading Multisyllable Words	186
Lesson 17.4	Proper and Common Nouns and Adjectives	187

Unit R

Lesson 18.0	Introduction of the Letter R/r	189
Lesson 18.1	Reading Words with the Letter R/r	189
Bonus Lesson	Reading Words with a Silent Letter "r"	190
Lesson 18.2	Reading Words with the Letter "r" Combinations: "br," "cr," "fr," "gr," "pr" and "tr"	191

| Lesson 18.3 | Reading Multisyllable Words | 192 |
| Lesson 18.4 | Proper and Common Nouns and Adjectives | 193 |

Unit S

Lesson 19.0	Introduction of the Letter S/s	195
Lesson 19.1	Reading Words with the Letter S/s	195
Lesson 19.2	Reading Words with the "sion," "sial" and "scious" Suffixes	198
Lesson 19.3	Reading Words with the "sh" and "sch" Letter Combinations	199
Lesson 19.4	Reading Words with the "scr," "shr," "spl," "spr" and "str" Letter Combinations	200
Lesson 19.5	Reading Words with the "sl" and "sle" Letter Combinations	201
Lesson 19.6	Reading Words with the "sm" Letter Combination	202
Lesson 19.7	Reading Words with the "ss" Letter Combination	203
Bonus Lesson	Reading Words with the "st" and "sw" Letter Combinations	204
Lesson 19.8	Reading Words with a Silent Letter "s"	205
Lesson 19.9	Reading Multisyllable Words	206
Lesson 19.10	Proper and Common Nouns and Adjectives	207

Unit T

Lesson 20.0	Introduction of the Letter T/t	209
Lesson 20.1	Reading Words with the Letter T/t	209
Lesson 20.2	Reading Words with the "th" and "thm" Letter Combinations	211
Lesson 20.3	Reading Words with the "tion," "tial" and "tious" Suffixes	212
Bonus Lesson	Reading Words with the "tience" and "tient" Suffixes	212
Lesson 20.4	Reading Words with the "tr" Letter Combination	213
Lesson 20.5	Reading Words with the "tle" Letter Combination	214
Lesson 20.6	Reading Words with the Letter "t" Sounds	215
Lesson 20.7	Reading Words with a Silent Letter "t"	217
Lesson 20.8	Reading Multisyllable Words	218
Lesson 20.9	Proper and Common Nouns and Adjectives	219

Unit U

Lesson 21.0	Introduction of the Letter U/u	221
Lesson 21.1	Reading Words with the Letter U/u	221
Lesson 21.2	Reading Words with the Short Vowel "u" Sound	222
Bonus Lesson	Reading Letter "u" Words	225
Lesson 21.3	Reading Words with the Long Vowel "u" Sound	226
Bonus Lesson	Reading Letter "u" Words	229
Lesson 21.4	Reading Words with Letter "u" Vowel Pairs	230
Lesson 21.5	Reading Words with the Final Letter "u"	232
Lesson 21.6	Reading Letter "u" Words with the Schwa Vowel Sound	233
Lesson 21.7	Reading Words with the "ur" Letter Combination	234
Lesson 21.8	Reading Words with the "ure" Letter Combination	235
Bonus Lesson	Reading Letter "u" Words with the /w/ Sound	235
Lesson 21.9	Reading Words with a Silent Letter "u"	236
Lesson 21.10	Reading Multisyllable Words	237
Lesson 21.11	Proper and Common Nouns and Adjectives	238

Unit V

Lesson 22.0	Introduction of the Letter V/v	241
Lesson 22.1	Reading Words with the Letter V/v	241
Lesson 22.2	Reading Multisyllable Words	243
Lesson 22.3	Proper and Common Nouns and Adjectives	244

Unit W

Lesson 23.0	Introduction of the Letter W/w	247
Lesson 23.1	Reading Words with the Letter W/w	247
Lesson 23.2	Reading Words with a Vowel Before the Letter "w"	249
Lesson 23.3	Reading Words with a Silent "w" and "wr" Letter Combination	251
Bonus Lesson	Reading Words with the "wh" Letter Combination	251
Lesson 23.4	Reading Multisyllable Words	252
Lesson 23.5	Proper and Common Nouns and Adjectives	253

Unit X

Lesson 24.0	Introduction of the Letter X/x	255
Lesson 24.1	Reading Words with the Letter X/x	255
Bonus Lesson	Reading Words with a Silent Letter "x"	257
Lesson 24.2	Reading Multisyllable Words	258
Lesson 24.3	Proper and Common Nouns and Adjectives	259

Unit Y

Lesson 25.0	Introduction of the Letter Y/y	261
Lesson 25.1	Reading Words with the Letter Y/y	261
Lesson 25.2	Reading Words with a Vowel Before the Letter "y"	264
Lesson 25.3	Reading Words with the "cy" Letter Combination	265
Lesson 25.4	Reading Words with the Final Letter "y"	266
Lesson 25.5	Reading Words with the "yr" Letter Combination	267
Lesson 25.6	Reading Letter "y" Words with the Schwa Vowel Sound	268
Lesson 25.7	Reading Words with a Silent Letter "y"	269
Lesson 25.8	Reading Multisyllable Words	270
Lesson 25.9	Proper and Common Nouns and Adjectives	271

Unit Z

Lesson 26.0	Introduction of the Letter Z/z	273
Lesson 26.1	Reading Words with the Letter Z/z	273
Lesson 26.2	Reading Words with a Silent Letter "z"	275
Bonus Lesson	Exploring an Exception to the "zz" Letter Combination	275
Lesson 26.3	Reading Multisyllable Words	276
Lesson 26.4	Proper and Common Nouns and Adjectives	277

My Cup of Water

A/a

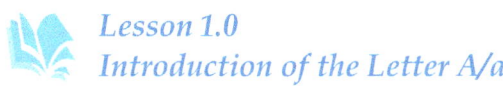

Lesson 1.0
Introduction of the Letter A/a

The letter "a" is a vowel. It is the 1st letter in the Roman alphabet of the English language. Letters are written as uppercase and lowercase letters.

	Uppercase Letter	Lowercase Letter
Print	A	a
Cursive	𝓐	𝒶
Computer Font	A	a

Lesson 1.1
Reading Words with the Letter A/a

The letter "a" is pronounced in <u>eleven</u> different ways.
- It represents the short vowel /ă/ sound, as in the word <u>apple</u>.
- It represents the long vowel /ā/ sound, as in the word <u>cake</u>.
- It represents the schwa vowel /ə/ sound, as in the word <u>sofa</u>.
- It represents the vowel /ô/ sound, as in the word <u>ball</u>.
- It represents the vowel /ä/ sound, as in the word <u>car</u>.
- It represents the vowel /â/ sound, as in the word <u>care</u>.
- It represents the short vowel /ĭ/ sound, as in the word <u>village</u>.
- It represents the short vowel /ĕ/ sound, as in the word <u>says</u>.
- It represents the long vowel /ō/ sound, as in the word <u>mauve</u>.
- It represents the short vowel /ŏ/ sound, as in the word <u>swamp</u>.
- It represents the short vowel /ŭ/ sound, as in the word <u>was</u>.
- At times it is silent, as in the word <u>boat</u>.

High Frequency, One Syllable Letter "a" Words
Short vowel words: act, add, am, as, ask, back, bag, bat, cat, dad, fan, gas, has, jam, lab, man, maps, nap, pan, pat, ran, sad, tab, van
Long vowel words: ate, bake, cake, came, date, face, game, mail, page, pain, rain, rake, rate, save, stage, tape, tale, wage, wave, way

Learn To Read English Textbook

Lesson 1.2
Reading Words with the Short Vowel "a" Sound

"a" represents the short vowel /ă/ sound

At the beginning of a word, the letter "a" usually represents the short vowel /ă/ sound, as in the word apple.

The letter "a" usually represents the short vowel /ă/ sound when it is the only vowel within a word or syllable.

When a consonant comes before and after the letter "a," it usually represents the short vowel /ă/ sound, as in the words cat, back and crack.

Beginning	Within	End
/ă/	/ă/	/ă/
apple	cat	

✎ Note: At the end of a word, the letter "a" does not represent the short vowel /ă/ sound.

✣ Short Vowel "a" Word Families

"ab" - "a" represents the short vowel /ă/ sound

The letter "a" in the "ab" word family represents the short vowel /ă/ sound, as in the word cab.

Word Box	blab, crab, dab, drab, fab, flab, gab, grab, jab, lab, nab, scab, slab, stab, tab
	Multisyllable Words:
	backstab, confab, minicab, pedicab, Punjab, rehab, skylab, taxicab

Word Box	abdomen, abduct, abhor, abnormal, absence, absent, absolutely, abstract, blabber, cabbage, cabin, cabinet, collaborate, grabbing, habitat, rabbits

"ack" - "a" represents the short vowel /ă/ sound

The letter "a" in the "ack" word family represents the short vowel /ă/ sound, as in the word back.

Word Box	back, black, clack, crack, flack, hack, jack, lack, pack, quack, rack, sack, shack, slack, smack, snack, stack, tack, track, whack
	Multisyllable Words:
	aback, attack, cutback, drawback, feedback, haystack, humpback, kickback

Word Box	acknowledge, background, crackers, crackle, hacker, hacking, jackal, jacket, lacking, mackerel, package, packed, packing, racket, shackled, snacking

"ad" - "a" represents the short vowel /ă/ sound

The letter "a" in the "ad" word family represents the short vowel /ă/ sound, as in the word sad.

Word Box	ad, bad, Brad, cad, Chad, clad, dad, fad, glad, grad, had, lad, mad, pad, rad, sad, tad
	Multisyllable Words:
	Bagdad, footpad, granddad, helipad, ironclad, keypad, kneepad, mousepad, nomad, notepad, postgrad, Trinidad, unclad, undergrad

Word Box	administer, admit, admonish, advance, advent, adventured, adverb, advice, adviser, advises, advisor, advisory, advocacy, advocate, Daddy, gladly

"ag" - "a" represents the short vowel /ă/ sound

The letter "a" in the "ag" word family represents the short vowel /ă/ sound, as in the word bag.

Word Box	bag, brag, crag, drag, flag, gag, hag, jag, lag, nag, rag, sag, shag, slag, snag, stag, swag, tag, wag, zag
	Multisyllable Words:
	airbag, beanbag, dishrag, handbag, hangtag, hashtag, jetlag, lollygag, moneybag, ragtag, saddlebag, zigzag

"am" - "a" represents the short vowel /ă/ sound

The letter "a" in the "am" word family represents the short vowel /ă/ sound, as in the word jam.

Word Box	am, bam, cam, clam, cram, dam, dram, flam, gram, ham, jam, Pam, ram, scam, scram, sham, slam, spam, swam, tam, tram, wham, yam
	Multisyllable Words:
	exam, kilogram, mammogram, milligram, monogram, radiogram, telegram

☞ Exception: bedlam - /ă/ sound

"amp" - "a" represents the short vowel /ă/ sound

The letter "a" in the "amp" word family represents the short vowel /ă/ sound, as in the word camp.

Word Box	amp, camp, champ, clamp, cramp, damp, lamp, ramp, stamp, tamp, tramp, vamp

☞ Exception: swamp - /ŏ/ sound or /ô/ sound

"an" - "a" represents the short vowel /ă/ sound

The letter "a" in the "an" word family represents the short vowel /ă/ sound, as in the word can.

Word Box	an, ban, bran, can, clan, Dan, fan, flan, Fran, man, Nan, pan, plan, ran, scan, span, Stan, tan, than, van
	Multisyllable Words: businessman, caravan, handyman, Japan, middleman, Milan, Pakistan, pecan, Sedan, Sudan, snowman, wingspan

☞ Exception: swan - /ŏ/ sound

"and" - "a" represents the short vowel /ă/ sound

The letter "a" in the "and" word family represents the short vowel /ă/ sound, as in the word land.

Word Box	and, band, bland, brand, gland, grand, hand, land, rand, sand, stand, strand
	Multisyllable Words: command, demand, expand, farmland, firsthand, mainland, offhand, quicksand, reprimand, Thailand, understand, wasteland

☞ Exceptions: Iceland, inland, Scotland - /ə/ sound

"ank" - "a" represents the short vowel /ă/ sound

The letter "a" in the "ank" word family represents the short vowel /ă/ sound, as in the word tank.

Word Box	bank, blank, clank, crank, dank, drank, flank, frank, hank, lank, plank, prank, rank, sank, shank, shrank, spank, swank, tank, thank, yank
	Multisyllable Words: embank, riverbank, sandbank

"ant" - "a" represents the short vowel /ă/ sound

The letter "a" in the "ant" word family represents the short vowel /ă/ sound, as in the word slant.

Word Box	ant, cant, chant, grant, pant, plant, rant, scant, slant
	Multisyllable Words: eggplant, replant, transplant

☞ Exceptions: croissant - /ä/ sound; want - /ŏ/ sound or /ô/ sound

"ap" - "a" represents the short vowel /ă/ sound

The letter "a" in the "ap" word family represents the short vowel /ă/ sound, as in the word map.

Word Box	cap, chap, clap, flap, gap, lap, map, nap, rap, sap, scrap, slap, snap, strap, tap, trap, wrap, yap, zap
	Multisyllable Words:
	bootstrap, burlap, catnap, entrap, enwrap, flytrap, handicap, icecap, kidnap, mayhap, mishap, overlap, skycap, snowcap, unwrap, whitecap

"ash" - "a" represents the short vowel /ă/ sound

The letter "a" in the "ash" word family represents the short vowel /ă/ sound, as in the word cash.

Word Box	ash, bash, brash, cash, clash, crash, dash, flash, gash, hash, lash, mash, rash, sash, slash, smash, splash, stash, thrash, trash
	Multisyllable Words:
	abash, backlash, balderdash, eyelash, whiplash

☞ Exceptions: brainwash, carwash, squash, wash - /ŏ/ sound or /ô/ sound

"at" - "a" represents the short vowel /ă/ sound

The letter "a" in the "at" word family represents the short vowel /ă/ sound, as in the word cat.

Word Box	at, bat, blat, brat, cat, chat, fat, flat, frat, hat, mat, pat, rat, sat, scat, slat, spat, splat, that, vat
	Multisyllable Words:
	acrobat, bureaucrat, democrat, diplomat, doormat, format, nonfat, thermostat

☞ Exceptions: somewhat, what - /ŏ/ sound or /ŭ/ sound or /ə/ sound

"atch" - "a" represents the short vowel /ă/ sound

The letter "a" in the "atch" word family represents the short vowel /ă/ sound, as in the word catch.

Word Box	batch, catch, hatch, latch, match, patch, scratch, snatch, thatch
	Multisyllable Words:
	crosshatch, dispatch, mismatch, unlatch

☞ Exceptions: swatch, watch - /ŏ/ sound

Lesson 1.3
Reading Words with the Long Vowel "a" Sound

"a" represents the long vowel /ā/ sound

The letter "a" can represent the long vowel /ā/ sound, as in the word cake. A long vowel is pronounced by its letter name.

Beginning	Within	End
/ā/	/ā/	/ā/
ape	cake	

✍ Note: At the end of a word, the letter "a" does not represent the long vowel /ā/ sound.

✤ **"a" + consonant + silent "e" word families**

The long vowel /ā/ sound has four pattern variations: VCe, CVCe, CCVCe and CCCVCe. The VCe pattern is at the end of many long vowel words.

"vowel + consonant + silent e" patterns	Target Words
VCe	ape
CVCe	cake
CCVCe	brave
CCCVCe	scrape

"ace" - "a" represents the long vowel /ā/ sound

When the "a" + consonant + "e" pattern is at the end of a word, the letter "a" usually represents the long vowel /ā/ sound, the consonant represents its sound while the vowel "e" is silent, as in the word pace.

Word Box	ace, brace, face, grace, lace, mace, pace, place, race, space, trace
	Multisyllable Words:
	boldface, disgrace, displace, embrace, fireplace, interface, misplace, shoelace

☞ Exceptions: surface - /ə/ sound; necklace, preface – /ĭ/ sound

"ade" - "a" represents the long vowel /ā/ sound

When the "a" + consonant + "e" pattern is at the end of a word, the letter "a" usually represents the long vowel /ā/ sound, the consonant represents its sound while the vowel "e" is silent, as in the word fade.

Word Box	blade, fade, glade, grade, jade, made, shade, spade, trade, wade

"ake" - "a" represents the long vowel /ā/ sound

When the "a" + consonant + "e" pattern is at the end of a word, the letter "a" usually represents the long vowel /ā/ sound, the consonant represents its sound while the vowel "e" is silent, as in the word <u>cake</u>.

Word Box	bake, brake, cake, drake, fake, flake, Jake, lake, make, quake, rake, sake, shake, snake, stake, take, wake *Multisyllable Words:* awake, cheesecake, cupcake, earthquake, forsake, handshake, hotcake, intake, keepsake, milkshake, mistake, rattlesnake, retake, snowflake

"ale" - "a" represents the long vowel /ā/ sound

When the "a" + consonant + "e" pattern is at the end of a word, the letter "a" usually represents the long vowel /ā/ sound, the consonant represents its sound while the vowel "e" is silent, as in the word <u>sale</u>.

Word Box	ale, bale, Dale, gale, kale, male, pale, sale, scale, stale, tale, whale, vale, Yale *Multisyllable Words:* downscale, female, folktale, impale, inhale, resale, upscale, wholesale

"ame" - "a" represents the long vowel /ā/ sound

When the "a" + consonant + "e" pattern is at the end of a word, the letter "a" usually represents the long vowel /ā/ sound, the consonant represents its sound while the vowel "e" is silent, as in the word <u>same</u>.

Word Box	blame, came, fame, flame, frame, game, lame, name, same, shame, tame *Multisyllable Words:* aflame, defame, inflame, nickname, overcame, reframe, rename, surname

"ane" - "a" represents the long vowel /ā/ sound

When the "a" + consonant + "e" pattern is at the end of a word, the letter "a" usually represents the long vowel /ā/ sound, the consonant represents its sound while the vowel "e" is silent, as in the word <u>cane</u>.

Word Box	bane, cane, crane, Dane, Jane, lane, mane, pane, plane, sane, vane, wane

"ape" - "a" represents the long vowel /ā/ sound

When the "a" + consonant + "e" pattern is at the end of a word, the letter "a" usually represents the long vowel /ā/ sound, the consonant represents its sound while the vowel "e" is silent, as in the word <u>cape</u>.

Word Box	ape, cape, drape, gape, grape, nape, scrape, shape, tape

"ase" - "a" represents the long vowel /ā/ sound

When the "a" + consonant + "e" pattern is at the end of a word, the letter "a" usually represents the long vowel /ā/ sound, the consonant represents its sound while the vowel "e" is silent, as in the word <u>case</u>.

Word Box	base, case, chase, phase, phrase

☞ Exception: vase - /ā/ sound or /ă/ sound or /ä/ sound

"ate" - "a" represents the long vowel /ā/ sound

When the "a" + consonant + "e" pattern is at the end of a word, the letter "a" usually represents the long vowel /ā/ sound, the consonant represents its sound while the vowel "e" is silent, as in the word <u>date</u>.

Word Box	ate, crate, date, fate, gate, grate, Kate, late, mate, plate, prate, rate, skate, state
	Multisyllable Words:
	advocate, classmate, debate, dilate, estate, generate, isolate, locate, mandate, migrate, negate, operate, populate, probate, rebate, rotate, vacate, vibrate

☞ Exceptions: accurate, climate, delicate, private - /ĭ/ sound

"ave" - "a" represents the long vowel /ā/ sound

When the "a" + consonant + "e" pattern is at the end of a word, the letter "a" usually represents the long vowel /ā/ sound, the consonant represents its sound while the vowel "e" is silent, as in the word <u>cave</u>.

Word Box	brave, cave, crave, Dave, gave, grave, pave, rave, save, shave, slave, wave
	Multisyllable Words:
	aftershave, behave, concave, deprave, enclave, engrave, enslave, forgave, microwave, misbehave

☞ Exceptions: have - /ă/ sound; octave - /ĭ/ sound or /ā/ sound

"ay" - "a" represents the long vowel /ā/ sound + silent "y"

When the "ay" letter combination is at the end of a word, the letter "a" represents the long vowel /ā/ sound while the letter "y" is silent, as in the word <u>day</u>.

Word Box	away, bay, birthday, clay, decay, delay, display, everyday, expressway, gray, hay, highway, holiday, jay, lay, may, Monday, nay, okay, pay, play, pray, ray, relay, say, slay, spray, stay, stray, subway, sway, today, tray, way

"ay" - "a" represents the long vowel /ā/ sound + silent "y"

When the "ay" letter combination is at the end of a syllable, the letter "a" represents the long vowel /ā/ sound while the letter "y" is silent, as in the word <u>crayons</u>.

Word Box	bricklayer, decaying, delayed, displayed, layer, maybe, mayonnaise, payment, player, playing, rayon, spraying, staying, straying, swayback, taxpayers

☞ Exceptions: says - /ĕ/ sound; kayak, bayou - /ī/ sound

"ay" represents the vowel /ä/ + /y/ sounds

When the "ay" letter combination is **divided** into two syllables, the letter "a" represents the vowel /ä/ sound and the letter "y" represents the /y/ sound, as in the words <u>Mayan</u> and <u>papaya</u>.

Reading Check Point
Assignment: Read the sentences.

1. I donated a cake for the bake sale.
2. Dain has a small cage in the basement.
3. The black chair and the vase are on sale.
4. I saw Dave's plane flying above the cave.
5. Kate and I are afraid to walk up the stairs.

Long Vowel "a" Cards		
"age"	"ake"	"ane"
cage stage wage	brake flake shake	cane crane plane
"ape"	"ate"	"ay"
drape grape shape	crate plate skate	gray stay way

Lesson 1.4
Reading Words with the "age" Letter Combination

In the "age" letter combination, the letter "a" is pronounced in <u>five</u> different ways.
- It represents the long vowel /ā/ sound, as in the word <u>cage</u>.
- It represents the short vowel /ĭ/ sound, as in the word <u>village</u>.
- It represents the vowel /ä/ sound, as in the word <u>massage</u>.
- It represents the schwa vowel /ə/ sound, as in the word <u>agenda</u>.
- It represents the short vowel /ă/ sound, as in the word <u>tragedy</u>.
- At times it is silent, as in the word <u>eager</u>.

"age" - "a" represents the long vowel /ā/ sound

In the "age" letter combination, the letter "a" can represent the long vowel /ā/ sound, as in the word <u>cage</u>.

Word Box	age, backstage, cage, disengaged, engage, enrage, gage, mage, page, pager, rage, sage, stage, stagehand, teenage, teenager, upstage, wage, webpage

"age" - "a" represents the short vowel /ĭ/ sound

When the "age" letter combination is at the end of a multisyllable word, the letter "a" can represent the short vowel /ĭ/ sound, as in the word <u>village</u>.

Word Box	average, advantage, bondage, cabbage, damage, encourage, hostage, image, linkage, manage, message, package, passage, percentage, usage, voyage

"age" - "a" represents the vowel /ä/ sound

In the "age" letter combination, the letter "a" can represent the vowel /ä/ sound, as in the word <u>massage</u>.

Word Box	barrage, barraged, camouflage, Cartagena, collage, corsage, entourage, flagellate, fuselage, garage, lager, massage, mirage, sabotage, triage

"age" - "a" represents the schwa vowel /ə/ sound

In the "age" letter combination, the letter "a" can represent the schwa vowel /ə/ sound, as in the word <u>agenda</u>.

Word Box	agenda, collagen, flagellum, magenta, mutagen

"age" - "a" represents the short vowel /ă/ sound

When the "age" letter combination is within a word, the letter "a" can represent the short vowel /ă/ sound, as in the words <u>tragedy</u> and <u>pageant</u>.

"age - "a" is silent

In the "age" letter combination, the vowel "a" can be silent, as in the words <u>eager</u> and <u>eagerly</u>.

Lesson 1.5
Reading Words with the "ai" Vowel Pair

When two vowels are **together** in a syllable or word, the first vowel usually represents the long vowel sound while the second vowel is silent.

"aid" - "a" represents the long vowel /ā/ sound

When the "ai" vowel combination is **together** in a word or syllable, the letter "a" usually represents the long vowel /ā/ sound while the letter "i" is silent, as in the word raid.

Word Box	afraid, aid, barmaid, braid, braiding, bridesmaid, laid, maid, Medicaid, mermaid, mislaid, overpaid, paid, prepaid, raid, raiding, unpaid, waylaid

☞ Exceptions: plaid - /ă/ sound; said - /ĕ/ sound

"ail" - "a" represents the long vowel /ā/ sound

When the "ai" vowel combination is **together** in a word or syllable, the letter "a" usually represents the long vowel /ā/ sound while the letter "i" is silent, as in the word sail.

Word Box	ail, bail, brail, fail, frail, hail, jail, mail, nail, pail, quail, rail, snail, tail, wail
	Multisyllable Words:
	Abigail, ailment, assail, avail, available, availability, bobtail, cocktail, curtail, derail, detail, detailing, doornail, entail, fingernail, foxtail, handrail, monorail, oxtail, prevail, prevailing, retailing, sailboat, sailing, sailor, tailor

"ain" and "aint" - "a" represents the long vowel /ā/ sound

When the "ai" vowel combination is **together** in a word or syllable, the letter "a" usually represents the long vowel /ā/ sound while the letter "i" is silent, as in the words rain and paint.

Word Box	brain, Cain, chain, drain, faint, gain, grain, main, pain, paint, plain, quaint, rain, saint, slain, Spain, sprain, stain, strain, taint, train, twain, vain, wain
	Multisyllable Words:
	attain, complain, constrain, constraint, contain, detain, detrain, domain, entertain, explain, ingrain, maintain, obtain, ordain, refrain, remain, retain

☞ Exceptions: porcelain - /ĭ/ sound; again, against - /ĕ/ sound

"ait" - "a" represents the long vowel /ā/ sound

When the "ai" vowel combination is **together** in a word or syllable, the letter "a" usually represents the long vowel /ā/ sound while the letter "i" is silent, as in the word await.

Word Box	await, awaiting, bait, faith, faithful, gait, interfaith, parfait, plait, strait, straiten, trait, traitor, unfaithful, wait, waiter, waiting, waitlist, waitress

☞ Exception: plait - /ā/ sound or /ă/ sound

Lesson 1.6
Reading Letter "a" Words with the Schwa Vowel Sound

"a" represents the schwa vowel /ə/ sound

The letter "a" can represent the schwa vowel /ə/ sound, as in the word <u>sofa</u>. The schwa vowel sounds like the short vowel /ŭ/ + /h/ sounds.

Schwa it!

Beginning	Within	End
/ə/	/ə/	/ə/
about	local	sofa

Word Box	*First letter "a"* abandon, about, above, abroad, account, across, adopt, adult, afloat, alarm, alert, allow, amend, amuse, annoy, around, await, awake, aware, away *Letter "a" within a word* alphabet, animal, atlas, balloon, calypso, canal, chemical, dollar, emphasize, local, nation<u>a</u>l, pleas<u>a</u>nt, relative, sal<u>a</u>d, sep<u>a</u>rate, sugar, thousand, vitamin *Final letter "a"* Africa, China, cobra, data, Dora, Kenya, Libya, okra, omega, opera, magma, pasta, plaza, peninsula, puma, Yoruba, Rebecca, scuba, sofa, yucca, zebra

"ag" - "a" represents the schwa vowel /ə/ sound

In multisyllable words, the vowel "a" in the "ag" letter combination can represent the schwa vowel /ə/ sound, as in the word <u>ago</u>.

Word Box	again, agape, agenda, aggression, aggressive, aggrieve, aghast, agleam, aglitter, aglow, agree, agreeable, agreement, hexagram, octagon, paragraph

"and" and "an" - "a" represents the schwa vowel /ə/ sound

In multisyllable words, the vowel "a" in the "and" letter combination and "an" letter combination can represent the schwa vowel /ə/ sound, as in the words <u>husband</u> and <u>organ</u>.

Word Box	bellman, Canadian, cardigan, congressman, garland, husband, Iceland, organ, pelican, Scotland, slogan, turban, urban, vegan, veteran, woman

"ant" - "a" represents the schwa vowel /ə/ sound

In multisyllable words, the vowel "a" in the "ant" letter combination can represent the schwa vowel /ə/ sound, as in the word <u>attendant</u>.

Word Box	applicant, assistant, defendant, distant, elegant, indignant, infant, infantry, informant, instant, jubilant, observant, participant, pleasant, relevant, servant, servants, significant, suppressant, tenant, unpleasant, vigilant

Lesson 1.7
Reading Words with the "ar" Letter Combination

In the "ar" letter combination, the letter "a" is pronounced in six different ways.
- It represents the vowel /ä/ sound, as in the word car.
- It represents the vowel /ô/ sound, as in the word war.
- It represents the short vowel /ă/ sound, as in the word Paris.
- It represents the schwa vowel /ə/ sound, as in the word dollar.
- It represents the vowel /â/ sound, as in the word care.
- It represents the short vowel /ĕ/ sound, as in the word library.
- At times it is silent, as in the word board.

"ar" represents the vowel /ä/ + /r/ sounds

The "ar" letter combination can represent the vowel /ä/ + /r/ sounds, as in the word car.

Word Box	arch, are, ark, arm, armor, art, artificial, artist, bar, car, carbon, carpet, cart, dark, disbar, seminar, shark, sharp, spark, star, start, starvation, starve, tar

"ar" represents the vowel /ô/ + /r/ sounds

The "ar" letter combination can represent the vowel /ô/ + /r/ sounds, as in the word war.

Word Box	quarantine, quark, quarrel, quarter, quartz, war, warble, warbler, ward, warden, wardrobe, warm, warmth, warn, warning, warp, warrant, warranty

"ar" represents the short vowel /ă/ + /r/ sounds

The "ar" letter combination can represent the short vowel /ă/ + /r/ sounds, as in the word Paris.

Word Box	Arab, barrel, barren, Carib, caricature, carrot, carry, character, marry, narrate, narrative, narrow, parachute, paragraph, parakeet, parallel, paralyze, tariff

"ar" represents the schwa vowel /ə/ + /r/ sounds

The "ar" letter combination can represent the schwa vowel /ə/ + /r/ sounds, as in the word dollar.

Word Box	altar, bursar, calendar, career, collar, curricular, declarative, forward, grammar, hangar, jeopardize, parade, particular, pillar, polar, regular

"are" - "a" represents the vowel /â/ sound

In the "are" letter combination, "ar" can represent the vowel /â/ +/r/ sounds, as in the word care.

Word Box	bare, barefoot, barely, blare, care, careful, carefully, dare, fare, flare, glare, hare, mare, pare, rare, rarely, scare, share, spare, square, stare, tare, ware

"ari" - "a" represents the vowel /â/ sound

In the "ari" letter combination, the vowel "a" can represent the vowel /â/ sound, as in the word caring.

Word Box	Aries, baring, barite, barium, blaring, caring, daring, flaring, garish, scenario, sharing, sparing, taring, variable, variant, variation, various

"ari" - "a" represents the short vowel /ă/ sound

In the "ari" letter combination, the vowel "a" can represent the short vowel /ă/ sound, as in the word Paris.

Word Box	arid, Arizona, chariot, charismatic, charitable, charity, clarify, clarity, irregularity, marinate, marital, maritime, Polaris, polarity, popularity, tariff

"ari" - "a" represents the schwa vowel /ə/ sound

In the "ari" letter combination, the vowel "a" can represent the schwa vowel /ə/ sound, as in the word charisma.

Word Box	arise, arisen, arising, arithmetic, burglarize, charisma, marine, nectarine, polarize, secularize, varietal, variety

"ari" - "a" represents the vowel /ä/ sound

In the "ari" letter combination, the vowel "a" can represent the vowel /ä/ sound, as in the words parish, mariachi and safari.

"ary" represents the schwa vowel /ə/ + /r/ + /ē/ sounds

The "ary" letter combination can represent the schwa vowel /ə/ + /r/ + /ē/ sounds, as in the words contrary, glossary and salary.

"ary" represents the short vowel /ĕ/ + /r/ + /ē/ sounds

The "ary" letter combination can represent the short vowel /ĕ/ + /r/ + /ē/ sounds, as in the word culinary.

Word Box	adversary, commentary, dictionary, disciplinary, inflationary, hereditary, intermediary, library, necessary, secretary, solitary, temporary, voluntary

"oar" - "a" is silent

In the "oar" letter combination, the vowel "a" is silent, as in the word board.

board	⟷	border	/ô/ + /r/ sounds
oar	⟷	or	/ô/ + /r/ sounds

Unit A Lesson 1.7

Bonus Lesson
Reading Words with the Variant Vowel "a"

"all" - "a" represents the vowel /ô/ sound

In the "all" letter combination, the vowel "a" represents the vowel /ô/ sound, as in the word ball.

Word Box	all, ball, call, fall, gall, hall, mall, pall, small, squall, stall, tall, thrall, wall rainfall, recall, reinstall, seawall, softball, stonewall, uninstall, waterfall

"alt" - "a" represents the vowel /ô/ sound

In the "alt" letter combination, the vowel "a" represents the vowel /ô/ sound, as in the word salt.

Word Box	alt, Balt, halt, malt, salt, altar, alter, alterative, altercate, alternate, although, altogether, asphalt, basalt, cobalt, exalt, exalts, gestalt, paltry, salty, unsalted

"au" represents the vowel /ô/ sound

The "au" vowel combination represents the vowel /ô/ sound, as in the word pause.

Word Box	audacity, daughter, daunt, exhaust, faucet, haul, inauguration, jaundice, laud, laundry, naughty, pauper, pause, sauce, sauna, sausage, slaughter

"aw" - "a" represents the vowel /ô/ sound

In the "aw" letter combination, the vowel "a" represents the vowel /ô/ sound, as in the word crawl.

Word Box	awful, hawk, jaw, jawbone, jigsaw, law, lawless, lawn, Lawrence, lawsuit, paw, pawl, pawn, Pawnee, raw, saw, sawfish, Sawyer, scrawl, scrawny

"a" represents the short vowel /ŏ/ sound

The letter "a" can represent the short vowel /ŏ/ sound, as in the word what.

Word Box	qualify, quality, quantity, quarrel, quarry, squad, squash, squat, swab, swamp, swan, swap, swat, tightwad, waffle, wallet, wallop, wander, want

"a" represents the vowel /ä/ sound

The letter "a" can represent the vowel /ä/ sound, as in the word car.

Word Box	alarm, ark, art, artist, Bahamas, dark, depart, farm, father, garbage, garden, garlic, garnish, guard, guitar, harm, hard, harp, large, start

Lesson 1.8
Reading Words with a Silent Letter "a"

"ai" - "a" is silent

When the "ai" vowel combination is **together** in a word or syllable, the vowel "a" can be silent, as in the word <u>aisle</u>.

Word Box	aisle, bonsai, Dubai, haiku, Mumbai, naira, Nairobi, porcelain, renaissance, samurai, Shanghai, Sinai, Tai, Taiga, Taipei, Taiwan, Taiwanese

"ea" - "a" is silent

When the "ea" vowel combination is **together** in a word or syllable, the vowel "a" is silent, as in the word <u>eat</u>.

Word Box	bead, beat, bread, cease, cheap, cheat, cream, deal, dream, each, east, eat, feast, feather, head, health, healthy, heavier, heavy, instead, leach, lead, league, leaf, leak, lean, leap, least, leave, mean, meant, meat, neat, read, ready, sea, seal, seat, spread, spreading, sweater, tea, teaching, treat, zeal

"oa" - "a" is silent

When the "oa" vowel combination is **together** in a word or syllable, the vowel "a" is silent, as in the word <u>goat</u>.

Word Box	boat, boar, broad, charcoal, coat, float, freeload, gloat, goad, goal, goalie, goat, groan, hoax, Joan, load, loaded, loaf, loam, loan, loath, loathing, moan

Silent Letter "a" at a Glance		
Letter	Sounds	Anchor Words
"a"	silent "a"	aisle
"a"	silent "a"	boat

Silent Letter "a" Cards		
"ead"	**"eap"**	**"eat"**
lead read spread	cheap leap reap	heat meat seat
"oach"	**"oan"**	**"oat"**
coach poach roach	Joan loan moan	boat coat float

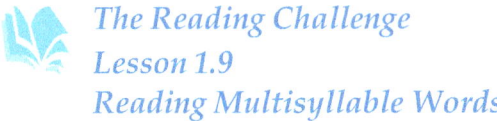

The Reading Challenge
Lesson 1.9
Reading Multisyllable Words

You can read a long word by dividing it into small parts called syllables. Each syllable has <u>one</u> <u>vowel</u> <u>sound</u> and usually one or more consonant sounds.

Three Ways to Divide Words into Syllables

1. A closed syllable ends with a consonant. When a closed syllable has one vowel, it usually has a short vowel.
   Example: dragon - drag + on

   When a closed syllable has two vowels, the first vowel is usually a long vowel while the second vowel is silent.
   Example: painting - paint + ing

2. An open syllable ends with a vowel. The vowel "a" at the end of an open syllable can be a long vowel.
   Example: cable - ca + ble

   The vowel "a" at the end of an open syllable can be the schwa vowel.
   Example: banana - ba + na + na

3. The "vowel + consonant + e" syllable is at the end of a word. The first vowel in this syllable pattern is usually a long vowel while the final "e" is silent.
   Example: blockade - block + ade

Multisyllable Word Lists

2 syllable words	3 syllable words	4 syllable words
abase	abandon	ability
above	absolute	absolution
accept	abundant	adaptation
access	acidic	adversity
acting	addressing	agitation
actor	adopting	alternative
adhere	adulthood	alligator
adjust	advancement	allocation
admire	Africa	aluminum
admit	agreement	amphibian
affirm	alignment	apology
afford	Amazon	avocado

Lesson 1.10
Reading Proper and Common Nouns and Adjectives
Capitalization Rules

Words are written with uppercase and/or lowercase letters. Proper nouns and proper adjectives begin with uppercase letters. Common nouns and common adjectives begin with lowercase letters.

A **proper noun** is a word that names a specific person, place, thing or concept.

A **common noun** is a word that names a general person, place, thing or concept.

	Proper Noun	Common Noun
Person	Anderson	astronaut
Place	Austria	arena
Thing	Apple, Inc.	apple
Concept		aspiration

A **proper adjective** is a word that describes a specific person, place, thing or concept.

A **common adjective** is a word that describes a general person, place, thing or concept.

Proper Adjective:	Common Adjective:
Person: Australian citizen	Person: attractive person
Thing: Apple computer	Thing: ambitious goals

Capitalization Rules

Uppercase Letter – "A"

- The first letter of the word that begins a sentence is capitalized.

- The first letter of the word that names a specific person, place, thing or concept is capitalized.

- The first letter of a person's title is capitalized.

- The first letter of each word in a title or subtitle is capitalized.

- As a pronoun, the letter "I" is capitalized.

✎ Note: Lowercase letters are generally used for all other words.

Lowercase Letter – "a"

- The first letter of a word that <u>does</u> <u>not</u> name a specific person, place, thing or concept is written with a lowercase letter.

- The first letter of a word that <u>does</u> <u>not</u> begin a sentence is written with a lowercase letter.

- All letters within and at the end of words are written with lowercase letters.

Reading Check Point
Assignment: Read the sentences.

1. In April, my aunt is going to Australia.
2. Anna said, "Africa is a large continent."
3. Mr. Ace Anderson is reading about Asia.
4. My sister, Annie, attends Acme Academy.
5. Alaska is located on the North American continent.

The Letter "a" at a Glance		
Letters	Sounds	Anchor Words
"a"	/ă/	apple
"a"	/ā/	cake
"a"	/ə/	sofa
"a"	/ô/	ball
"a"	/ä/	car
"a"	/â/	care
"a"	/ĭ/	village
"a"	/ĕ/	says
"au"	/ō/	mauve
"a"	/ŏ/	swamp
"a"	/ŭ/ or /ŏ/ or /ə/	was
"a"	silent "a"	boat

Learn To Read English Textbook

Unit A
Lesson 1.10

Unit B

B/b

Lesson 2.0
Introduction of the Letter B/b

The letter "b" is a consonant. It is the 2nd letter in the Roman alphabet of the English language. Letters are written as uppercase and lowercase letters.

	Uppercase Letter	Lowercase Letter
Print	B	b
Cursive	*B*	*b*

Lesson 2.1
Reading Words with the Letter B/b

The letter "b" is pronounced in <u>one</u> way.
- It represents the /b/ sound, as in the word <u>bat</u>.
- At times it is silent, as in the word <u>comb</u>.

High Frequency Letter "b" Words
baby, back, bad, ball, band, bath, be, bean, bear, because, become, bee, before, bell, best, big, bike, black, blue, board, boat, book, bone, born, both, box, boy, breathe, bring, brother, but, buy, by

At the beginning, within and end of a word, the letter "b" represents the /b/ sound, as in the words <u>bat</u>, <u>number</u> and <u>tab</u>.

Beginning	Within	End
/b/	/b/	/b/
bat	assembly	absorb
better	keyboard	bathtub
billing	library	club
bottle	number	disturb
boxer	portable	proverb
broken	possible	superb
bronze	umbrella	tab
burger	website	verb

Word Box	bib, Bob, bulb, cab, crab, climb, club, cob, crab, crib, cub, fib, grab, herb, hub, jab, job, lab, mob, nab, rib, rob, rub, scrub, sob, stub, sub, tab, tub, verb, web

Learn To Read English Textbook

Reading Words with the Letter B/b

Short Vowel Blending Table for the Letter B/b

/ă/ apple	/ĕ/ egg	/ĭ/ insect	/ŏ/ octopus	/ŭ/ up
b a g	b e t	b i t	b o p	b u g
ba g	be t	bi t	bo p	bu g
bag	bet	bit	bop	bug

Long Vowel Blending Table for the Letter B/b

/ā/ ape	/ē/ eagle	/ī/ ice	/ō/ open	/yōō/ cube
b a k e	b e e p	b i k e	b oa t	b u g l e
ba ke	bee p	bi ke	boa t	bu gle
bake	beep	bike	boat	bugle

Reading Check Point
Assignment: Read the sentences.

1. The baby's bib is blue.
2. The boy has big blocks.
3. Brad has a baseball bat.
4. Ben baked banana bread.
5. Bob and Bill are in a blue cab.

Letter "b" Parts of Speech Table

Nouns	Verbs	Adjectives
baby	babysit	backward
baboon	baked	bad
bachelor	beat	bold
back	become	barefoot
background	beautify	barren
badger	believe	bashful
bag	belong	basic
ball	bend	becoming
balcony	biting	best
ballet	blame	better
balloon	blocking	big
beaver	blow	bimonthly
biceps	boiling	binary
bookmark	bounce	biweekly

Unit B Lesson 2.1

Learn To Read English Textbook

Lesson 2.2
Reading Words with the "br" Letter Combination

"br" represents the /b/ + /r/ sounds

In the "br" letter combination, the letter "b" represents the /b/ sound and the letter "r" represents the /r/ sound, as in the word brat.

Short Vowel Blending Table for the "br" Letter Combination

/ă/ apple	/ĕ/ egg	/ĭ/ insect	/ŏ/ octopus	/ŭ/ up
br a n d	Br e n t	br i m	br o n ze	br u n t
bra nd	Bre nt	bri m	bro nze	bru nt
brand	Brent	brim	bronze	brunt

Long Vowel Blending Table for the "br" Letter Combination

/ā/ ape	/ē/ eagle	/ī/ ice	/ō/ open	/o͞o/ glue
br ai n	br ee ch	br i de	br o ke	br u te
brai n	bree ch	bri de	bro ke	bru te
brain	breech	bride	broke	brute

Word Box	brace, brag, braid, brain, brake, bran, branch, brand, brass, brave, brawl, brazen, bread, break, breakage, breast, breathe, breed, breeze, brew, bribe, brick, bridal, bride, bridge, brief, briefing, brim, bring, brisk, broad, broil, broke, brook, broom, bronze, broom, brother, brow, brown, bruise, brush

Letter "br" Parts of Speech Table

Nouns	Verbs	Adjectives
bracelet	brag	brash
brainwash	bragging	brave
brake	braid	bravery
branches	braise	bridal
brass	brake	brief
Brazil	break	bright
bread	breathe	brilliant
breeze	breed	brisk
brick	brew	British
Britain	brighten	broad
brochure	bruise	brutal
Brooklyn	bruising	brute
briefcase		

Learn To Read English Textbook

Lesson 2.3
Reading Words with the "bl" and "ble" Letter Combinations

"bl" represents the /b/ + /l/ sounds

In the "bl" letter combination, the letter "b" represents the /b/ sound and the letter "l" represents the /l/ sound, as in the word black.

Word Box	black, bladder, blame, blanch, bland, blank, blanket, blare, blast, blaze, blight, blimp, blind, blink, blinker, blip, bliss, blister, blitz, blizzard, block, blockage, blog, blood, bloom, blooper, blossom, blotch, blowing, blue, bluff, blunder

"ble" represents the /b/ + /l/ + /ĕ/ sounds

The "ble" letter combination can represent the /b/ + /l/ + /ĕ/ sounds, as in the word blemish.

Word Box	bled, blemish, blend, blender, blending, blessed, blessings, sublet, subletting

"ble" represents the /b/ + /l/ + /ē/ sounds

The "ble" letter combination can represent the /b/ + /l/ + /ē/ sounds, as in the word bleed.

Word Box	bleach, bleachers, bleaching, bleak, bleakly, bleed, bleeder, bleeding, bleep, bleeping

"ble" represents the /b/ + /l/ + /ə/ sounds

When the "ble" letter combination is within a word, it can represent the /b/ + /l/ + /ə/ sounds, as in the word problem.

Word Box	emblem, emblematic, emblematically, problem, problematic, problems

"ble" represents the /b/ + /ə/ + /l/ sounds + silent "e"

When the "ble" letter combination is at the end of a word, it represents the /b/ + /ə/ + /l/ sounds + silent "e," as in the word table.

Word Box	able, accessible, assemble, bubble, cable, disable, double, edible, fable, feeble, fumble, humble, incredible, noble, possible, ramble, stable, taxable, trouble

"bler" represents the /b/ + /ə/ + /l/ + /ə/ + /r/ sounds

When the "bler" letter combination is at the end of a word, it represents the /b/ + /ə/ + /l/ + /ə/ + /r/ sounds, as in the word enabler.

Word Box	assembler, babbler, cobbler, dribbler, enabler, gambler, nimbler, rambler, scrambler, troubler, tumbler

Lesson 2.4
Reading Words with the "mb" and "bt" Letter Combinations

"mb" represents the /m/ sound + silent "b"

When the "mb" letter combination is **together** in one syllable, the letter "m" represents the /m/ sound while the letter "b" is silent, as in the word comb. The "mb" letter combination is usually found at the end of a word or syllable.

Word Box	catacomb, climb, climber, climbing, comb, combing, combs, crumb, dumb, entomb, lamb, limb, numb, numbness, plumb, plumber, thumb, tomb, womb

"mb" represents the /m/ + /b/ sounds

When the "mb" letter combination is **divided** into two syllables, the letter "m" represents the /m/ sound and the letter "b" represents the /b/ sound, as in the word number. The letter "m" is in one syllable and the letter "b" is in the other syllable.

Word Box	ambition, ambivalence, amble, ambulance, assemble, bombard, combine, crumble, gumbo, jumbo, number, remember, slumber, symbol, thrombus

"bt" has a silent "b" + /t/ sound

When the "bt" letter combination is **together** in one syllable, the letter "b" is silent while the letter "t" represents the /t/ sound, as in the word debt. The "bt" letter combination is usually found at the end of a word or syllable.

Word Box	debt, debtor, doubt, doubting, indebted, subtle, subtleness, subtlety, subtly

"bt" represents the /b/ + /t/ sounds

When the "bt" letter combination is **divided** into two syllables, the letter "b" represents the /b/ sound and the letter "t" represents the /t/ sound, as in the word obtain. The letter "b" is in one syllable and the letter "t" is in the other syllable.

Word Box	bobtail, obtain, obtained, obtrude, obtrusively, obtuse, subterranean, subtext, subtitles, subtotal, subtract, subtracting, subtraction, subtrahend, subtropics

Reading Check Point
Assignment: Read the sentences.

1. Student loan debt is accelerating at a fast pace.
2. The ambulance drove by my house at a high speed.
3. The subtitles clearly indicate the key ideas of the text.
4. My students are learning to subtract three-digit numbers.
5. The skilled plumber installs, maintains and repairs our pipes.

Lesson 2.5
Reading Words with a Silent Letter "b"

The letter "b" can be silent, as in the word subpoena.

✦ **Reading Words with the "mb" and "bt" Letter Combinations**

When the "mb" letter combination or "bt" letter combination is **together** in one syllable, the letter "b" is silent, as in the words comb and debt.

Word Box	climb, comb, combs, crumb, debt, debtor, doubt, dumb, dumbbell, entomb, lamb, limb, plumb, plumber, subtle, subtleness, subtly, thumb, tomb, womb

"mb" represents the /m/ sound + silent "b"	
comb	climb
crumb	lamb
limb	womb

"bt" has a silent "b" + /t/ sound	
debt	debtor
doubt	doubting
indebted	subtle

✦ **Reading Words with the "bb" Letter Combination**

"bb" represents the /b/ sound + silent "b"

When the "bb" letter combination is **together** in one syllable, the first letter "b" represents the /b/ sound while the second letter "b" is silent, as in the word rabbit.

Word Box	babble, blubber, bubble, cabbage, chubby, dabble, dribble, ebb, gobble, grubby, hobble, hobby, jabber, lobby, nibble, rabbit, ribbon, shabby, stubborn

"bb" represents the /b/ + /b/ sounds

When the "bb" letter combination is **divided** into two syllables, the first letter "b" represents the /b/ sound and the second letter "b" also represents the /b/ sound, as in the word subbasement.

Word Box	subbase, subbasement, subbranch

Silent Letter "b" at a Glance		
Letter(s)	Sound	Anchor Words
"b"	silent "b"	subpoena
"mb"	silent "b"	comb
"bt"	silent "b"	debt
"bb"	/b/ + silent "b"	rabbit

The Reading Challenge
Lesson 2.6
Reading Multisyllable Words

You can read a long word by dividing it into small parts called syllables. Each syllable has <u>one</u> <u>vowel</u> <u>sound</u> and usually one or more consonant sounds.

Three Ways to Divide Words into Syllables

1. A closed syllable ends with a consonant. When a closed syllable has one vowel, it usually has a short vowel.
   Example: bedbug - bed + bug

   When a closed syllable has two vowels, the first vowel is usually a long vowel while the second vowel is silent.
   Example: beading - bead + ing

2. An open syllable ends with a vowel. The vowel at the end of the syllable is usually a long vowel.
   Example: behind - be + hind

3. The "vowel + consonant + e" syllable is at the end of a word. The first vowel in this syllable pattern is usually a long vowel while the final "e" is silent.
   Example: beehive - bee + hive

Multisyllable Word Lists

2 syllable words	3 syllable words	4 syllable words
backdrop	bakery	bacterium
balance	Bahamas	ballerina
bedroom	balcony	barometer
beehive	baritone	beautifully
below	beautify	belligerent
birdie	becoming	benevolent
blackout	behavior	bicarbonate
bobsled	Bermuda	bilateral
bringing	bicycle	biography
British	bimonthly	biology
broaden	blogosphere	bodybuilder
broker	bravery	brokenhearted
bulky	bulletin	bureaucracy

Lesson 2.7
Reading Proper and Common Nouns and Adjectives
Capitalization Rules

Words are written with uppercase and/or lowercase letters. Proper nouns and proper adjectives begin with uppercase letters. Common nouns and common adjectives begin with lowercase letters.

A proper noun is a word that names a specific person, place, thing or concept.

A common noun is a word that names a general person, place, thing or concept.

	Proper Noun	Common Noun
Person	Bobby	barber
Place	Barbados	beach
Thing	Barbie doll	beagle
Concept	Buddhism	beauty

A proper adjective is a word that describes a specific person, place, thing or concept.

A common adjective is a word that describes a general person, place, thing or concept.

Proper Adjective:	Common Adjective:
Person: Brazilian citizen Thing: British literature	Person: bold speaker Thing: big bags

Capitalization Rules

Uppercase Letter – "B"

- The first letter of a word that begins a sentence is capitalized.

- The first letter of a word that names a specific person, place, thing or concept is capitalized.

- The first letter of a person's title is capitalized.

- The first letter of each word in a title or subtitle is capitalized.

- As a pronoun, the letter "I" is capitalized.

✎ Note: Lowercase letters are generally used for all other words.

Lowercase Letter – "b"

- The first letter of a word that <u>does</u> <u>not</u> name a specific person, place, thing or concept is written with a lowercase letter.

- The first letter of a word that <u>does</u> <u>not</u> begin a sentence is written with a lowercase letter.

- All letters within and at the end of words are written with lowercase letters.

Reading Check Point
Assignment: Read the sentences.

1. Bruce is a brave boy.
2. The bikers are at the bay.
3. Bess is busy baking loaves of bread.
4. Bobby's baseball bat is in the basket.
5. Benjamin is the best basketball player.

The Letter "b" at a Glance		
Letter	Sound	Anchor Words
"b"	/b/	bat
"b"	silent "b"	comb

Unit C

C/c

 **Lesson 3.0**
Introduction of the Letter C/c

The letter "c" is a consonant. It is the 3rd letter in the Roman alphabet of the English language. Letters are written as uppercase and lowercase letters.

	Uppercase Letter	Lowercase Letter
Print	C	c
Cursive	𝒞	𝒸

 Lesson 3.1
Reading Words with the Hard Letter "c"

The letter "c" does not have its own sound. It borrows the /k/ sound from the letter "k" and the /s/ sound from the letter "s."

The letter "c" is pronounced in four different ways.
- It represents the /k/ sound, as in the word cat.
- It represents the /s/ sound, as in the word city.
- It represents the /ch/ sound, as in the word cello.
- It represents the /sh/ sound, as in the word ocean.
- At times it is silent, as in the word back.

High Frequency Letter "c" Words
call, called, came, can, can't, car, care, carry, cat, catch, certain, chair, change, child, children, city, class, clean, clock, close, clothes, cloud, cold, come, coming, complete, could, country, couple, cozy

The letter "c" represents the hard "c" sound and the soft "c" sound.

The hard "c" represents one sound.	The soft "c" represents three sounds.
• /k/ sound	• /s/ sound • /sh/ sound • /ch/ sound

Learn To Read English Textbook

❖ Reading Words with the Hard Letter "c"

"c" represents the /k/ sound

The hard "c" represents the /k/ sound. When the letter "c" is before the vowel "a," "o" or "u," it usually represents the /k/ sound, as in the words <u>cap</u>, <u>cop</u> and <u>cup</u>.

Short Vowel Blending Table for the Hard C/c

/ă/ apple	/ĕ/ egg	/ĭ/ insect	/ŏ/ octopus	/ŭ/ up
c a p			c o p	c u p
ca p			co p	cu p
cap			cop	cup

Long Vowel Blending Table for the Hard C/c

/ā/ ape	/ē/ eagle	/ī/ ice	/ō/ open	/yōō/ cube
c a k e			c oa t	c u t e
ca ke			coa t	cu te
cake			coat	cute

"ca" - "c" represents the /k/ sound

In the "ca" letter combination, the letter "c" represents the /k/ sound, as in the word <u>cast</u>.

Word Box	cab, cage, cake, call, camp, candle, cane, cap, cape, car, cart, case, cask, cat, catch, application, duplicate, education, historical, local, significant, technical

"co" - "c" represents the /k/ sound

In the "co" letter combination, the letter "c" represents the /k/ sound, as in the word <u>cold</u>.

Word Box	account, coach, coat, coast, cob, code, come, con, cop, corn, cost, cot, country, cow, decode, ecology, income, mascot, peacock, scope, secondly, welcome

"cu" - "c" represents the /k/ sound

In the "cu" letter combination, the letter "c" represents the /k/ sound, as in the word <u>cute</u>.

Word Box	cub, cube, cubic, cue, cuff, cup, curb, cure, curl, curves, custom, cut, cute, cuts, acute, difficult, discuss, incur, focus, locust, occupy, occur, scuba, secure, talcum

"c" represents the /k/ sound

When the letter "c" is at the end of a word, it represents the /k/ sound, as in the words <u>basic</u>, <u>panic</u> and <u>zinc</u>.

Lesson 3.2
Reading Words with the Soft Letter "c"

"c" represents the /s/ sound

When the letter "c" is before the vowel "e," "i" or "y," it usually represents the /s/ sound, as in the words cell, city and cyst.

The soft "c" is pronounced in three different ways.
- It represents the /s/ sound, as in the word city.
- It represents the /ch/ sound, as in the word cello.
- It represents the /sh/ sound, as in the word chef.

Short Vowel Blending Table for the Soft C/c

/ă/ apple	/ĕ/ egg	/ĭ/ insect	/ŏ/ octopus	/ŭ/ up	/ĭ/ gym
	c e ll	c i t y			c y st
	ce ll	ci t y			cy st
	cell	city			cyst

Long Vowel Blending Table for the Soft C/c

/ā/ ape	/ē/ eagle	/ī/ ice	/ō/ open	/ōō/ glue	/ī/ cycle
	c ea se	c i te			c y cle
	cea se	ci te			cy cle
	cease	cite			cycle

"ce" - "c" represents the /s/ sound

In the "ce" letter combination, the letter "c" represents the /s/ sound, as in the word face.

Word Box	ace, announce, celery, cell, censure, center, cents, cereal, dance, face, grace, ice, incense, lace, peace, place, price, process, race, receive, rice, stance, tolerance

"ci" - "c" represents the /s/ sound

In the "ci" letter combination, the letter "c" represents the /s/ sound, as in the word acid.

Word Box	accident, acid, cider, cinch, cinema, circle, circuit, circus, cite, citizen, city, civil, excited, facility, incident, incite, pacific, participant, pencil, recipe, society

"cy" - "c" represents the /s/ sound

In the "cy" letter combination, the letter "c" represents the /s/ sound, as in the word icy.

Word Box	accuracy, agency, bicycle, currency, cycle, cyst, dependency, discrepancy, icy, emergency, fancy, frequency, literacy, policy, tendency, urgency, vacancy

Learn To Read English Textbook

Lesson 3.3
Reading Words with the "cr" Letter Combination

"cr" represents the /k/ + /r/ sounds

In the "cr" letter combination, the letter "c" represents the /k/ sound and the letter "r" represents the /r/ sound, as in the word <u>cross</u>.

Short Vowel Blending Table for the "cr" Letter Combination

/ă/ apple	/ĕ/ egg	/ĭ/ insect	/ŏ/ octopus	/ŭ/ up
cr a b	cr e p t	cr i b	cr o p	cr u m b
cra b	cre p t	cri b	cro p	cru mb
crab	crept	crib	crop	crumb

Long Vowel Blending Table for the "cr" Letter Combination

/ā/ ape	/ē/ eagle	/ī/ ice	/ō/ open	/o͞o/ glue
cr a ne	cr ee p	cr i me	cr oa k	cr ue l
cra ne	cree p	cri me	croa k	crue l
crane	creep	crime	croak	cruel

"cr" represents the /k/ + /r/ sounds

When the "cr" letter combination is at the beginning of a word, it represents the /k/ + /r/ sounds, as in the word <u>crush</u>.

Word Box	crab, crack, craft, cream, create, creative, credence, credential, credit, creep, crew, crime, crisis, crisp, crispy, critic, cross, crucial, crumble, crunch, crust

"cr" represents the /k/ + /r/ sounds

When the "cr" letter combination is within a word, it represents the /k/ + /r/ sounds, as in the word <u>concrete</u>.

Word Box	across, ascribe, decrease, discretion, discrimination, hypocrite, increase, microbe, prescription, recreation, secret, secretary, subscription, transcript

Reading Check Point
Assignment: Read the sentences.

1. I have a craving for candy.
2. The cats ate the bread crumbs.
3. My baby crawls on the carpet.
4. We like to drink cranberry juice.
5. Cindy's ice cream cone is very sweet.

Lesson 3.4
Reading Words with the "cl" and "cle" Letter Combinations

"cl" represents the /k/ + /l/ sounds

In the "cl" letter combination, the letter "c" represents the /k/ sound and the letter "l" represents the /l/ sound, as in the word <u>club</u>.

Short Vowel Blending Table for the "cl" Letter Combination

/ă/ apple	/ĕ/ egg	/ĭ/ insect	/ŏ/ octopus	/ŭ/ up
cl a p	cl e f	cl i p	cl o p	cl u b
cla p	cle f	cli p	clo p	clu b
clap	clef	clip	clop	club

Long Vowel Blending Table for the "cl" Letter Combination

/ā/ ape	/ē/ eagle	/ī/ ice	/ō/ open	/ōō/ glue
cl ai m	cl ea n	cl ie nt	cl o se	cl u e
clai m	clea n	clie nt	clo se	cl ue
claim	clean	client	close	clue

"cle" represents the /k/ + /l/ + /ĕ/ sounds

When the "cle" letter combination is at the beginning or within a word, it can represent the /k/ + /l/ + /ĕ/ sounds, as in the word <u>cleft</u>.

Word Box	cleanliness, cleanse, cleansed, cleanser, cleansing, clef, clemency, clement, clench, cleric, clerical, clever, clevis, inclemency, inclement, inclemently

"cle" represents the /k/ + /l/ + /ē/ sounds

When the "cle" letter combination is at the beginning or within a word, it can represent the /k/ + /l/ + /ē/ sounds, as in the word <u>clean</u>.

Word Box	clean, cleaned, cleaner, cleanest, cleanly, cleans, cleats, cleavage, cleave, cleaver, nuclear, nucleate, nucleic acid, nucleolus, nucleon, nucleus

☞ Exceptions: clergy - /k/+/l/+/û/ sounds; circlet - /k/+/l/+/ĭ/ sounds; clear - /k/+/l/+/î/ sounds

"cle" represents the /k/ + /ə/ + /l/ sounds + silent "e"

When the "cle" letter combination is at the end of a word, it represents the /k/ + /ə/ + /l/ sounds + silent "e," as in the word <u>bicycle</u>. It is important to note that the schwa vowel /ə/ sound is inserted between the /k/ and /l/ sounds.

Word Box	article, chronicle, circle, cubicle, cycle, follicle, icicle, miracle, obstacle, pinnacle, particle, spectacle, tabernacle, tentacle, tubercle, uncle, vehicle, ventricle

Lesson 3.5
Reading Words with the "ct" Letter Combination

"ct" represents the /k/ + /t/ sounds

In the "ct" letter combination, the letter "c" represents the /k/ sound while the letter "t" usually represents the /t/ sound, as in the word fact.

Word Box	actor, adjunct, cactus, compact, conjunct, conflict, conflictive, connect, connective, contact, contract, effective, expect, expectancy, fact, factor, pact

Assignment: Read the words in the two columns. Listen carefully for the /k/ sound made by the letter "c."

Letter "t" represents /t/ sound	"ct" letter combination represents /k/ + /t/ sounds
pat	compact, impact, pact
fat	fact, factor, factory
jet	object, deject, inject
let	collect, electric, electricity
pet	aspect, inspect, respect
lit	afflict, conflict, inflict

"ct" has a silent "c" + /t/ sound

In the "ct" letter combination, the letter "c" can be silent while the letter "t" represents the /t/ sound, as in the word indict.

Word Box	Connecticut, indict, indictable, indicted, indictee, indictment, victual, victuals

"ct" represents the /k/ + /ch/ sounds

When the "ct" letter combination is before the vowel "u," the letter "c" represents the /k/ sound and the letter "t" represents the /ch/ sound, as in the word picture.

Word Box	actual, actuality, actualize, actuary, actuate, conjectural, conjecture, contractual, effectual, factual, fluctuate, lecture, manufacture, puncture, structure

"ct" represents the /k/ + /sh/ sounds

When the "ction" letter combination is **divided** into two syllables, the letter "c" represents the /k/ sound and the "tion" suffix represents the /sh/ + /ə/ + /n/ sounds, as in the word action.

Word Box	abstraction, action, conjunction, connection, contraction, diction, dictionary, fraction, induction, intersection, reaction, satisfaction, section, transaction

Lesson 3.6
Reading Soft Letter "c" Words

"c" represents the /sh/ sound

When the letter "c" is before the vowel "e" or "i," it can represent the /sh/ sound, as in the words ocean and glacier.

"cean" represents the /sh/ + /ə/ + /n/ sounds

In the "cean" letter combination, the letter "c" represents the /sh/ sound, as in the word ocean.

Word Box	caducean, cetacean, crustacean, gallinacean, ocean, oceanic, oceanarium

"cian" represents the /sh/ + /ə/ + /n/ sounds

In the "cian" letter combination, the letter "c" represents the /sh/ sound, as in the word musician.

Word Box	beautician, clinician, cosmetician, dietician, electrician, logician, magician, musician, optician, pediatrician, physician, politician, statistician, technician

"cial" represents the /sh/ + /ə/ + /l/ sounds

In the "cial" letter combination, the letter "c" represents the /sh/ sound, as in the word crucial.

Word Box	artificial, commercial, crucial, crucially, especially, facial, financial, interracial, official, provincial, racial, social, special, specialist, specialization, superficial

"cious" represents the /sh/ + /ə/ + /s/ sounds

In the "cious" letter combination, the letter "c" represents the /sh/ sound, as in the word capricious.

Word Box	capricious, capriciously, capriciousness, conscious, delicious, ferocious, judicious, precious, spacious, specious, unconscious, unconsciously

"cient" represents the /sh/ + /ə/ + /n/ + /t/ sounds

In the "cient" letter combination, the letter "c" represents the /sh/ sound, as in the word efficient.

Word Box	ancient, ancients, coefficient, deficient, deficiently, efficient, efficiently, insufficient, omniscient, proficient, proficiently, sufficient, sufficiently

☞ Exceptions: scientific, scientist – silent "c"

Lesson 3.7
Reading Words with the "ch" Letter Combination

The "ch" letter combination is pronounced in four different ways.
- It represents the /ch/ sound, as in the word chicken.
- It represents the /k/ sound, as in the word ache.
- It represents the /sh/ sound, as in the word chef.
- It represents the /k/+/w/ sounds, as in the word choir.
- At times it is silent, as in the word yacht.

"ch" – Pronunciation Table

"ch" - /ch/ chicken	"ch" - /k/ chaos	"ch" - /sh/ chef	"ch" - silent yacht
couch	chasm	brochure	fuchsia
voucher	anchor	chic	yachting
chance	school	Chicago	yachtsman

"ch" represents the /ch/ sound

The "ch" letter combination usually represents the /ch/ sound, as in the word chicken.

Word Box	*"ch" at the beginning of a word* chain, chair, chalk, chance, change, chapter, charge, chart, chatter, cheap, cheat, check, cherry, chess, chest, chicken, child, children, chin, chip, chose, chosen *"ch" at the end of a word* bench, branch, clinch, crunch, each, inch, lunch, peach, pinch, porch, punch, ranch, reach, research, rich, sandwich, search, stretch, such, teach, touch, trench

"ch" represents the /k/ sound

The "ch" letter combination can represent the /k/ sound, as in the word ache.

Word Box	ache, anchor, chameleon, chaos, character, charisma, chemical, chemist, chemistry, chord, chorus, echo, echogram, orchestra, psych, school, stomach

"ch" represents the /sh/ sound

The "ch" letter combination can represent the /sh/ sound, as in the word chef.

Word Box	brochure, cache, champagne, chef, chic, Chicago, chiffon, chute, crochet, machine, machinery, machines, parachute, parachutes, parachutist, ricochet

"ch" represents the /k/+/w/ sounds

The "ch" letter combination can represent the /k/+/w/ sounds, as in the word choir.

"ch" is silent

The "ch" letter combination can be silent, as in the words yacht and fuchsia.

Lesson 3.8
Reading Words with the "cc" Letter Combination

"cc" represents the /k/ sound + silent "c"

When the "cc" letter combination is **together** in one syllable, the first letter "c" represents the /k/ sound while the second letter "c" is silent, as in the word <u>occupy</u>.

Word Box	acclaim, accommodate, accomplished, account, accustom, broccoli, hiccup, Morocco, occasion, occur, occurrence, raccoon, soccer, stucco, yucca

"cc" represents the /sh/ sound or /ch/ sound

When the "cc" letter combination is **together** in one syllable, it can represent the /sh/ sound, as in the word <u>pasticcio</u> or the /ch/ sound, as in the word <u>carpaccio</u>.

Word Box	/sh/ sound – pasticcio /ch/ sound – capriccio, carpaccio, fettuccine

"cc" represents the /k/ + /s/ sounds

When the "cc" letter combination is **divided** into two syllables, the first letter "c" represents the /k/ sound and the second letter "c" represents the /s/ sound, as in the word <u>accept</u>.

Word Box	accede, accelerant, accelerate, accelerator, accent, accentuate, accept, acceptable, acceptance, accepted, access, accessible, accessory, accident, accidental, occiput, succeed, successfully, succinct, vaccinate, vaccination

Letter "cc" Parts of Speech Table

Nouns	Verbs	Adjectives
accelerant	accede	acceptable
acceptance	accelerate	accepted
accessory	accept	accessible
broccoli	acclaim	accidental
hiccup	acclimate	accurate
occasion	accommodate	accusative
soccer	accompany	accustomed
success	occupied	occasional
successful	occupy	occipital
succession	occur	successive
successor	succeed	succinct
yucca	succumb	succulent

Lesson 3.9
Reading Words with a Silent Letter "c"

"c" is silent

The letter "c" can be silent, as in the words czar and Tucson.

"cc" represents the /k/ sound + silent "c"

When the "cc" letter combination is **together** in one syllable, the first letter "c" represents the /k/ sound while the second letter "c" is silent, as in the word occupy.

Word Box	acclaim, accommodate, accomplished, account, accountant, accustom, broccoli, hiccup, Morocco, occasion, occur, raccoon, soccer, stucco, yucca

"ck" has a silent "c" + /k/ sound

In the "ck" letter combination, the letter "c" is silent, as in the word sack.

Word Box	back, black, deck, dock, docket, duck, jack, kick, lack, lock, luck, lucky, neck, pack, padlock, pick, pocket, quick, rack, rock, rocket, rocky, sick, stock, ticket

"ct" has a silent "c" + /t/ sound

In the "ct" letter combination, the letter "c" can be silent while the letter "t" represents the /t/ sound, as in the word indict.

Word Box	Connecticut, indict, indictable, indicted, indictee, indictment, victual, victuals

"acqu" - "c" is silent

In the "acqu" letter combination, the letter "c" is silent, as in the word acquit.

Word Box	acquaint, acquaintance, acquiesce, acquiescence, acquire, acquired, acquirement, acquisition, acquisitive, acquit, acquittal, acquitted, acquitting

"sc" represents the /s/ sound + silent "c"

In the "sc" letter combination, the letter "c" can be silent, as in the word science.

Word Box	ascend, ascendant, ascent, ascertain, fascinate, miscellaneous, obscene, scenario, scene, scenery, scenography, scent, scepter, scientist, sci-fi, scissors

"ch" is silent

The "ch" letter combination is silent, as in the words fuchsia and yacht.

"scle" – "c" is silent

In "scle" letter combination, the letter "c" is silent, as in the words muscle and corpuscle.

The Reading Challenge
Lesson 3.10
Reading Multisyllable Words

You can read a long word by dividing it into small parts called syllables. Each syllable has <u>one</u> <u>vowel</u> <u>sound</u> and usually one or more consonant sounds.

Three Ways to Divide Words into Syllables

1. A closed syllable ends with a consonant. When a closed syllable has one vowel, it usually has a short vowel.
   Example: catnap - cat + nap

   When a closed syllable has two vowels, the first vowel is usually a long vowel while the second vowel is silent.
   Example: cleaning - clean + ing

2. An open syllable ends with a vowel. The vowel at the end of the syllable is usually a long vowel.
   Example: cement - ce + ment

3. The "vowel + consonant + e" syllable is at the end of a word. The first vowel in this syllable pattern is usually a long vowel while the final "e" is silent.
   Example: combine - com + bine

Multisyllable Word Lists

2 syllable words	3 syllable words	4 syllable words
cabin	calendar	calculator
cable	camera	caterpillar
cadet	Canada	cauliflower
camping	capital	celebration
cellar	celebrate	ceremony
chamber	cellular	circulation
changing	cereal	community
chaplain	character	concentration
China	chemical	conceptual
climate	citizen	consequences
cricket	clinical	constellation
concrete	coloring	criminalize
corner	cultivate	criterion
culture	cucumber	custodian
cutting	cylinder	customary

Learn To Read English Textbook

Lesson 3.11
Reading Proper and Common Nouns and Adjectives
Capitalization Rules

Words are written with uppercase and/or lowercase letters. Proper nouns and proper adjectives begin with uppercase letters. Common nouns and common adjectives begin with lowercase letters.

A **proper noun** is a word that names a specific person, place, thing or concept.

A **common noun** is a word that names a general person, place, thing or concept.

	Proper Noun	Common Noun
Person	Mr. Carson	commuter
Place	Canada	café
Thing	Cadbury	cabinet
Concept	Christianity	compassion

A **proper adjective** is a word that describes a specific person, place, thing or concept.

A **common adjective** is a word that describes a general person, place, thing or concept.

Proper Adjective:	Common Adjective:
Person: Canadian citizen Thing: Christian music	Person: clever student Thing: clean cabinets

Capitalization Rules

Uppercase Letter – "C"

- The first letter of a word that begins a sentence is capitalized.

- The first letter of a word that names a specific person, place, thing or concept is capitalized.

- The first letter of a person's title is capitalized.

- The first letter of each word in a title or subtitle is capitalized.

- As a pronoun, the letter "I" is capitalized.

✎ Note: Lowercase letters are generally used for all other words.

Lowercase Letter – "c"

- The first letter of a word that <u>does</u> <u>not</u> name a specific person, place, thing or concept is written with a lowercase letter.

- The first letter of a word that <u>does</u> <u>not</u> begin a sentence is written with a lowercase letter.

- All letters within and at the end of words are written with lowercase letters.

 Reading Check Point
Assignment: Read the sentences.

1. Cleveland is not a capital city.
2. The Clement Circus does not have clowns.
3. Chad is a member of the Celtic Football Club.
4. The cougar is commonly known as a catamount.
5. Central America is a subcontinent of the Americas.

The Letter "c" at a Glance		
Letter(s)	Sounds	Anchor Words
"c"	/k/	cat
"c"	/s/	city
"c"	/sh/	ocean
"c"	/ch/	cello
"c"	silent "c"	czar
"cc"	silent "c"	occupy
"ck"	silent "c"	back
"ct"	silent "c"	Connecticut
"acqu"	silent "c"	acquit
"sc"	silent "c"	science
"ch"	silent "c"	yacht
"scle"	silent "c"	muscle

Unit D

D/d

Lesson 4.0
Introduction of the Letter D/d

The letter "d" is a consonant. It is the 4th letter in the Roman alphabet of the English language. Letters are written as uppercase and lowercase letters.

	Uppercase Letter	Lowercase Letter
Print	D	d
Cursive	𝒟	𝒹

Lesson 4.1
Reading Words with the Letter D/d

The letter "d" is pronounced in <u>three</u> different ways.
- It represents the /d/ sound, as in the word <u>dog</u>.
- It represents the /j/ sound, as in the word <u>schedule</u>.
- It represents the /t/ sound, as in the word <u>walked</u>.
- At times it is silent, as in the word <u>judge</u>.

High Frequency, One Syllable Letter "d" Words
dad, dance, dark, date, day, dear, deck, deep, deer, den, dent, desk, did, dip, dish, disk, do, does, dog, doll, done, dot, dove, down, drag, dream, dress, drink, drive, drop, drum, dry, duck

At the beginning, within and end of a word, the letter "d" represents the /d/ sound, as in the words <u>dog</u>, <u>adapt</u> and <u>bed</u>.

Beginning	Within	End
/d/	/d/	/d/
dog	adapt	bed
dish	order	bend
duck	medal	card
dance	model	sand
dream	wedding	seed

Learn To Read English Textbook   Copyrighted Material

Reading Words with the Letter D/d

Short Vowel Blending Table for the Letter D/d

/ă/ apple	/ĕ/ egg	/ĭ/ insect	/ŏ/ octopus	/ŭ/ up
d a d	d e ck	d i g	d o t	d u g
da d	de ck	di g	do t	du g
dad	deck	dig	dot	dug

Long Vowel Blending Table for the Letter D/d

/ā/ ape	/ē/ eagle	/ī/ ice	/ō/ open	/o͞o/ glue
d a y	d ee p	d i m e	d o m e	d u n e
da y	dee p	di me	do me	du ne
day	deep	dime	dome	dune

"d" represents the /d/ sound

The letter "d" usually represents the /d/ sound, as in the word <u>dog</u>.

Word Box	dad, daily, damp, dance, dark, dash, date, dawn, day, dear, deep, deer, den, dent, desk, did, dig, dill, dime, dirt, disk, dock, doll, door, down, dump, dusk

Reading Check Point

Assignment: Read the sentences.

1. The ditch is deep and dark.
2. The driver drove to Denmark.
3. Donna ate a donut for dessert.
4. David drew doves, dogs and ducks.
5. After dinner, Dan drove to the store.

Letter "d" Parts of Speech Table

Nouns	Verbs	Adjectives
daffodil	dabble	daffy
deacon	daring	daily
decimal	dealing	dainty
detergent	debate	damp
directory	decay	degenerate
domino	decided	different
dragon	decorate	discrete
drifter	driving	dressy

Lesson 4.2
Reading Letter "d" Words with the /d/ Sound and /j/ Sound

"d" represents the /j/ sound

The letter "d" can represent the /j/ sound, as in the word <u>cordially</u>.

Word Box	cordial, cordiality, educate, education, gradually, graduation, grandeur, modulation, modulator, pendulous, procedure, soldier, undulant, undulation

"du" - "d" represents the /d/ sound or /j/ sound

In the "du" letter combination, the letter "d" can represent the /d/ sound, as in the word <u>duck</u> or the /j/ sound, as in the word <u>schedule</u>.

"du" "d" represents the /d/ sound	"du" "d" represents the /j/ sound
dump	educate
duct	gradual
dug	undulate

When the "du" letter combination is at the beginning of a word or syllable, the letter "d" usually represents the /d/ sound, as in the word <u>duck</u>.

Word Box	*"du" at the beginning of a word* dual, due, dug, duke, dull, duly, dump, dunk, duplex, during, dusk, dust, duty *"du" within a word* adult, conduct, conduit, deduct, induce, induct, indulge, kudu, product, reduce

When the "du" letter combination is within a word, the letter "d" can represent the /j/ sound, as in the word <u>schedule</u>.

Word Box	educable, educated, education, educative, glandular, graduate, individual, modulate, module, nodule, pendular, pendulum, procedure, verdure

"dure" - "d" represents the /d/ sound or /j/ sound

In the "dure" letter combination, the letter "d" can represent the /d/ sound, as in the word <u>endure</u> or the /j/ sound, as in the word <u>procedure</u>.

"dure" "d" represents the /d/ sound	"dure" "d" represents the /j/ sound
duress	verdure
endure	procedure

Lesson 4.3
Reading Words with the "ed" Suffix/ Past Tense Verbs

"ed" represents the short vowel /ĭ/ + /d/ sounds

When the "ed" suffix is added to a verb ending with the /d/ or /t/ sound, it represents the short vowel /ĭ/ + /d/ sounds.

Word Box	attended, blended, confounded, connected, decided, departed, ended, exploded, halted, handed, intended, knitted, landed, melted, nested, nodded

"ed" has a silent "e" + /d/ sound

When the "ed" suffix is added to a verb ending with the /b/, /g/, /ī/, /j/, /l/, /m/, /n/, /ng/ or /ō/ sound, it has a silent "e" + /d/ sound. This rule also applies to the following sounds: /ou/, /r/, /v/ and /z/.

Word Box		
	/b/:	absorbed, ascribed, described, disturbed, grabbed, robbed, robed, stubbed
	/g/:	begged, bragged, bugged, clogged, defogged, hugged, nagged, tugged
	/ī/:	amplified, cried, denied, fried, glorified, multiplied, notified, tied, tried
	/j/:	dodged, encouraged, exchanged, judged, merged, paged, purged, staged
	/l/:	assembled, called, chilled, circled, drilled, filed, filled, settled, stilled
	/m/:	alarmed, blamed, combed, entombed, framed, named, numbed, tamed
	/n/:	abandoned, attained, cleaned, declined, defined, earned, fanned, gained
	/ng/:	banged, belonged, challenged, changed, clanged, hanged, prolonged
	/ō/:	bestowed, flowed, mowed, rowed, shadowed, sowed, snowed, towed
	/ou/:	allowed, avowed, bowed, endowed, meowed, plowed, vowed, wowed
	/r/:	acquired, allured, answered, cared, delivered, hammered, purred, tired
	/v/:	achieved, arrived, loved, perceived, relieved, saved, served, shelved
	/z/:	actualized, agonized, amazed, burglarized, criticized, gazed, raised

"ed" has a silent "e" + /t/ sound

When the "ed" suffix is added to a verb ending with the /ch/, /f/, /k/, /k/+/s/, /p/, /s/ or /sh/ sound, it has a silent "e" + /t/ sound.

Word Box		
	/ch/:	approached, attached, launched, matched, pinched, reached, watched
	/f/:	bluffed, coughed, fluffed, huffed, laughed, sniffed, staffed, surfed
	/k/:	asked, baked, blocked, checked, cooked, kicked, liked, picked, ticked
	/k/+/s/:	axed, deflexed, fixed, inflexed, mixed, relaxed, remixed, taxed, vexed
	/p/:	beeped, capped, cropped, dropped, equipped, hopped, mapped
	/s/:	advised, advanced, bused, dressed, exercised, faced, glimpsed
	/sh/:	accomplished, crashed, dashed, finished, mashed, polished, washed

Lesson 4.4
Reading Words with a Silent Letter "d"

"d" is silent

The letter "d" can be silent, as in the word handsome.

Word Box	handkerchief, handsome, Wednesday, Windsor

"dge" - "d" is silent

In the "dge" letter combination, the letter "d" is silent, as in the word judge.

Word Box	acknowledge, badge, bridge, cartridge, dislodge, dodge, drawbridge, drudge, edge, fledge, fridge, fudge, hedge, judge, knowledge, ledge, lodge, misjudge, nudge, nudged, porridge, ridge, sedge, sledge, wedge

"adj" - "d" is silent

In the "adj" letter combination, the letter "d" is silent, as in the word adjust.

Word Box	adjacent, adjacency, adjective, adjectives, adjoin, adjourn, adjournment, adjudge, adjudicate, adjunct, adjunctive, adjuration, adjure, adjured, adjuring, adjust, adjusted, adjusting, adjustment, adjustments, adjusts, adjutancy

✤ *Reading Words with the "dd" Letter Combination*

"dd" represents the /d/ sound + silent "d"

When the "dd" letter combination is **together** in one syllable, the first letter "d" represents the /d/ sound while the second letter "d" is silent, as in the word add.

Word Box	add, adds, addend, addendum, adder, addict, addiction, addition, address, adduce, backslidden, bidding, bladder, bobsledding, buddy, cuddle, downtrodden, fiddle, forbidden, hidden, huddle, griddle, ladder, meddle, muddle, nodding, oddball, oddly, odds, paddock, paddle, pudding, puddle, riddle, saddle, shredding, sudden, swaddle, toddler, trodden, wedding

"dd" represents the /d/ + /d/ sounds

When the "dd" letter combination is **divided** into two syllables, the first letter "d" represents the /d/ sound and the second letter "d" also represents the /d/ sound, as in the word granddad.

Word Box	granddad, granddaughter, headdress, midday

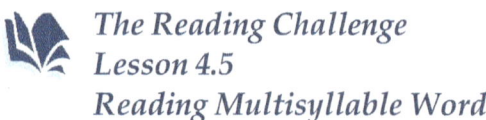

The Reading Challenge
Lesson 4.5
Reading Multisyllable Words

You can read a long word by dividing it into small parts called syllables. Each syllable has <u>one</u> <u>vowel</u> <u>sound</u> and usually one or more consonant sounds.

Three Ways to Divide Words into Syllables

1. A closed syllable ends with a consonant. When a closed syllable has one vowel, it usually has a short vowel.
   Example: discuss - dis + cuss

   When a closed syllable has two vowels, the first vowel is usually a long vowel while the second vowel is silent.
   Example: deeply - deep + ly

2. An open syllable ends with a vowel. The vowel at the end of the syllable is usually a long vowel.
   Example: debug - de + bug

3. The "vowel + consonant + e" syllable is at the end of a word. The first vowel in this syllable pattern is usually a long vowel while the final "e" is silent.
   Example: debate - de + bate

Multisyllable Word Lists

2 syllable words	3 syllable words	4 syllable words
daisy	dangerous	declaration
damage	decimal	dedication
damper	demanding	delivery
dancing	dentistry	democracy
danger	diamond	denotation
debate	diminish	destination
decal	diploma	development
dreaming	disconnect	dictionary
dressy	donations	discovery
drinking	downwardly	disposable
drying	dreadfulness	disappointment
dual	duplicate	diversity
dumping	dynamic	dormitory
dwelling	dynasty	duplicity

Lesson 4.6
Reading Proper and Common Nouns and Adjectives
Capitalization Rules

Words are written with uppercase and/or lowercase letters. Proper nouns and proper adjectives begin with uppercase letters. Common nouns and common adjectives begin with lowercase letters.

A proper noun is a word that names a specific person, place, thing or concept.

A common noun is a word that names a general person, place, thing or concept.

	Proper Noun	Common Noun
Person	Dad (when used as a name)	dad (not when used as a name)
Place	Denmark	dorm
Thing	Danish	diamond
Concept		determination

A proper adjective is a word that describes a specific person, place, thing or concept.

A common adjective is a word that describes a general person, place, thing or concept.

Proper Adjective:	Common Adjective:
Person: Danish citizens Thing: Dutch language	Person: delightful children Thing: delicious donuts

Capitalization Rules

Uppercase Letter – "D"

- The first letter of a word that begins a sentence is capitalized.

- The first letter of a word that names a specific person, place, thing or concept is capitalized.

- The first letter of a person's title is capitalized.

- The first letter of each word in a title or subtitle is capitalized.

- As a pronoun, the letter "I" is capitalized.

✎ Note: Lowercase letters are generally used for all other words.

Lowercase Letter – "d"

- The first letter of a word that <u>does</u> <u>not</u> name a specific person, place, thing or concept is written with a lowercase letter.

- The first letter of a word that <u>does</u> <u>not</u> begin a sentence is written with a lowercase letter.

- All letters within and at the end of words are written with lowercase letters.

Reading Check Point
Assignment: Read the sentences.

1. My duplex is next to Denny's Diner.
2. Last December, I drove to Delaware.
3. The diagram was drawn by the doctor.
4. Dr. Dan Douglas has a degree in dentistry.
5. Dr. Dennis lives in Copenhagen, Denmark.

The Letter "d" at a Glance		
Letter	Sounds	Anchor Words
"d"	/d/	dog
"d"	/j/	schedule
"d"	/t/	walked
"d"	silent "d"	judge

Unit D
Lesson 4.6

E/e

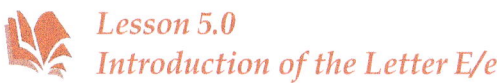

Lesson 5.0
Introduction of the Letter E/e

The letter "e" is a vowel. It is the 5th letter in the Roman alphabet of the English language. Letters are written as uppercase and lowercase letters.

	Uppercase Letter	Lowercase Letter
Print	E	e
Cursive	$\mathcal{E}$	e

Lesson 5.1
Reading Words with the Letter E/e

The letter "e" is pronounced in <u>fourteen</u> different ways.
- It represents the short vowel /ĕ/ sound, as in the word <u>egg</u>.
- It represents the long vowel /ē/ sound, as in the word <u>me</u>.
- It represents the schwa vowel /ə/ sound, as in the word <u>item</u>.
- It represents the long vowel /ā/ sound, as in the word <u>beta</u>.
- It represents the short vowel /ĭ/ sound, as in the word <u>pretty</u>.
- It represents the long vowel /yōō/ sound, as in the word <u>few</u>.
- It represents the vowel /û/ sound, as in the word <u>diversion</u>.
- It represents the vowel /ōō/ sound, as in the word <u>screw</u>.
- It represents the vowel /ä/ sound, as in the word <u>genre</u>.
- It represents the vowel /î/ sound, as in the word <u>peer</u>.
- It represents the vowel /â/ sound, as in the word <u>where</u>.
- It represents the long vowel /ō/ sound, as in the word <u>sew</u>.
- It represents the /y/+/ĕ/ sounds, as in the word <u>vignette</u>.
- It represents the short vowel /ŏ/ sound, as in the word <u>ensemble</u>.
- At times it is silent, as in the word <u>great</u>.

High Frequency, One Syllable Letter "e" Words

Short vowel words: bed, bent, bet, den, egg, fed, fence, gem, get, hen, jet, leg, let, men, met, neck, pen, red, rent, set, ten, vet, yet, wet

Long vowel words: beat, bee, beef, cheese, deal, deep, each, east, eat, fee, feel, feet, free, green, keep, leaf, sea, see, street, tea, these, wheat

Learn To Read English Textbook

Lesson 5.2
Reading Words with the Short Vowel "e" Sound

"e" represents the short vowel /ĕ/ sound

At the beginning of a word, the letter "e" usually represents the short vowel /ĕ/ sound, as in the word egg.

When a consonant comes before and after the letter "e," it usually represents the short vowel /ĕ/ sound, as in the words bed and press.

Beginning	Within	End
/ĕ/	/ĕ/	/ĕ/
egg	bed	

✎ Note: At the end of a word, the letter "e" does not represent the short vowel /ĕ/ sound.

✤ **Short Vowel "e" Word Families**

"eck" - "e" represents the short vowel /ĕ/ sound

The vowel "e" in the "eck" word family represents the short vowel /ĕ/ sound, as in the word neck.

Word Box	beck, check, deck, neck, peck, speck, wreck
	Multisyllable Words:
	paycheck, shipwreck, turtleneck

"ed" - "e" represents the short vowel /ĕ/ sound

The vowel "e" in the "ed" word family represents the short vowel /ĕ/ sound, as in the word wed.

Word Box	bed, bled, bred, fed, fled, Fred, led, red, sled, sped, Ted, wed

Word Box	bedlam, bedroom, educate, educating, federal, federate, federation, ledge, medical, pedal, peddle, pedicure, redwood, sediment, sledding, wedding

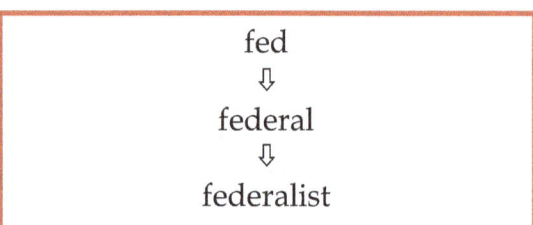

"edge" - "e" represents the short vowel /ĕ/ sound

The first vowel "e" in the "edge" word family represents the short vowel /ĕ/ sound, as in the word <u>ledge</u>.

Word Box	dredge, edge, fledge, hedge, ledge, pledge, sedge, sledge, wedge

"eg" - "e" represents the short vowel /ĕ/ sound

The vowel "e" in the "eg" word family represents the short vowel /ĕ/ sound, as in the word <u>nutmeg</u>.

Word Box	beg, keg, leg, Meg, peg

Word Box	legacy, legend, legging, leghorn, legible, legislate, legwork, mega, megabit, pregnancy, pregnant, regimen, register, regular, segment, segregate, segue

"ell" - "e" represents the short vowel /ĕ/ sound

The vowel "e" in the "ell" word family represents the short vowel /ĕ/ sound, as in the word <u>cell</u>.

Word Box	bell, cell, dell, dwell, fell, sell, shell, smell, spell, swell, tell, well, yell *Multisyllable Words:* doorbell, eggshell, farewell, foretell, indwell, inkwell, misspell, nutshell, retell, seashell, stairwell

"elt" - "e" represents the short vowel /ĕ/ sound

The vowel "e" in the "elt" word family represents the short vowel /ĕ/ sound, as in the word <u>melt</u>.

Word Box	belt, Celt, dwelt, felt, knelt, melt, pelt *Multisyllable Words:* heartfelt, indwelt, Roosevelt, snowmelt, Sunbelt

"em" - "e" represents the short vowel /ĕ/ sound

The vowel "e" in the "em" word family represents the short vowel /ĕ/ sound, as in the word <u>hem</u>.

Word Box	gem, hem, stem, them

Unit E
Lesson 5.2

"en" - "e" represents the short vowel /ĕ/ sound

The vowel "e" in the "en" word family represents the short vowel /ĕ/ sound, as in the word <u>men</u>.

Word Box	Ben, den, hen, Ken, men, pen, ten, then, when, wren, yen

"end" - "e" represents the short vowel /ĕ/ sound

The vowel "e" in the "end" word family represents the short vowel /ĕ/ sound, as in the word <u>lend</u>.

Word Box	bend, blend, end, fend, lend, mend, rend, send, spend, tend, trend, wend
	Multisyllable Words:
	amend, append, attend, commend, comprehend, depend, expend, extend, intend, offend, pretend, recommend, stipend, subtend, suspend

Reading Multisyllable Words

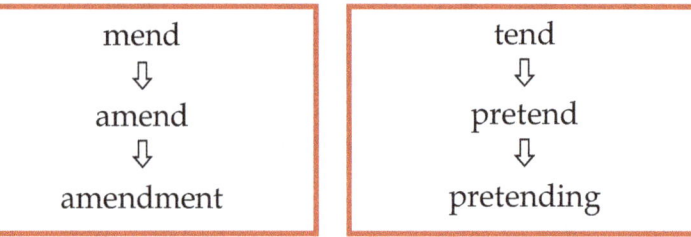

"ent" - "e" represents the short vowel /ĕ/ sound

The vowel "e" in the "ent" word family represents the short vowel /ĕ/ sound, as in the word <u>dent</u>.

Word Box	bent, Brent, cent, dent, lent, pent, rent, scent, sent, spent, tent, vent, went
	Multisyllable Words:
	accident, agent, cement, comment, consent, content, event, indent, invent, prevent, recent, relent, repent, resent

Reading Multisyllable Words

"esh" - "e" represents the short vowel /ĕ/ sound

The vowel "e" in the "esh" word family represents the short vowel /ĕ/ sound, as in the word refresh.

Word Box	flesh, fresh, mesh, thresh

"ess" - "e" represents the short vowel /ĕ/ sound

The vowel "e" in the "ess" word family can represent the short vowel /ĕ/ sound, as in the word mess.

Word Box	Bess, bless, chess, cress, dress, fess, guess, Jess, less, mess, press, stress, Tess access, address, compress, depress, excess, nevertheless, success, oppress

"ess" - "e" represents the short vowel /ĭ/ sound

The vowel "e" in the "ess" word family can represent the short vowel /ĭ/ sound, as in the word endless.

Word Box	actress, brightness, congress, endless, eyewitness, faceless, fadeless, fitness, mattress, regardless, seamstress, speechless, weightless, wilderness, witness

Reading Multisyllable Words

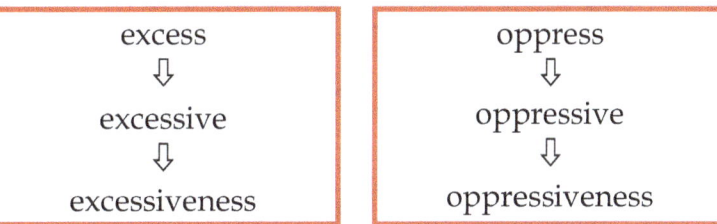

"est" - "e" represents the short vowel /ĕ/ sound

The vowel "e" in the "est" word family represents the short vowel /ĕ/ sound, as in the word rest.

Word Box	best, chest, crest, jest, nest, pest, quest, rest, test, vest, west, zest

Reading Multisyllable Words

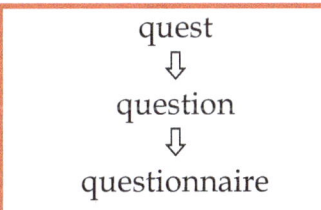

quest ⇩ question ⇩ questionnaire

zest ⇩ zestful ⇩ zestfully

✤ *Reading Words with the "et" Letter Combination*

In the "et" letter combination, the letter "e" is pronounced in <u>three</u> different ways.
- It represents the short vowel /ĕ/ sound, as in the word <u>set</u>.
- It represents the short vowel /ĭ/ sound, as in the word <u>ticket</u>.
- It represents the long vowel /ā/ sound, as in the word <u>buffet</u>.

"et" represents the short vowel /ĕ/ + /t/ sounds

When the "et" letter combination is at the end of a one syllable word, the letter "e" represents the short vowel /ĕ/ sound and the letter "t" represents the /t/ sound, as in the word <u>set</u>.

Word Box	bet, get, jet, let, met, net, pet, set, vet, wet, yet

"et" represents the short vowel /ĭ/ + /t/ sounds

When the "et" letter combination is at the end of a multisyllable word, the letter "e" can represent the short vowel /ĭ/ sound and the letter "t" represents the /t/ sound, as in the word <u>ticket</u>.

Word Box	anklet, basket, blanket, booklet, bucket, bullet, cabinet, carpet, casket, closet, couplet, covet, cricket, docket, doublet, driblet, droplet, facet, fidget, goblet, market, nugget, planet, pocket, secret, thicket, trumpet, velvet, violet

"et" represents the long vowel /ā/ sound + silent "t"

When the "et" letter combination is at the end of a multisyllable word, the letter "e" can represent the long vowel /ā/ sound while the letter "t" is silent, as in the word <u>buffet</u>.

Word Box	ballet, buffet, cachet, crochet, filet, gourmet, sorbet, valet

"et" represents the long vowel /ā/ + /t/ sounds

When the "et" letter combination is within a word, the letter "e" can represent the long vowel /ā/ sound and the letter "t" represents the /t/ sound, as in the words <u>beta</u> and <u>betatron</u>.

Reading Check Point
Assignment: Read the sentences.

1. I have a ticket to the ballet.
2. The crickets are in the bucket.
3. The five-page booklet has crochet tips.
4. The vet tells Shelly how to care for her pets.
5. Brett read a dynamic account of Harriet Tubman.

Lesson 5.3
Reading Words with the Long Vowel "e" Sound

"e" represents the long vowel /ē/ sound

The letter "e" can represent the long vowel /ē/ sound, as in the word <u>eat</u>. A long vowel is pronounced by its letter name.

Beginning	Within	End
/ē/	/ē/	/ē/
eat	cheap	bee

✤ "e" + consonant + silent "e" word families

The long vowel /ē/ sound has four pattern variations: VCe, CVCe, CCVCe and CCCVCe. The VCe pattern is at the end of many long vowel words.

"vowel + consonant + silent e" patterns	Target Words
VCe	Eve
CVCe	Pete
CCVCe	theme
CCCVCe	scheme

"ede" - "e" represents the long vowel /ē/ sound

When the "e" + consonant + "e" pattern is at the end of a word, the first vowel "e" usually represents the long vowel /ē/ sound, the consonant represents its sound while the final vowel "e" is silent, as in the word <u>Swede</u>.

Word Box	Bede, cede, Mede, Swede *Multisyllable Words:* accede, centipede, concede, impede, intercede, millipede, precede, recede, secede, stampede, supersede

"eme" - "e" represents the long vowel /ē/ sound

When the "e" + consonant + "e" pattern is at the end of a word, the first vowel "e" usually represents the long vowel /ē/ sound, the consonant represents its sound while the final vowel "e" is silent, as in the word <u>supreme</u>.

Word Box	scheme, theme *Multisyllable Words:* academe, blaspheme, extreme, morpheme, phoneme, supreme

"ene" - "e" represents the long vowel /ē/ sound

When the "e" + consonant + "e" pattern is at the end of a word, the first vowel "e" usually represents the long vowel /ē/ sound, the consonant represents its sound while the final vowel "e" is silent, as in the words scene and gene.

Word Box	*Multisyllable Words:* benzene, carotene, convene, ethylene, gangrene, intervene, Irene, kerosene, obscene, reconvene, Pentene, scalene, serene, supervene

"ese" - "e" represents the long vowel /ē/ sound

When the "e" + consonant + "e" pattern is at the end of a word, the first vowel "e" usually represents the long vowel /ē/ sound, the consonant represents its sound while the final vowel "e" is silent, as in the words cheese and these.

Word Box	*Multisyllable Words:* Bengalese, Bhutanese, Burmese, Cantonese, Chinese, Congolese, diocese, Guyanese, Japanese, Lebanese, legalese, Maltese, manganese, Nepalese, obese, Portuguese, Senegalese, Sinhalese, Siamese, Sudanese, Taiwanese, Togolese, Vietnamese

"ete" - "e" represents the long vowel /ē/ sound

When the "e" + consonant + "e" pattern is at the end of a word, the first vowel "e" usually represents the long vowel /ē/ sound, the consonant represents its sound while the final vowel "e" is silent, as in the word Pete.

Word Box	*Multisyllable Words:* athlete, compete, complete, concrete, delete, deplete, discrete, excrete, incomplete, obsolete, replete, secrete

Bonus Lesson
Reading Words with the "age" Letter Combination

When the "age" letter combination is at the beginning of a word, the letter "e" is not silent.

In the "age" letter combination, the letter "e" is pronounced in three different ways.
- It represents the short vowel /ĭ/ sound, as in the word aged.
- It represents the schwa vowel /ə/ sound, as in the word agent.
- It represents the short vowel /ĕ/ sound, as in the word agenda.

"age" letter combination	Sounds
aged, agedly	/ā/ + /j/ + /ĭ/ sounds
agency, agent	/ā/ + /j/ + /ə/ sounds
agenda, agendas	/ə/ + /j/ + /ĕ/ sounds

Lesson 5.4
Reading Words with Letter "e" Vowel Pairs

When two vowels are **together** in a word or syllable, the first vowel usually represents the long vowel sound while the second vowel is silent.

"ea" represents the long vowel /ē/ sound + silent "a"

When the "ea" vowel combination is **together** in a word or syllable, the letter "e" usually represents the long vowel /ē/ sound while the letter "a" is silent, as in the word eat.

Word Box	bead, beat, cease, cheap, cheat, cream, deal, dream, each, east, eat, feast, grease, heal, heap, heat, heave, leach, lead, league, leaf, leak, lean, leap, least, leave, mean, meat, neat, read, sea, seal, seat, tea, teach, treat, zeal
	Multisyllable Words: beacon, creamer, decrease, defeat, disease, easy, feature, increase, leader, leaving, peacock, peanut, repeat, reason, revealing, season, speaker, teachers

"ea" represents the short vowel /ĕ/ sound + silent "a"

When the "ea" vowel combination is **together** in a word or syllable, the letter "e" can represent the short vowel /ĕ/ sound while the letter "a" is silent, as in the word head.

Word Box	bread, feather, head, header, health, healthy, heavier, heavy, instead, leather, meant, read, ready, spread, spreading, sweater, thread, wealth, wealthy

"ea" has a silent "e" + long vowel /ā/ sound

When the "ea" vowel combination is **together** in a word or syllable, the letter "e" can be silent while the letter "a" represents the long vowel /ā/ sound, as in the words break and great.

"ee" represents the long vowel /ē/ sound + silent "e"

When the "ee" vowel combination is **together** in a word or syllable, the first letter "e" usually represents the long vowel /ē/ sound while the second letter "e" is silent, as in the word feet.

Word Box	bee, breed, cheese, creep, deed, deem, deep, fee, feed, feel, feet, flee, fleet, free, greed, Greek, green, greet, heel, jeep, keep, keen, Lee, meet, need, peep, queen, reef, reel, screen, see, seed, seek, seem, seen, sheep, sheet, sleep, sleeps, speed, spleen, squeeze, steel, street, sweet, tee, three, tree, wheel
	Multisyllable Words: agree, between, coffee, esteem, freedom, freely, needle, proceed, redeem, referee, refugee, seeing, seeking, sleepy, speeding, succeed, teenager, toffee

✤ Reading Words with Letter "ei" Vowel Pair

"ei" represents the long vowel /ē/ sound + silent "i"

When the "ei" vowel combination is **together** in a word or syllable, the letter "e" can represent the long vowel /ē/ sound while the letter "i" is silent, as in the word ceiling.

Word Box	caffeine, ceiling, conceive, deceit, deceitful, deceive, deceiving, either, leisure, leisurely, neither, perceive, protein, receive, receiving, seize, seizure

"ei" has a silent "e" + long vowel /ā/ sound

When the "ei" vowel combination is **together** in a word or syllable, it can represent the long vowel /ā/ sound, as in the word eight.

Word Box	beige, Beijing, Beirut, deign, eighteen, eighty, freight, freighter, neighbor, reign, reindeer, surveillance, veil, vein, weigh, weight, weighty, unveil

"ei" has a silent "e" + long vowel /ī/ sound

When the "ei" vowel combination is **together** in a word or syllable, the letter "e" can be silent while the letter "i" represents the long vowel /ī/ sound, as in the words height and heighten.

✤ Reading Words with Letter "eo" Vowel Pair

"eo" represents the long vowel /ē/ sound + silent "o"

When the "eo" vowel combination is **together** in a word or syllable, the letter "e" can represent the long vowel /ē/ sound while the letter "o" is silent, as in the word people.

"eo" represents the short vowel /ĕ/ sound + silent "o"

When the "eo" vowel combination is **together** in a word or syllable, the letter "e" can represent the short vowel /ĕ/ sound while the letter "o" is silent, as in the words jeopardize and jeopardy.

"eo" represents the long vowel /ē/ + /ō/ sounds

When the "eo" vowel combination is **divided** into two syllables, the letter "e" can represent the long vowel /ē/ sound and the letter "o" represents the long vowel /ō/ sound, as in the words stereo and video.

✤ Reading Words with Letter "ie" Vowel Pair

"ie" has a silent "i" + long vowel /ē/ sound

When the "ie" vowel combination is **together** in a word or syllable, it can represent the long vowel /ē/ sound, as in the word cookies.

Word Box	babies, belief, believe, believing, berries, besiege, brief, brownie, chief, cities, outfield, parties, pennies, relief, siege, shield, shielding, thief, yielding

Lesson 5.5
Reading Words with the Final Letter "e"

"e" represents the long vowel /ē/ sound

When the letter "e" is at the end of a word, it can represent the long vowel /ē/ sound, as in the word me.

Word Box	acne, be, he, me, she, we

"e" represents the schwa vowel /ə/ sound

When the letter "e" is at the end of a word, it can represent the schwa vowel /ə/ sound, as in the words genre and the.

"e" represents the long vowel /ē/ sound

When the letter "e" is at the end of the first syllable, it can represent the long vowel /ē/ sound, as in the word hero.

Word Box	debar, decaffeinated, decelerate, department, detox, detrain, devitalize, preamble, preapproved, precept, precinct, preempt, preexist, prefix, react, reactor, reassure, rebate, rebirth, rebound, recap, region, secret, zero

"e" represents the short vowel /ĭ/ sound

When the letter "e" is at the end of the first syllable, it can represent the short vowel /ĭ/ sound, as in the word become.

Word Box	became, becloud, becoming, before, began, begin, behind, below, cement, depend, devise, devoted, prefer, prepare, prescribe, rebel, rebuff, rebuke, recalling, recant, records, recover, recruiting, refer, refresh, reverse, secure

"e" is silent

When the "vowel + consonant + e" pattern is at the end of a word, the final vowel "e" is silent, as in the word cake.

Word Box	ate, bone, brake, fine, have, hide, mice, note, pane, pine, pipe, plane, rate, rice, ripe, robe, rope, sale, site, slide, slope, snake, state, stone, there, tone, twice, use

Silent Letter "e" Cards

"ake"	"ete"	"ice"	"ope"	"ute"
make	complete	nice	hope	chute
rake	concrete	price	rope	flute
take	delete	slice	slope	mute

Learn To Read English Textbook

Lesson 5.6
Reading Letter "e" Words with the Schwa Vowel Sound

"e" represents the schwa vowel /ə/ sound

The vowel "e" can represent the schwa vowel /ə/ sound, as in the word <u>item</u>. The schwa vowel sounds like the short vowel /ŭ/ + /h/ sounds.

Schwa it!

Beginning	Within	End
/ə/	/ə/	/ə/
	item	the

Word Box	*Letter "e" within a word* ben<u>e</u>fit, calendar, cel<u>e</u>brate, cinema, elephant, enemy, peninsula, tel<u>e</u>phone *Final letter "e"* the, genre

"em" - "e" represents the schwa vowel /ə/ sound

At the end of a multisyllable word, the vowel "e" in the "em" word family can represent the schwa vowel /ə/ sound, as in the word <u>system</u>.

Word Box	anthem, Bethlehem, diadem, ecosystem, emblem, Harlem, item, mayhem, modem, poem, problem, system, tandem, theorem, totem

"en" - "e" represents the schwa vowel /ə/ sound

At the end of a multisyllable word, the vowel "e" in the "en" word family can represent the schwa vowel /ə/ sound, as in the word <u>chicken</u>.

Word Box	blacken, broken, children, chicken, chosen, dozen, estrogen, fasten, forgiven, happen, hydrogen, ibuprofen, mistaken, nitrogen, proven, quicken

"el" - "e" represents the schwa vowel /ə/ sound

At the end of a multisyllable word, the vowel "e" in the "el" word family can represent the schwa vowel /ə/ sound, as in the word <u>bagel</u>.

Word Box	angel, bagel, barrel, bowel, camel, easel, gavel, hazel, jewel, label, level, marvel, navel, novel, panel, pixel, revel, sorrel, tassel, towel, vowel

"er" - "e" represents the schwa vowel /ə/ sound

At the end of a multisyllable word, the vowel "e" in the "er" word family can represent the schwa vowel /ə/ sound, as in the word <u>fever</u>.

Word Box	after, baker, bigger, buffer, cover, enter, fiber, later, lower, marker, meter, never, offer, other, order, layer, liver, paper, power, river, tiger, water

Lesson 5.7
Reading Words with the "er" Letter Combination

In the "er" letter combination, the letter "e" is pronounced in six different ways.
- It represents the vowel /û/ sound, as in the word perks.
- It represents the short vowel /ĕ/ sound, as in the word peril.
- It represents the schwa vowel /ə/ sound, as in the word letter.
- It represents the vowel /î/ sound, as in the word superior.
- It represents the short vowel /ĭ/ sound, as in the word berate.
- It represents the vowel /â/ sound, as in the word where.

"e" + "r" sounds	Word Box
"er" represents the /û/ + /r/	certain, certainly, certification, certified, certify, cervix, clerk, ferment, germ, her, infer, infernal, inferno, infertile, merge, were
"er" represents the /ĕ/ + /r/	berry, beryl, cerebral, ceremony, ferry, ferret, perigee, peril, periscope, perish, perishable, peristalsis, peristyle, periwig, Perry
"er" represents the /ə/ + /r/	baker, driver, her, hotter, intercept, interval, lawyer, letter, number, offer, opera, packer, ponder, teacher, toaster, wider
"er" represents the /î/ + /r/	anterior, Bering Sea, cereal, exterior, feral, inferior, interior, period, periodic, periodical, posterior, superior, ulterior

"ever" represents the short vowel /ĕ/ + /v/ + /ə/ + /r/ sounds

When the "ever" letter combination is at the end of a word, the first letter "e" can represent the short vowel /ĕ/ sound, the letter "v" represents the /v/ sound and the letters "e" and "r" represent the schwa vowel /ə/ + /r/ sounds, as in the word never.

Word Box	clever, ever, forever, however, lever, never, sever, whatever, whenever, whoever, whomever

☞ Exception: fever – /ē/ + /v/ + /ə/ + /r/ sounds

"ere" represents the /î/ + /r/ sounds + silent "e"

When the "ere" letter combination is at the end of a word, it can represent the vowel /î/ + /r/ sounds + silent "e," as in the word here.

Word Box	adhere, atmosphere, biosphere, cashmere, hemisphere, interfere, mere, microsphere, persevere, revere, severe, sincere, sphere, troposphere

"ere" represents the /â/ + /r/ sounds + silent "e"

When the "ere" letter combination is at the end of a word, it can represent the vowel /â/ + /r/ sounds + silent "e," as in the word where.

Word Box	elsewhere, everywhere, nowhere, somewhere, there, therefore, where

Lesson 5.8
Reading Words with the "eu" and "ew" Letter Combinations

✥ "eu" Letter Combination

"eu" represents the long vowel /yōō/ sound

When the "eu" vowel combination is **together** in a word or syllable, it can represent the long vowel /yōō/ sound or /ōō/ sound, as in the word <u>maneuver</u>.

Word Box	eucalyptus, eugenics, Eugene, eulogize, eulogy, euphemism, euphoria, maneuver, neuter, neutral, neutron, therapeutic

"eu" represents the vowel /yŏŏ/ sound

When the "eu" vowel combination is **together** in a word or syllable, it can represent the vowel /yŏŏ/ sound, as in the word <u>Europe</u>.

Word Box	Eurasia, eureka, Euripides, euro, Eurocentric, Eurocurrency, Eurodollar, Europa, Europe, European, europium, Eurydice, neuron, neurosis, neurotic

✥ "ew" Letter Combination

"ew" represents the long vowel /ōō/ sound

When the "ew" letter combination is **together** in a word or syllable, it can represent the long vowel /ōō/ sound, as in the word <u>new</u>.

Word Box	blew, brew, cashew, chew, chewing, crew, dew, drew, grew, jewel, jewelry, knew, mildew, new, newly, newlywed, renew, screw, stew, threw, withdrew

"ew" represents the long vowel /yōō/ sound

When the "ew" letter combination is **together** in a word or syllable, it can represent the long vowel /yōō/ sound, as in the word <u>few</u>.

Word Box	curfew, dew, few, fewer, knew, mildew, nephew, new, newly, newlywed, renew, renewal, renewing, renews, stew, steward, stewardship

"ew" represents the long vowel /ō/ sound

When the "ew" letter combination is **together** in a word or syllable, it can represent the long vowel /ō/ sound, as in the words <u>sew</u>, <u>sewing</u> and <u>sewn</u>.

Reading Check Point
Assignment: Read the sentences.

1. The airplane flew directly over Europe.
2. Yes, Newton ate his slice of streusel cake.
3. My dog, Eugene, likes to chew old shoes.
4. The neutron does not have an electrical charge.
5. Matthew has strong views about that political issue.

Lesson 5.9
Reading Words with the "ey" Letter Combination

"ey" represents the long vowel /ē/ sound

When the "ey" letter combination is at the end of a word, the letter "e" can represent the long vowel /ē/ sound while the letter "y" is silent, as in the word <u>key</u>.

Word Box	alley, attorney, barley, chimney, donkey, honey, jersey, jockey, journey, key, kidney, medley, money, monkey, pricey, pulley, trolley, valley, volley

"ey" represents the long vowel /ā/ sound

When the "ey" letter combination is at the end of a word or syllable, it can represent the long vowel /ā/ sound, as in the word <u>they</u>.

Word Box	convey, conveyance, conveying, disobey, grey, greyhound, hey, heyday, obey, obeyed, obeying, prey, purvey, survey, surveyor, they, trey, whey

Reading Check Point
Assignment: Read the sentences.

1. Jeffery did not obey Audrey's rules.
2. Shirley cooks with fresh parsley and cheese.
3. It is difficult to climb out of the steep valley.
4. Sydney is eating kidney beans and rice for dinner.
5. My attorney deposits money into a bank account.

Bonus Lesson
Reading Words with the Vowel "e"

"e" represents the short vowel /ŏ/ sound

At the beginning of a word, the letter "e" can represent the short vowel /ŏ/ sound, as in the word <u>ensemble</u>.

Word Box	encore, en masse, ensemble, entente, entourage, entrée, entrepreneur

"e" represents the short vowel /ĭ/ sound

At the beginning of a word, the letter "e" can represent the short vowel /ĭ/ sound, as in the word <u>example</u>.

Word Box	eclipse, effect, efficient, eject, elective, electric, electron, eleven, elicit, eliminate, ellipse, elusive, elute, emancipate, emergency, emotion, England, English, equate, equation, equator, equip, equipment, errant, erupt, escape

Lesson 5.10
Reading Words with a Silent Letter "e"

"e" is silent

The vowel "e" can be silent, as in the word <u>forfeit</u>.

Word Box	feud, feudal, feudalism, forfeit, forfeiture, great, greater, greatest, greatly, greatness, height, heighten, heist, neutron, neutrons, yeoman, yeomanry

"e" is silent

The second vowel in a vowel pair is usually silent, as in the word <u>ties</u>.

Word Box	allied, argue, blue, cried, cries, die, does, dried, dries, flies, fries, goes, hue, lied, lies, pie, relied, relies, shoe, spied, spies, tie, toe, tried, tries, true, Tuesday

"ed" - "e" is silent

When the "ed" letter combination is at the end of a verb, the letter "e" can be silent, as in the word <u>saved</u>.

Word Box	absorbed, allowed, checked, circled, cleaned, clogged, confused, deplaned, deposed, fried, impaired, laughed, merged, named, prolonged, relaxed, refused, removed, saved, served, staged, towed, tried, washed, watched

"vowel + consonant + silent e"

When the "vowel + consonant + e" pattern is at the end of a word, the final vowel "e" is silent, as in the word <u>cake</u>.

Word Box	*"a" + consonant + silent "e"* ate, bake, base, cage, came, date, fade, game, lake, lane, late, pale, rake, snake *"e" + consonant + silent "e"* athlete, complete, concrete, delete, extreme, intercede, Pete, scene, supreme *"i" + consonant + silent "e"* bike, bite, fire, five, hide, hike, hive, kite, life, lime, mile, mine, pile, side, slide *"o" + consonant + silent "e"* bone, code, cone, hole, hose, mole, nose, note, poke, robe, role, rope, stone *"u" + consonant + silent "e"* brute, cube, cute, dude, duke, fluke, fume, huge, minute, mule, rule, tune *"y" + consonant + silent "e"* byte, enzyme, gigabyte, hype, megabyte, rhyme, style, terabyte, thyme, type

The Reading Challenge
Lesson 5.11
Reading Multisyllable Words

You can read a long word by dividing it into small parts called syllables. Each syllable has <u>one</u> <u>vowel</u> <u>sound</u> and usually one or more consonant sounds.

Three Ways to Divide Words into Syllables

1. A closed syllable ends with a consonant. When a closed syllable has one vowel, it usually has a short vowel.
   Example: bedbug - bed + bug

   When a closed syllable has two vowels, the first vowel is usually a long vowel while the second vowel is silent.
   Example: seedlings - seed + lings

2. An open syllable ends with a vowel. The vowel at the end of the syllable is usually a long vowel.
   Example: behind - be + hind

3. The "vowel + consonant + e" syllable is at the end of a word. The first vowel in this syllable pattern is usually a long vowel while the final "e" is silent.
   Example: stampede - stam + pede

Multisyllable Word Lists

2 syllable words	3 syllable words	4 syllable words
eardrum	edible	ecology
earful	elastic	ecosystem
earthly	elephant	educated
easel	eleven	elevator
eastward	emotions	embroidery
easy	endangered	emergency
eating	energy	emotional
eject	envelope	entertainer
elbow	ethical	engineering
elect	equipment	everlasting
elope	everything	environment
email	example	exacerbate
embark	excellence	experiment
embrace	exercise	explanation
emerge	excitement	evasively
every	expression	evolution

Lesson 5.12
Reading Proper and Common Nouns and Adjectives
Capitalization Rules

Words are written with uppercase and/or lowercase letters. Proper nouns and proper adjectives begin with uppercase letters. Common nouns and common adjectives begin with lowercase letters.

A **proper noun** is a word that names a specific person, place, thing or concept.

A **common noun** is a word that names a general person, place, thing or concept.

	Proper Noun	Common Noun
Person	Mr. Eastward	engineer
Place	England	eatery
Thing	Exxon Mobil	elephant
Concept		excitement

A **proper adjective** is a word that describes a specific person, place, thing or concept.

A **common adjective** is a word that describes a general person, place, thing or concept.

Proper Adjective:	Common Adjective:
Person: English citizen	Person: educational specialist
Thing: English tea	Thing: eagle eyes

Capitalization Rules

Uppercase Letter – "E"

- The first letter of the word that begins a sentence is capitalized.

- The first letter of the word that names a specific person, place, thing or concept is capitalized.

- The first letter of a person's title is capitalized.

- The first letter of each word in a title or subtitle is capitalized.

- As a pronoun, the letter "I" is capitalized.

✎ Note: Lowercase letters are generally used for all other words.

Lowercase Letter – "e"

- The first letter of a word that <u>does</u> <u>not</u> name a specific person, place, thing or concept is written with a lowercase letter.

- The first letter of a word that <u>does</u> <u>not</u> begin a sentence is written with a lowercase letter.

- All letters within and at the end of words are written with lowercase letters.

The Letter "e" at a Glance

Letter(s)	Sounds	Anchor Words
"e"	/ĕ/	egg
"e"	/ē/	me
"e"	/ə/	item
"ue"	/ā/	beta
"e"	/ĭ/	pretty
"ew"	/yo͞o/	few
"e"	/û/	diversion
"e"	/o͞o/	screw
"e"	/ä/	genre
"e"	/î/	peer
"e"	/ō/	sew
"e"	/â/	where
"e"	/ŏ/	ensemble
"e"	/y/+/ĕ/	vignette
"e"	silent "e"	great

Unit F

F/f

 Lesson 6.0
Introduction of the Letter F/f

The letter "f" is a consonant. It is the 6th letter in the Roman alphabet of the English language. Letters are written as uppercase and lowercase letters.

	Uppercase Letter	Lowercase Letter
Print	F	f
Cursive	𝓕	𝓯

 Lesson 6.1
Reading Words with the Letter F/f

The letter "f" is pronounced in <u>two</u> different ways.
- It represents the /f/ sound, as in the word <u>fan</u>.
- It represents the /v/ sound, only in the word <u>of</u>.
- At times it is silent, as in the word <u>coffee</u>.

High Frequency, One Syllable Letter "f" Words
face, fact, fall, false, fan, far, farm, fast, fat, fee, feel, few, field, fig, fight, fill, fire, firm, fish, fist, fit, five, fix, flag, flame, flesh, flip, flour, flow, flute, fly, food, fool, for, form, friend, from, front, frost, fruit, fund, fur, fuse

At the beginning, within and end of a word, the letter "f" represents the /f/ sound, as in the words <u>fox</u>, <u>often</u> and <u>leaf</u>.

Beginning	Within	End
/f/	/f/	/f/
false	afford	chef
family	before	leaf
flesh	office	myself
flush	suffer	proof
fruit	wafer	yourself

Learn To Read English Textbook

✤ *Reading Words with the Letter F/f*

Short Vowel Blending Table for the Letter F/f

/ă/ apple	/ĕ/ egg	/ĭ/ insect	/ŏ/ octopus	/ŭ/ up
f a t	f e ll	f i g	f o g	f u n
fa t	fe ll	fi g	fo g	fu n
fat	fell	fig	fog	fun

Long Vowel Blending Table for the Letter F/f

/ā/ ape	/ē/ eagle	/ī/ ice	/ō/ open	/yōō/ cube
f a c e	f e e t	f i r e	f o c u s	f u m e
fa ce	fee t	fi re	foc u s	fu me
face	feet	fire	focus	fume

Reading Check Point
Assignment: Read the sentences.

1. Fish cannot fly.
2. The fruit is very fresh.
3. Fred is my best friend.
4. The fox is a fast runner.
5. Fred said, "The frog is fat."

Letter "f" Parts of Speech Table

Nouns	Verbs	Adjectives
fabric	facilitate	fabulous
factory	faded	factual
family	failed	faithful
fence	farming	fearful
festival	fasten	festive
fever	feasting	fervent
fingerprint	featured	fictional
fixture	feeding	figurative
florist	finished	Finnish
footstep	fishing	flaky
fraction	fitting	flowery
function	flourished	foolish
funnel	forgiving	formative
furnace	freezing	frosty
furniture	fussing	futuristic

Lesson 6.2
Reading Words with the "fr" Letter Combination

"fr" represents the /f/ + /r/ sounds

In the "fr" letter combination, the letter "f" represents the /f/ sound and the letter "r" represents the /r/ sound, as in the word frog.

Short Vowel Blending Table for the "fr" Letter Combination

/ă/ apple	/ĕ/ egg	/ĭ/ insect	/ŏ/ octopus	/ŭ/ up
fr a t	fr e t	fr i ll	fr o g	fr um p
fra t	fre t	fri ll	fro g	fru mp
frat	fret	frill	frog	frump

Long Vowel Blending Table for the "fr" Letter Combination

/ā/ ape	/ē/ eagle	/ī/ ice	/ō/ open	/oō/ glue
fr a m e	fr ee z e	fr i ght	fr o z en	fr ui t
fra me	free ze	fri ght	fro ze n	frui t
frame	freeze	fright	frozen	fruit

Word Box	frail, fragment, frame, France, frank, free, freeze, French, fresh, Friday, friend, frill, frizz, frock, frog, from, front, frosty, frown, frozen, fruit, frustrated, fry

Letter "fr" Parts of Speech Table

Nouns	Verbs	Adjectives
fraction	freeload	fragile
fragment	freeze	frail
freckle	freezing	frank
freestyle	frighten	free
friends	frizzle	French
fruits	frozen	fresh

 Reading Check Point
Assignment: Read the sentences.

1. Frantz was born in France.
2. My friends are very funny.
3. I fried fish in a deep frying pan.
4. On Friday, I am traveling to Finland.
5. The fruits in the bowl are fresh and juicy.

Lesson 6.3
Reading Words with the "fl" and "fle" Letter Combinations

"fl" represents the /f/ + /l/ sounds

In the "fl" letter combination, the letter "f" represents the /f/ sound and the letter "l" represents the /l/ sound, as in the word <u>flag</u>.

Short Vowel Blending Table for the "fl" Letter Combination

/ă/ apple	/ĕ/ egg	/ĭ/ insect	/ŏ/ octopus	/ŭ/ up
fl a g	fl e sh	fl i p	fl o g	fl u ff
fla g	fle sh	fli p	flo g	flu ff
flag	flesh	flip	flog	fluff

Long Vowel Blending Table for the "fl" Letter Combination

/ā/ ape	/ē/ eagle	/ī/ ice	/ō/ open	/ōō/ glue
fl a r e	fl ee t	fl i gh t	fl o a t	fl u k e
fla re	flee t	fli ght	floa t	flu ke
flare	fleet	flight	float	fluke

Word Box	flag, flame, flat, flee, fleet, flesh, fling, flint, flip, flock, flog, flop, florist, floss, flossy, flounce, flounder, flour, flow, flower, fluff, fluid, fluke, flung, flush

"fle" represents the /f/ + /l/ + /ĕ/ sounds

When the "fle" letter combination is at the beginning or within a word, it can represent the /f/ + /l/ + /ĕ/ sounds, as in the word <u>flex</u>.

Word Box	circumflex, deflected, deflector, fleck, fledging, flesh, fleshly, flex, flexible, flexure, inflect, inflection, inflexible, reflect, reflection, reflector, reflex

"fle" represents the /f/ + /l/ + /ē/ sounds

When the "fle" letter combination is at the beginning of a word, it can represent the /f/ + /l/ + /ē/ sounds, as in the word <u>flee</u>.

Word Box	flea, fleas, flee, fleece, fleeced, fleecing, fleeing, fleet, fleeting, fleets

"fle" represents the /f/ + /ə/ + /l/ sounds + silent "e"

When the "fle" letter combination is at the end of a word, it represents the /f/ + /ə/ + /l/ sounds + silent "e," as in the word <u>raffle</u>.

Word Box	baffle, duffle, muffle, raffle, riffle, rifle, ruffle, scuffle, shuffle, sniffle, stifle, trifle, truffle, waffle

Lesson 6.4
Reading Words with the "ft," "lf" and "ff" Letter Combinations

"ft" represents the /f/ + /t/ sounds

In the "ft" letter combination, the letter "f" represents the /f/ sound and the letter "t" represents the /t/ sound, as in the word <u>craft</u>.

Short Vowel Blending Table for the "ft" Letter Combination

/ă/ apple	/ĕ/ egg	/ĭ/ insect	/ŏ/ octopus	/ŭ/ up
r a f t	l e f t	l i f t	l o f t	t u f t
ra f t	le f t	li f t	lo f t	tu f t
raft	left	lift	loft	tuft

Word Box	after, afterward, aircraft, airlift, aloft, cleft, craft, craftsmanship, draft, drift, fifteen, fifth, fifty, forklift, gift, graft, halftime, left, lift, loft, often, raft, shaft, shift, shifts, shoplift, sift, soft, softly, software, swift, theft, thrift, thrifty

"lf" represents the /l/ + /f/ sounds

In the "lf" letter combination, the letter "l" represents the /l/ sound and the letter "f" represents the /f/ sound, as in the word <u>golf</u>.

Word Box	bookshelf, elf, fulfill, fulfillment, golf, gulf, malformed, malfunction, myself, olfaction, olfactory, pelf, self, shelf, sulfate, sulfur, sulfuric, wolf, yourself

"ff" represents the /f/ sound + silent "f"

In the "ff" letter combination, the letter "f" represents the /f/ sound, as in the word <u>off</u>.

Word Box	affirm, affix, affluent, afford, bluff, buffalo, buffet, chiffon, cliff, coffee, differ, different, difficult, diffuse, effort, fluffy, jiffy, offer, puff, scoff, staff, stuff

Lesson 6.5
Reading Words with a Silent Letter "f"

"ff" represents the /f/ sound + silent "f"

In the "ff" letter combination, the first letter "f" represents the /f/ sound while the second letter "f" is silent, as in the word <u>cliff</u>.

Word Box	affiliates, buffalo, buffer, buffet, caffeine, cliff, daffodils, different, effect, effective, effort, graffiti, off, official, raffle, ruffle, staff, stiff, suffer, suffocate

Lesson 6.6
Reading Singular and Plural Forms of Words Ending in "-f" and "-fe"

When a singular word ends with "-f" or "-fe," the ending can change to "-ves" to make the word plural.

	Singular words ending in "-f" and "-fe"	Plural words ending in "-ves"

Word Box	calf
	half
	knife
	life
	loaf
	self: himself
	      herself
	      yourself
	shelf
	thief
	wife
		calves
		halves
		knives
		lives
		loaves
		selves: themselves
		      themselves
		      yourselves
		shelves
		thieves
		wives

When a singular word ends with "-f" or "-fe," the letter "-s" can be added to make the word plural.

	Singular words ending in "-f" and "-fe"	Plural words ending in "-s"
Word Box	roof dwarf safe	roofs dwarfs safes

Reading Check Point
Assignment: Read the sentences.

1. Wolves are dangerous animals.
2. The five wives have fancy dresses.
3. Elves are small, imaginary people.
4. During the flight, the boys sat by themselves.
5. The fans were placed on two wooden shelves.

Bonus Lesson
Exploring an Exception to the Letter "f"

The letter "f" represents the /v/ sound, only in the word <u>of</u>.

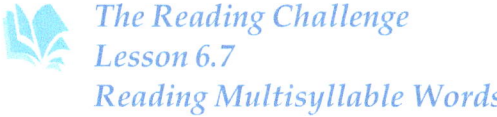

The Reading Challenge
Lesson 6.7
Reading Multisyllable Words

You can read a long word by dividing it into small parts called syllables. Each syllable has one vowel sound and usually one or more consonant sounds.

Three Ways to Divide Words into Syllables

1. A closed syllable ends with a consonant. When a closed syllable has one vowel, it usually has a short vowel.
   Example: finish - fin + ish

   When a closed syllable has two vowels, the first vowel is usually a long vowel while the second vowel is silent.
   Example: feasting - feast + ing

2. An open syllable ends with a vowel. The vowel at the end of the syllable is usually a long vowel.
   Example: female - fe + male

3. The "vowel + consonant + e" syllable is at the end of a word. The first vowel in this syllable pattern is usually a long vowel while the final "e" is silent.
   Example: fertile - fer + tile

Multisyllable Word Lists

2 syllable words	3 syllable words	4 syllable words
fable	factory	fabulously
fading	family	facility
famous	fanatic	facsimile
fencing	fatally	fashionable
ferry	fervently	favorable
fertile	fibula	favoritism
festive	fictitious	festivity
fiber	filament	fettuccine
figure	filtration	flagellation
filing	fingerprint	flamboyantly
finger	flabbergast	fluctuation
foothill	flatulent	fluoridation
forgive	focusing	foreseeable
fortress	foliage	formality
fracture	forensics	fortunately
future	functional	fragmentary

Learn To Read English Textbook

Lesson 6.8
Reading Proper and Common Nouns and Adjectives
Capitalization Rules

Words are written with uppercase and/or lowercase letters. Proper nouns and proper adjectives begin with uppercase letters. Common nouns and common adjectives begin with lowercase letters.

A **proper noun** is a word that names a specific person, place, thing or concept.

A **common noun** is a word that names a general person, place, thing or concept.

	Proper Noun	Common Noun
Person	Frederick	father
Place	Finland	farm
Thing	February	festival
Concept		freedom

A **proper adjective** is a word that describes a specific person, place, thing or concept.

A **common adjective** is a word that describes a general person, place, thing or concept.

Proper Adjective:	Common Adjective:
Person: French citizens Thing: Finnish language	Person: funny friends Thing: flat surface

Capitalization Rules

Uppercase Letter – "F"

- The first letter of a word that begins a sentence is capitalized.

- The first letter of a word that names a specific person, place, thing or concept is capitalized.

- The first letter of a person's title is capitalized.

- The first letter of each word in a title or subtitle is capitalized.

- As a pronoun, the letter "I" is capitalized.

✎ Note: Lowercase letters are generally used for all other words.

Lowercase Letter – "f"

- The first letter of a word that <u>does</u> <u>not</u> name a specific person, place, thing or concept is written with a lowercase letter.

- The first letter of a word that <u>does</u> <u>not</u> begin a sentence is written with a lowercase letter.

- All letters within and at the end of words are written with lowercase letters.

The Letter "f" at a Glance		
Letter	**Sounds**	**Anchor Words**
"f"	/f/	fan
"f"	/v/	of
"f"	silent "f"	coffee

Unit G

G/g

Lesson 7.0
Introduction of the Letter G/g

The letter "g" is a consonant. It is the 7th letter in the Roman alphabet of the English language. Letters are written as uppercase and lowercase letters.

	Uppercase Letter	Lowercase Letter
Print	G	g
Cursive	*G*	*g*

Lesson 7.1
Reading Words with the Hard Letter "g"

The letter "g" is pronounced in <u>four</u> different ways.
- It represents the /g/ sound, as in the word <u>gum</u>.
- It represents the /j/ sound, as in the word <u>gem</u>.
- It represents the /zh/ sound, as in the word <u>massage</u>.
- It represents the /f/ sound, as in the word <u>laugh</u>.
- At times it is silent, as in the word <u>light</u>.

High Frequency, One Syllable Letter "g" Words
gain, game, gang, gap, garb, gate, gem, gene, get, gift, girl, give, glance, globe, glow, glue, go, goal, goat, gold, golf, grade, grand, grant, grape, great, gross, ground, group, grow, grows, guest, guide

The letter "g" represents the hard "g" sound or the soft "g" sound.

The hard "g" represents <u>one</u> sound.	The soft "g" represents <u>two</u> sounds.
• /g/ sound	• /j/ sound • /zh/ sound

Learn To Read English Textbook

✦ Reading Words with the Hard Letter "g"

The hard "g" represents the /g/ sound. When the letter "g" is before the vowel "a," "o" or "u," it usually represents the /g/ sound, as in the words <u>gate</u>, <u>goat</u> and <u>gum</u>.

Short Vowel Blending Table for the Hard G/g

/ă/ apple	/ĕ/ egg	/ĭ/ insect	/ŏ/ octopus	/ŭ/ up
g a s			g o b	g u m
ga s			go b	gu m
gas			gob	gum

Long Vowel Blending Table for the Hard G/g

/ā/ ape	/ē/ eagle	/ī/ ice	/ō/ open	/ōō/ glue
g a t e			g o a t	gr ue l
ga t e			goa t	gr uel
gate			goat	gruel

"ga" - "g" represents the /g/ sound

In the "ga" letter combination, the letter "g" represents the /g/ sound, as in the word <u>mega</u>.

Word Box	congregation, extravagant, gab, gain, galaxy, game, gang, gap, gas, gash, gasp, gate, gave, gaze, investigate, legal, magazine, organize, regards, segregation

"go" - "g" represents the /g/ sound

In the "go" letter combination, the letter "g" represents the /g/ sound, as in the word <u>bingo</u>.

Word Box	category, flamingo, forgot, go, goal, goat, goes, gold, golf, gone, gong, good, goose, got, gown, negotiate, outgoing, pentagon, scapegoat, vigorous, wagon

"gu" - "g" represents the /g/ sound

In the "gu" letter combination, the letter "g" represents the /g/ sound, as in the word <u>guide</u>.

Word Box	ambiguous, configure, distinguish, extinguish, guard, guess, guest, guide, guilt, gulf, gulp, gum, gush, gust, guy, inauguration, language, regular, yogurt

"g" represents the /g/ sound

When the letter "g" is at the end of a word, it represents the /g/ sound, as in the word <u>bag</u>.

Lesson 7.2
Reading Words with the Soft Letter "g"

When the letter "g" is before the vowel "e," "i" or "y," it usually represents the /j/ sound, as in the words gel, gin and gym.

The soft "g" is pronounced in two different ways.
- It represents the /j/ sound, as in the word gem.
- It represents the /zh/ sound, as in the word regime.

Short Vowel Blending Table for the Soft G/g

/ă/ apple	/ĕ/ egg	/ĭ/ insect	/ŏ/ octopus	/ŭ/ up	"y" - /ĭ/ gym
	g e l	g i n			g y m
	ge l	gi n			gy m
	gel	gin			gym

Long Vowel Blending Table for the Soft G/g

/ā/ ape	/ē/ eagle	/ī/ ice	/ō/ open	/o͞o/ glue	"y" - /ī/ gyro
	g e n e	g i a n t			g y r o
	ge ne	gia n t			gy ro
	gene	giant			gyro

"ge" - "g" represents the /j/ sound

In the "ge" letter combination, the letter "g" represents the /j/ sound, as in the word gem.

Word Box	age, agency, agenda, contingency, digest, edge, emerge, garage, gem, general, genetics, genius, gentle, geometry, ingested, intelligent, judge, large, rage, stage

"gi" - "g" represents the /j/ sound

In the "gi" letter combination, the letter "g" represents the /j/ sound, as in the word gin.

Word Box	apologize, cardiologist, changing, digital, eligible, engine, fragile, giant, giblets, gigantic, gin, ginger, giraffe, imagine, logical, register, registry, vigil, vigilant

"gy" - "g" represents the /j/ sound

In the "gy" letter combination, the letter "g" represents the /j/ sound, as in the word gym.

Word Box	allergy, analogy, apology, biology, clergy, energy, gym, gymnastics, gypsum, gypsy, gyrate, ideology, liturgy, psychology, stingy, technology, trilogy, zoology

"dge" – "g" represents the /j/ sound

When the "dge" letter combination is at the end of a word, the letter "g" represents the /j/ sound while the letters "d" and "e" are silent, as in the word judge.

Word Box	badge, bridge, cartridge, dodge, edge, fudge, grudge, judge, ledge, lodge, nudge, pledge, porridge, prejudge, ridge, sedge, sledge, sludge, smudge, wedge

"ge" - "g" represents the /zh/ sound

In the "ge" letter combination, the letter "g" can represent the /zh/ sound, as in the word massage.

Word Box	beige, camouflage, collage, concierge, corsage, cortege, entourage, fuselage, garage, loge, massage, mirage, rouge, sabotage, triage

"ge" - "g" represents the /zh/ sound

In the "ge" letter combination, the letter "g" can represent the /zh/ sound, as in the word genre.

✦ Exceptions to the hard "g" and soft "g" rules

The letter "g" in the "ge" and "gi" letter combinations can represent the /g/ sound, as in the words get and girl.

Letter Combinations	Words	Sound
"ge"	gear geese	/g/
"gi"	gill give gift	/g/

✦ Reading Words with the "ger" Letter Combination

"ger" - "g" represents the /g/ sound

When the "ger" letter combination is at the end of a word, the letter "g" can represent the /g/ sound, as in the word burger.

Word Box	anger, bigger, blogger, chigger, defogger, digger, eager, finger, jogger, hamburger, linger, slugger, stagger, stronger, swagger, tiger, trigger

"ger" - "g" represents the /j/ sound

When the "ger" letter combination is at the end of a word, the letter "g" can represent the /j/ sound, as in the word passenger.

Word Box	astrologer, challenger, charger, danger, encourager, exchanger, ginger, larger, ledger, messenger, plunger, ranger, scavenger, teenager, villager

Lesson 7.3
Reading Words with the "gr" Letter Combination

"gr" represents the /g/ + /r/ sounds

In the "gr" letter combination, the letter "g" represents the /g/ sound and the letter "r" represents the /r/ sound, as in the word <u>grass</u>.

Short Vowel Blending Table for the "gr" Letter Combination

/ă/ apple	/ĕ/ egg	/ĭ/ insect	/ŏ/ octopus	/ŭ/ up
gr a b		gr i n		gr u b
gra b		gri n		gru b
grab		grin		grub

Long Vowel Blending Table for the "gr" Letter Combination

/ā/ ape	/ē/ eagle	/ī/ ice	/ō/ open	/o͞o/ glue
gr a pe	gr ee n	gr i p e	gr o w	gr ue l
gra pe	gree n	gri pe	gr ow	grue l
grape	green	gripe	grow	gruel

Letter "gr" Parts of Speech Table

Nouns	Verbs	Adjectives
grace	grabbed	gracious
grackle	grading	gradual
graduation	graduate	grand
grade	granulate	grandiose
graffiti	graphing	granular
grain	grasp	graphic
grammar	greet	greedy
grandstand	grieve	green
grease	grill	grizzly
groups	grinding	gross

 Reading Check Point
Assignment: Read the sentences.

1. Our English grammar class is great.
2. My grandchild is going to Grenada.
3. This cereal is made with whole grains.
4. The flowers are growing in the garden.
5. The new group of students will pass my class.

Lesson 7.4
Reading Words with the "gl" and "gle" Letter Combinations

"gl" represents the /g/ + /l/ sounds

In the "gl" letter combination, the letter "g" represents the /g/ sound and the letter "l" represents the /l/ sound, as in the word glue.

Short Vowel Blending Table for the "gl" Letter Combination

/ă/ apple	/ĕ/ egg	/ĭ/ insect	/ŏ/ octopus	/ŭ/ up
gl a ss	Gl e nn	gl i nt	gl o ss	gl u t
gla ss	Gle nn	gli nt	glo ss	glu t
glass	Glenn	glint	gloss	glut

Long Vowel Blending Table for the "gl" Letter Combination

/ā/ ape	/ē/ eagle	/ī/ ice	/ō/ open	/ōō/ glue
gl a z e	gl ea n	gl i d e	gl o b e	gl u e
gla ze	glea n	gli de	glo be	gl ue
glaze	glean	glide	globe	glue

"gle" represents the /g/ + /l/ + /ĕ/ sounds

When the "gle" letter combination is at the beginning or within a word, it can represent the /g/ + /l/ + /ĕ/ sounds, as in the words glen and neglectful.

"gle" represents the /g/ + /l/ + /ē/ sounds

When the "gle" letter combination is at the beginning or within a word, it can represent the /g/ + /l/ + /ē/ sounds, as in the words agleam and glean.

"gle" represents the /g/ + /ə/ + /l/ sounds + silent "e"

When the "gle" letter combination is at the end of a word, it represents the /g/ + /ə/ + /l/ sounds + silent "e," as in the word Google.

Word Box	angle, bangle, beagle, cringle, dangle, disentangle, eagle, entangle, giggle, goggle, jingle, jungle, mingle, rectangle, single, struggle, tangle, triangle

Reading Check Point
Assignment: Read the sentences.

1. Gloria has reading glasses.
2. I saw a glimpse of a gazelle.
3. Grace glued the box together.
4. When it's cold, I wear gloves.
5. Glenn's triangle has three equal angles.

Lesson 7.5
Reading Words with the "gh" Letter Combination

The "gh" letter combination is pronounced in two different ways.
- It represents the /g/ sound, as in the word ghetto.
- It represents the /f/ sound, as in the word laugh.
- At times it is silent, as in the word sigh.

"gh" represents /g/ sound as in the word ghetto	"gh" represents /f/ sound as in the word laugh	"gh" is silent as in the word sigh
Ghana gherkin ghost ghastly ghetto	cough enough laughter rough tough	sigh thigh thought through weigh

"gh" represents the /g/ sound + silent "h"

In the "gh" letter combination, the letter "g" can represent the /g/ sound while the letter "h" is silent, as in the word ghetto.

Word Box	Ghana, Ghanaian, ghastly, gherkin, ghetto, ghost, ghostly, ghoul, spaghetti

"gh" represents the /f/ sound

The "gh" letter combination can represent the /f/ sound, as in the word laugh.

Word Box	cough, coughed, coughing, coughs, enough, laugh, laughing, laughs, laughter, rough, roughly, tough, trough

"gh" is silent

The "gh" letter combination can be silent, as in the word sigh.

Word Box	although, breakthrough, dough, high, higher, neighborhood, slough, thigh, though, thoroughbred, thoroughly, through, throughout, weigh, weighed

"ght" - "gh" is silent

In the "ght" letter combination, the letters "g" and "h" are silent while the letter "t" represents the /t/ sound, as in the word light.

Word Box	bought, bright, caught, daughter, eight, fight, knight, light, might, night, ought, plight, right, sight, slightly, straight, taught, thought, tight, weight, weighty

Lesson 7.6
Reading Words with the "gn" Letter Combination

The "gn" letter combination is pronounced in two different ways.
- It represents the /g/ + /n/ sounds, as in the word ignite.
- It represents the /n/ sound, as in the word sign.

"gn" represents the /g/ + /n/ sounds

When the "gn" letter combination is **divided** into two syllables, the letter "g" represents the /g/ sound and the letter "n" represents the /n/ sound, as in the word ignite. The letter "g" is in one syllable and the letter "n" is in the other syllable.

Word Box	cognitive, diagnosed, dignify, dignitary, dignity, ignites, ignition, ignore, magnetic, magnify, pregnant, recognition, recognized, signal, signature

"gn" has a silent "g" + /n/ sound

When the "gn" letter combination is **together** in a word or syllable, the letter "g" is silent while the letter "n" represents the /n/ sound, as in the word sign.

Word Box	align, benign, champagne, cologne, design, designer, designing, foreign, foreigner, malign, realign, realigned, reign, resign, resigning, resigns, vignette

Letter "gn" Parts of Speech Table

Nouns	Verbs	Adjectives
magnet	designing	cognate
magnitude	diagnose	cognitive
ignition	dignify	diagnostic
pregnancy	dignified	diamagnetic
cognition	dignifying	igneous
diagnosis	ignite	ignoble
dignitary	ignited	ignorant
dignity	igniting	magnetic
recognition	ignore	magnificent
signal	recognize	pregnable
signature	recognized	recognizable
signet	recognizing	recognizant
vignette	signals	signatory
designer	signalize	signatories
willingness	signify	significant

Lesson 7.7
Reading Words with a Silent Letter "g"

"g" is silent
The letter "g" can be silent, as in the words <u>diaphragm</u> and <u>phlegm</u>.

"gg" represents the /g/ sound + silent "g"
When the "gg" letter combination is **together** in a syllable, the first letter "g" can represent the /g/ sound while the second letter "g" is silent, as in the word <u>goggle</u>.

Word Box	aggregate, aggressive, boggle, clogged, dagger, egg, giggle, goggle, hugged, jiggle, joggle, juggle, logged, nugget, plugged, plugging, sluggard, smuggle, snuggle, straggle, struggle, toboggan, toggle, tugged, wiggle, unplugged

"gg" represents the /j/ sound + silent "g"
When the "gg" letter combination is **together** in a syllable, the first letter "g" can represent the /j/ sound while the second letter "g" is silent, as in the word <u>suggest</u>.

Word Box	exaggerate, exaggeration, suggest, suggested, suggestion, suggestive, suggests

"gg" represents the /g/ + /j/ sounds
When the "gg" letter combination is **divided** into two syllables, the first letter "g" represents the /g/ sound and the second letter "g" represents the /j/ sound, as in the words <u>suggest</u> and <u>suggestive</u>.

"ght" - "gh" is silent
In the "ght" letter combination, the letters "g" and "h" are silent, as in the word <u>light</u>.

Word Box	bought, bright, caught, daughter, eight, fight, knight, light, might, night, ought, plight, right, sight, slightly, straight, taught, thought, tight, weight, weighty

"gn" has a silent "g" + /n/ sound
In the "gn" letter combination, the letter "g" can be silent, as in the word <u>sign</u>.

Word Box	align, aligning, alignment, assign, assigned, bologna, campaign, design, designer, foreign, gnash, gnat, gnaw, gnome, gnu, malign, reign, reigned

Reading Multisyllable Words

assign ⇩ assignment

design ⇩ designer

Learn To Read English Textbook

The Reading Challenge
Lesson 7.8
Reading Multisyllable Words

You can read a long word by dividing it into small parts called syllables. Each syllable has one vowel sound and usually one or more consonant sounds.

Three Ways to Divide Words into Syllables

1. A closed syllable ends with a consonant. When a closed syllable has one vowel, it usually has a short vowel.

   Example: ginger - gin + ger

   When a closed syllable has two vowels, the first vowel is usually a long vowel while the second vowel is silent.

   Example: goalie - goal + ie

2. An open syllable ends with a vowel. The vowel at the end of the syllable is usually a long vowel.

   Example: giant - gi + ant

3. The "vowel + consonant + e" syllable is at the end of a word. The first vowel in this syllable pattern is usually a long vowel while the final "e" is silent.

   Example: zygote - zy + gote

Multisyllable Word Lists

2 syllable words	3 syllable words	4 syllable words
gainful	galaxy	generation
gallant	gallbladder	generator
gallop	gallery	geranium
gamer	gasoline	glaciation
garage	gathering	gladiator
garbage	gazebo	glamorizer
garden	generous	gloriously
garland	genesis	glycogenic
ghetto	genetics	gradually
giblets	gentleman	graduation
gimmick	gingerly	grammatical
grateful	glorious	graphically
greatly	grasshopper	gravitation
greedy	gravity	Guatemala

Lesson 7.9
Reading Proper and Common Nouns and Adjectives
Capitalization Rules

Words are written with uppercase and/or lowercase letters. Proper nouns and proper adjectives begin with uppercase letters. Common nouns and common adjectives begin with lowercase letters.

A **proper noun** is a word that names a specific person, place, thing or concept.

A **common noun** is a word that names a general person, place, thing or concept.

	Proper Noun	Common Noun
Person	Grandmother (when used as a name)	grandmother (not when used as a name)
Place	Germany	ground
Thing	Google, LLC	goat
Concept	Gnosticism	generosity

A **proper adjective** is a word that describes a specific person, place, thing or concept.

A **common adjective** is a word that describes a general person, place, thing or concept.

Proper Adjective:	Common Adjective:
Person: German citizens Thing: Greek root words	Person: generous parents Thing: gigantic bag of chips

Capitalization Rules

Uppercase Letter – "G"

- The first letter of a word that begins a sentence is capitalized.

- The first letter of a word that names a specific person, place, thing or concept is capitalized.

- The first letter of a person's title is capitalized.

- The first letter of each word in a title or subtitle is capitalized.

- As a pronoun, the letter "I" is capitalized.

✎ Note: Lowercase letters are generally used for all other words.

Lowercase Letter – "g"

- The first letter of a word that <u>does</u> <u>not</u> name a specific person, place, thing or concept is written with a lowercase letter.

- The first letter of a word that <u>does</u> <u>not</u> begin a sentence is written with a lowercase letter.

- All letters within and at the end of words are written with lowercase letters.

The Letter "g" at a Glance		
Letter(s)	Sound	Anchor Words
"g"	/g/	gum
"g"	/j/	gem
"g"	/zh/	massage
"gh"	/f/	laugh
"g"	silent "g"	light

H/h

Lesson 8.0
Introduction of the Letter H/h

The letter "h" is a consonant. It is the 8th letter in the Roman alphabet of the English language. Letters are written as uppercase and lowercase letters.

	Uppercase Letter	Lowercase Letter
Print	H	h
Cursive	*H*	*h*

Lesson 8.1
Reading Words with the Letter H/h

The letter "h" is pronounced in one way.
- It represents the /h/ sound, as in the word hat.
- At times it is silent, as in the word cheetah.

High Frequency, One Syllable Letter "h" Words
had, hail, hair, half, hall, ham, hand, hang, hard, hat, hatch, have, he, head, heal, heart, heat, help, hen, her, here, hide, high, hike, hill, hit, hits, hold, hole, home, hop, hope, horn, horse, hose, hot, hut

At the beginning and within a word, the letter "h" represents the /h/ sound, as in the words hat and ahead.

Beginning	Within	End
/h/	/h/	/h/
hat	ahead	

Short Vowel Blending Table for the Letter H/h

/ă/ apple	/ĕ/ egg	/ĭ/ insect	/ŏ/ octopus	/ŭ/ up
h a ck	h e l p	h i t ch	h o g	h u g
ha ck	hel p	hi tch	ho g	hu g
hack	help	hitch	hog	hug

❖ Reading Words with the Letter H/h

Long Vowel Blending Table for the Letter H/h

/ā/ ape	/ē/ eagle	/ī/ ice	/ō/ open	/yōō/ cube
h ai l	h ee l	h i d e	h o l e	h u g e
hai l	hee l	hi de	ho le	hu ge
hail	heel	hide	hole	huge

Letter "h" Parts of Speech Table

Nouns	Verbs	Adjectives
hammer	hacked	hairy
hardship	hampered	half
headache	harbored	happy
headquarter	healed	harsh
helicopter	helped	healthy
highway	hesitates	helpful
historian	hiding	herbal
holiday	hiking	hidden
hopscotch	hitting	hilarious
hospital	holding	holistic
humanist	honored	homesick
hunger	hopping	honest
hustler	humbled	huge
hybrid	hurdled	husky
hypocrite	hyphenate	hygienic

  Reading Check Point
   Assignment: Read the sentences.

1. He could not lift the heavy hammer.
2. Howard placed the harness on his horse.
3. Harry's horse ate a hardy amount of hay.
4. A huge helicopter hovered over my house.
5. They played their harps in perfect harmony.

Lesson 8.2
Reading Words with the Letter "h" Combinations:
"ch," "gh," "ph," "rh," "sch," "sh," "th" and "wh"

Each letter in the letter "h" combination is pronounced quickly. The letters can blend together to make a distinct consonant sound. The chart shows sounds made by the letter "h" combinations.

Letter Combinations	Sounds	Anchor Words
"ch"	/ch/	chess, chicken
"ch"	/k/	chaos, character
"ch"	/sh/	brochure, machine
"ch"	silent "ch"	fuchsia, yacht
"gh"	/g/ + silent "h"	Ghana, ghetto
"gh"	/f/	enough, laugh
"gh" / "ght"	silent "gh"	sigh, sight
"ph"	/f/	elephant, telephone
"ph"	/p/ + /h/	uphill, haphazard
"rh"	/r/ + silent "h"	rhinestone, rhino
"rh"	/r/ + /h/	neighborhood, perhaps
"sch"	/s/ + /k/	school, scholar
"sch"	/sh/	schilling, schwa
"sh"	/sh/	fish, she, show
"th"	soft /th/	teeth, thin
"th"	hard /th/	brother, the
"th"	/t/ + silent "h"	Thailand, thyme
"th"	silent "th"	asthma, northeaster
"wh"	/hw/	whale, wheat
"wh"	/w/	whale, wheat
"wh"	silent "w" + /h/	who, wholesome

✤ Reading Words with the "shh" and "thh" Letter Combinations

"shh" represents the /sh/ + /h/ sounds

When the "shh" letter combination is **divided** into two syllables, the "sh" letter combination represents the /sh/ sound and the letter "h" represents the /h/ sound, as in the word fishhook.

"thh" represents the /th/ + /h/ sounds

When the "thh" letter combination is **divided** into two syllables, the "th" letter combination represents the /th/ sound and the letter "h" represents the /h/ sound, as in the word withhold.

Word Box	/sh/ + /h/ sounds: fishhook, fishhooks /th/ + /h/ sounds: bathhouse, withheld, withhold

Bonus Lesson
The Position of the Letter "h"

At the beginning of a word, "h" represents the /h/ sound	Within a word, "h" represents the /h/ sound	At the end of a word, "h" is silent in the "ah," "oh" and "uh" letter combinations
habitation	apprehension	cheetah
habitual	apprehensive	Gullah
habituate	beforehand	huh
hairspray	behavior	hurrah
Haitian	carbohydrate	matzoh
hamburger	dehumidify	menorah
handicap	dehydration	messiah
headlight	exhibition	mitzvah
helicopter	inhabitant	oh
highlights	inheritance	Oprah
histogram	policyholder	pharaoh
horizontal	prehistoric	pooh
hummingbird	prohibition	savannah
hydroelectric	stockholder	Yeshivah

✓ Reading Check Point
Assignment: Read the sentences.

1. Whitney is dancing in the savannah.
2. The child's tricycle has three wheels.
3. The chemist works in the science lab.
4. Everyone laughed at the funny jokes.
5. Student athletes play many competitive sports.

Lesson 8.3
Reading Words with a Silent Letter "h"

"h" is silent
The letter "h" can be silent, as in the word hour.

Word Box	annihilate, Bahrain, Bhutan, biorhythm, cirrhosis, Cohen, Delhi, diarrhea, exhibit, exhume, graham, Gullah, heir, hemor<u>r</u>hage, herb, honest, honestly, honor, hour, hourly, hurrah, John, khaki, rhinoceros, rhubarb, rhyme, rhyming, rhythm, silhouette, shep<u>h</u>erd, shep<u>h</u>erdess, spaghetti, vehement, vehicle, yeah

"h" is silent
The letter "h" can be silent in the following letter combinations: "ph," "th," "gh," "ch," "rh" and "wh."

Word Box	"ph" shepherd, shepherdess "th" Thai, Thailand, Thais, Thames, thyme "gh" aghast, ghastly, ghetto, ghost, fight, light, night, right, sigh, sight "ch" fuchsia, yacht, yachtsman, yachtsmen, yachtswoman, yachtswomen "rh" rhetoric, rheumatic, rhinestone, rhinoceros, rhubarb, rhyme, rhythm "wh" whale, whether, which, whine, whirl, whisker, whisper, white, whiz

"h" is silent
The letter "h" can be silent at the end of a word or syllable, as in the word cheetah.

Word Box	annihilate, bah, blah, cheetah, Fa<u>h</u>renheit, hah, hurrah, messiah, oh, ooh, pharaoh, pooh, Sarah, savannah, Shiloh, Torah, Utah, verandah, yeah

"exh" - "h" is silent
In the "exh" letter combination, the letter "h" is usually silent, as in the word exhibit.

Word Box	exhaust, exhaustion, exhaustive, exhibit, exhibition, exhibitor, exhilarate, exhilarating, exhort, exhortation, exhume, exhumed, exhuming, inexhaustible

☞ Exception: exhale - /h/ sound

Reading Check Point
Assignment: Read the sentences.

1. My sister, Hattie, is in her high chair.
2. Harvey dug a large hole behind the house.
3. Hope Hotel has a fabulous Thai restaurant.
4. Honestly, the sound of Hazel's harp is beautiful.
5. I have a flight from Bangkok, Thailand to Savannah, Georgia.

The Reading Challenge
Lesson 8.4
Reading Multisyllable Words

You can read a long word by dividing it into small parts called syllables. Each syllable has <u>one</u> <u>vowel</u> <u>sound</u> and usually one or more consonant sounds.

Three Ways to Divide Words into Syllables

1. A closed syllable ends with a consonant. When a closed syllable has one vowel, it usually has a short vowel.
   Example: habit - hab + bit

   When a closed syllable has two vowels, the first vowel is usually a long vowel while the second vowel is silent.
   Example: heater - heat + er

2. An open syllable ends with a vowel. The vowel at the end of the syllable is usually a long vowel.
   Example: hero - he + ro

3. The "vowel + consonant + e" syllable is at the end of a word. The first vowel in this syllable pattern is usually a long vowel while the final "e" is silent.
   Example: humanize - hu + man + ize

Multisyllable Word Lists

2 syllable words	3 syllable words	4 syllable words
habit	hairdresser	habitual
happen	hamburger	harmonica
happy	happily	hectometer
hazel	headquarters	helicopter
helping	holiday	heredity
hero	Honduras	homogenous
hidden	honeycomb	horizontal
himself	hospital	hospitalize
honors	however	hostility
hopping	hurricane	humidity
hugging	hydration	Hungarian
human	hydraulic	hysterical
humble	hyphenate	hypertension

Lesson 8.5
Reading Proper and Common Nouns and Adjectives
Capitalization Rules

Words are written with uppercase and/or lowercase letters. Proper nouns and proper adjectives begin with uppercase letters. Common nouns and common adjectives begin with lowercase letters.

A proper noun is a word that names a specific person, place, thing or concept.

A common noun is a word that names a general person, place, thing or concept.

	Proper Noun	Common Noun
Person	Hausa	husband
Place	Henry St.	house
Thing	Hausa	hat
Concept	Hinduism	humor

A proper adjective is a word that describes a specific person, place, thing or concept.

A common adjective is a word that describes a general person, place, thing or concept.

Proper Adjective:	Common Adjective:
Person: Hungarian citizens Thing: Hebrew language	Person: healthy patients Thing: heavy bag

Capitalization Rules

Uppercase Letter – "H"

- The first letter of a word that begins a sentence is capitalized.

- The first letter of a word that names a specific person, place, thing or concept is capitalized.

- The first letter of a person's title is capitalized.

- The first letter of each word in a title or subtitle is capitalized.

- As a pronoun, the letter "I" is capitalized.

✎ Note: Lowercase letters are generally used for all other words.

Lowercase Letter – "h"

- The first letter of a word that <u>does</u> <u>not</u> name a specific person, place, thing or concept is written with a lowercase letter.

- The first letter of a word that <u>does</u> <u>not</u> begin a sentence is written with a lowercase letter.

- All letters within and at the end of words are written with lowercase letters.

The Letter "h" at a Glance		
Letter	**Sound**	**Anchor Words**
"h"	/h/	hat
"h"	silent "h"	cheeta<u>h</u>

I/i

Lesson 9.0
Introduction of the Letter I/i

The letter "i" is a vowel. It is the 9th letter in the Roman alphabet of the English language. Letters are written as uppercase and lowercase letters.

	Uppercase Letter	Lowercase Letter
Print	I	i
Cursive	*I*	*i*

Lesson 9.1
Reading Words with the Letter I/i

The letter "i" is pronounced in <u>seven</u> different ways.
- It represents the short vowel /ĭ/ sound, as in the word <u>insect</u>.
- It represents the long vowel /ī/ sound, as in the word <u>bike</u>.
- It represents the schwa vowel /ə/ sound, as in the word <u>pencil</u>.
- It represents the long vowel /ē/ sound, as in the word <u>taxi</u>.
- It represents the vowel /û/ sound, as in the word <u>girl</u>.
- It represents the vowel /î/ sound, as in the word <u>nirvana</u>.
- It represents the short vowel /ă/ sound, as in the word <u>meringue</u>.
- At times it is silent, as in the word <u>maid</u>.

High Frequency, One Syllable Letter "i" Words
Short vowel words:
if, in, is, it, big, bin, bit, did, dig, dim, dip, drift, drill, flip, fish, fit, fix, flint, flip, hill, him, hit, kid, lid, lip, pin, pit, sit, tin, tip, win
Long vowel words:
bite, drive, kite, file, fine, hide, high, ice, lime, line, mile, mine, nine, pine, rice, ride, side, size, slice, tide, tile, time, wife, wise

Lesson 9.2
Reading Words with the Short Vowel "i" Sound

"i" represents the short vowel /ĭ/ sound

At the beginning of a word, the letter "i" usually represents the short vowel /ĭ/ sound, as in the word in.

When a consonant comes before and after the letter "i," it usually represents the short vowel /ĭ/ sound, as in the words big and dish.

Beginning	Within	End
/ĭ/	/ĭ/	/ĭ/
in	dish	

✎ Note: At the end of a word, the letter "i" does not represent the short vowel /ĭ/ sound.

✤ **Short Vowel "i" Word Families**

"ib" - "i" represents the short vowel /ĭ/ sound

The letter "i" in the "ib" word family represents the short vowel /ĭ/ sound, as in the word bib.

Word Box	bib, crib, fib, glib, nib, rib *Multisyllable Words:* Carib, sparerib

"ick" - "i" represents the short vowel /ĭ/ sound

The letter "i" in the "ick" word family represents the short vowel /ĭ/ sound, as in the word sick.

Word Box	brick, chick, click, flick, kick, lick, Nick, pick, prick, quick, Rick, sick, slick, stick, thick, tick, trick, wick *Multisyllable Words:* broomstick, candlestick, chopstick, drumstick, gimmick, handpick, homesick, lovesick, maverick, sidekick, toothpick, yardstick

Word Box	kicker, licker, licking, nickel, nickelodeon, nickname, picket, picking, pickle, picky, sickle, slicker, sticker, sticking, ticker, ticket, tickle, ticklish, wicker

"id" - "i" represents the short vowel /ĭ/ sound

The letter "i" in the "id" word family represents the short vowel /ĭ/ sound, as in the word did.

Word Box	bid, did, hid, grid, id, kid, lid, rid, slid, squid

"ift" - "i" represents the short vowel /ĭ/ sound

The letter "i" in the "ift" word family represents the short vowel /ĭ/ sound, as in the word lift.

Word Box	gift, lift, rift, sift, shift, swift, thrift

"ig" - "i" represents the short vowel /ĭ/ sound

The letter "i" in the "ig" word family represents the short vowel /ĭ/ sound, as in the word wig.

Word Box	big, brig, dig, fig, gig, grig, jig, pig, rig, swig, twig, wig, zig

"ill" - "i" represents the short vowel /ĭ/ sound

The letter "i" in the "ill" word family represents the short vowel /ĭ/ sound, as in the word fill.

Word Box	bill, chill, dill, drill, fill, frill, gill, grill, hill, ill, Jill, mill, pill, sill, skill, spill, still, thrill, till, will

"im" - "i" represents the short vowel /ĭ/ sound

The letter "i" in the "im" word family represents the short vowel /ĭ/ sound, as in the word dim.

Word Box	brim, dim, grim, him, Jim, Kim, prim, rim, skim, slim, swim, Tim, trim, whim

"imp" - "i" represents the short vowel /ĭ/ sound

The letter "i" in the "imp" word family represents the short vowel /ĭ/ sound, as in the word chimp.

Word Box	blimp, chimp, limp, primp, scrimp, shrimp, skimp

"in" - "i" represents the short vowel /ĭ/ sound

The letter "i" in the "in" word family represents the short vowel /ĭ/ sound, as in the word tin.

Word Box	bin, chin, din, fin, gin, grin, in, kin, pin, skin, spin, thin, tin, twin, win

Word Box	coincidence, incapable, incompetent, inconsistent, incumbent, indent, index, infant, infer, inflate, inner, mince, minister, ministry, ringer, window, windy

"ing" - "i" represents the short vowel /ĭ/ sound

The letter "i" in the "ing" word family represents the short vowel /ĭ/ sound, as in the word sing.

Word Box	Bing, bring, cling, ding, fling, king, Ming, ping, ring, sing, sling, spring sting, string, swing, thing, wing, wring, zing

"ink" - "i" represents the short vowel /ĭ/ sound

The letter "i" in the "ink" word family represents the short vowel /ĭ/ sound, as in the word sink.

Word Box	blink, brink, chink, clink, dink, drink, fink, ink, jink, kink, link, mink, pink, plink, prink, rink, shrink, sink, slink, stink, think, wink

"ip" - "i" represents the short vowel /ĭ/ sound

The letter "i" in the "ip" word family represents the short vowel /ĭ/ sound, as in the word zip.

Word Box	blip, chip, clip, dip, drip, flip, grip, hip, lip, nip, pip, rip, ship, sip, skip, slip, strip, tip, trip, whip, zip

"is" - "i" represents the short vowel /ĭ/ sound

The letter "i" in the "is" word family represents the short vowel /ĭ/ sound, as in the words his and this.

"it" - "i" represents the short vowel /ĭ/ sound

The letter "i" in the "it" word family represents the short vowel /ĭ/ sound, as in the word sit.

Word Box	bit, fit, flit, hit, it, kit, knit, lit, pit, quit, sit, skit, slit, spit, split, twit, wit

"iz" - "i" represents the short vowel /ĭ/ sound

The letter "i" in the "iz" word family represents the short vowel /ĭ/ sound, as in the words quiz and whiz.

Lesson 9.3
Reading Words with the Long Vowel "i" Sound

"i" represents the long vowel /ī/ sound

The letter "i" can represent the long vowel /ī/ sound, as in the word ice. A long vowel is pronounced by its letter name.

Beginning	Within	End
/ī/	/ī/	/ī/
ice	tie	hi

✤ **"i" + consonant + silent "e" word families**

The long vowel /ī/ sound has four pattern variations: VCe, CVCe, CCVCe and CCCVCe. The VCe pattern is at the end of many long vowel words.

"vowel + consonant + silent e" patterns	Target Words
VCe	ice
CVCe	bike
CCVCe	smile
CCCVCe	strike

"ice" - "i" represents the long vowel /ī/ sound

When the "i" + consonant + "e" pattern is at the end of a word, the vowel "i" usually represents the long vowel /ī/ sound, the consonant represents its sound while the vowel "e" is silent, as in the word mice.

Word Box	dice, ice, mice, nice, price, rice, slice, spice, splice, thrice, twice, vice

☞ Exception: service - /ĭ/ sound

"ide" - "i" represents the long vowel /ī/ sound

When the "i" + consonant + "e" pattern is at the end of a word, the vowel "i" usually represents the long vowel /ī/ sound, the consonant represents its sound while the vowel "e" is silent, as in the word side.

Word Box	bide, bride, glide, hide, pride, ride, side, slide, stride, tide, wide *Multisyllable Words:* aside, beside, collide, confide, decide, divide, inside, outside, provide, seaside

"ife" - "i" represents the long vowel /ī/ sound

When the "i" + consonant + "e" pattern is at the end of a word, the vowel "i" usually represents the long vowel /ī/ sound, the consonant represents its sound while the vowel "e" is silent, as in the word life.

Word Box	fife, knife, life, strife, wife

"ile" - "i" represents the long vowel /ī/ sound

When the "i" + consonant + "e" pattern is at the end of a word, the vowel "i" usually represents the long vowel /ī/ sound, the consonant represents its sound while the vowel "e" is silent, as in the word file.

Word Box	bile, file, mile, Nile, pile, smile, stile, tile, vile, while *Multisyllable Words:* agile, awhile, compile, fragile, hostile, juvenile, mobile, reptile, volatile

☞ Exceptions: agile, docile, fragile, hostile - /ī/ sound or /ə/ sound

"ime" - "i" represents the long vowel /ī/ sound

When the "i" + consonant + "e" pattern is at the end of a word, the vowel "i" usually represents the long vowel /ī/ sound, the consonant represents its sound while the vowel "e" is silent, as in the word sublime.

Word Box	chime, clime, crime, dime, grime, lime, mime, prime, slime, time, rime

"ine" - "i" represents the long vowel /ī/ sound

When the "i" + consonant + "e" pattern is at the end of a word, the vowel "i" usually represents the long vowel /ī/ sound, the consonant represents its sound while the vowel "e" is silent, as in the word pine.

Word Box	brine, chine, cline, dine, fine, line, mine, nine, pine, sine, shine, shrine, spine, swine, tine, trine, twine, vine, whine, wine

"ine" - "i" represents the long vowel /ē/ sound

When the "i" + consonant + "e" pattern is at the end of a word, the vowel "i" can represent the long vowel /ē/ sound, as in the words machine and magazine.

"ine" - "i" represents the short vowel /ĭ/ sound

When the "i" + consonant + "e" pattern is at the end of a word, the vowel "i" can represent the short vowel /ĭ/ sound, as in the words discipline and engine.

"ire" - "i" represents the long vowel /ī/ sound

When the "i" + consonant + "e" pattern is at the end of a word, the vowel "i" usually represents the long vowel /ī/ sound, the consonant represents its sound while the vowel "e" is silent, as in the word fire.

Word Box	fire, hire, mire, shire, spire, tire, wire *Multisyllable Words:* acquire, admire, aspire, attire, backfire, bonfire, campfire, conspire, desire, empire, entire, esquire, expire, hardwire, inspire, retire, sapphire, satire, umpire

"ite" - "i" represents the long vowel /ī/ sound

When the "i" + consonant + "e" pattern is at the end of a word, the vowel "i" usually represents the long vowel /ī/ sound, the consonant represents its sound while the vowel "e" is silent, as in the word kite.

Word Box	bite, cite, kite, lite, mite, quite, rite, site, spite, sprite, white, write *Multisyllable Words:* despite, dynamite, excite, ignite, incite, invite, polite, recite, satellite

☞ Exceptions: definite, hypocrite - /ĭ/ sound

"ive" - "i" represents the long vowel /ī/ sound

When the "i" + consonant + "e" pattern is at the end of a word, the vowel "i" usually represents the long vowel /ī/ sound, the consonant represents its sound while the vowel "e" is silent, as in the word live.

Word Box	dive, drive, five, live, strive *Multisyllable Words:* alive, arrive, archive, beehive, contrive, deprive, revive, survive

☞ Exceptions: defensive, exclusive, progressive - /ĭ/ sound

"ild" - "i" represents the long vowel /ī/ sound

In the "ild" letter combination, the letter "i" can represent the long vowel /ī/ sound, as in the words child and mild.

Word Box	childish, mild, milder, mildest, mildly, wild, wilder, wildest, wildly, wildness

☞ Exceptions: children, wilderness - /ĭ/ sound

"ind" - "i" represents the long vowel /ī/ sound

In the "ind" letter combination, the letter "i" can represent the long vowel /ī/ sound, as in the words find and kind.

"ight" - "i" represents the long vowel /ī/ sound

In the "ight" letter combination, the letter "i" represents the long vowel /ī/ sound, as in the word bright.

Word Box	blight, fight, flight, fright, knight, light, might, night, right, sight, slight, tight
	Multisyllable Words:
	alright, brighten, delight, flashlight, highlight, overnight, playwright, tonight

☞ Exception: straight - silent "i"

"eight" - "ei" represents the long vowel /ā/ sound

In the "eight" letter combination, the letters "e" and "i" represent the long vowel /ā/ sound, as in the word eight.

Word Box	eight, eighteen, eighteenth, eightieth, eighty, freight, freighter, weight, weightless, weightlessly, weightlessness, weightlifter, weightlifting, weighty

☞ Exception: height – /ī/ sound

Long Vowel "i" Cards

"ibe"	"ice"	"ide"
bribe	price	bride
scribe	slice	glide
tribe	twice	pride

"ipe"	"ite"	"ive"
stripe	sprite	drive
swipe	white	strive
tripe	write	thrive

  Reading Check Point
Assignment: Read the sentences.

1. The heat intensifies at lunchtime.
2. I have nine pencils inside my desk.
3. The intern puts raisins on his cereal.
4. I read an interesting book about pilgrims.
5. The speed limit is fifty-five miles per hour.

Lesson 9.4
Reading Words with Letter "i" Vowel Pairs

When two vowels are **together** in a word or syllable, the first vowel usually represents the long vowel sound while the second vowel is silent.

When two vowels are **divided** into two syllables, each vowel represents an individual sound.

"ia" represents the long vowel /ī/ sound

When the "ia" vowel combination is **together** in a word or syllable, the letter "i" represents the long vowel /ī/ sound while the letter "a" is silent, as in the word <u>dial</u>.

Word Box	dial, dialing, diaper, redial, trial

It is important to note that the words in the word box can be pronounced in two ways:
- long vowel /ī/ sound
- long vowel /ī/ + /ə/ sounds

Word Box	/ī/ sound	/ī/ + /ə/ sounds
dial	✓	✓
trial	✓	✓
diaper	✓	✓

"ia" represents the long vowel /ī/ + /ə/ sounds

When the "ia" vowel combination is **divided** into two syllables, the letter "i" represents the long vowel /ī/ sound while the vowel "a" can represent the schwa vowel /ə/ sound, as in the word <u>bias</u>.

Word Box	appliance, bias, compliance, defiant, denial, diabetes, diabetic, diabolical, diagram, dial, dialect, diamond, diaper, diary, diatom, giant, liability, liable, podiatry, psychiatrist, psychiatry, reliable, reliant, undeniable, viable

☞ Exception: dialysis - /ī/ + /ă/ sounds

"ie" represents the long vowel /ī/ sound

When the "ie" vowel combination is **together** in a word or syllable, the letter "i" can represent the long vowel /ī/ sound while the letter "e" is silent, as in the word <u>tie</u>.

Word Box	cried, cries, die, dried, dries, flies, fried, fries, hie, lie, lied, lies, pie, pied, pies, spied, spies, tie, tied, ties, tried, tries, vie, vied allied, applied, certified, classified, diversified, edified, fortified, identified, justified, modified, occupied, qualified, relied, satisfied, signified, supplied

"ie" has a silent "i" + long vowel /ē/ sound

When the "ie" vowel combination is **together** in a word or syllable, the letter "i" can be silent while the letter "e" can represent the long vowel /ē/ sound, as in the word cookies.

Word Box	babies, belief, believe, berries, brief, brownie, chief, cities, cookies, copies, families, field, grief, hobbies, niece, parties, pennies, relief, shield, thief, yield

"ie" represents the long vowel /ī/ + /ə/ sounds

When the "ie" vowel combination is **divided** into two syllables, the letter "i" can represent the long vowel /ī/ sound, and the letter "e" can represent the schwa vowel /ə/ sound, as in the word science.

Word Box	client, clientele, hierarchy, hieratic, hieroglyph, hieroglyphic, science, scientific, scientists

"ie" represents the long vowel /ī/ + /ĭ/ sounds

When the "ie" vowel combination is **divided** into two syllables, the letter "i" can represent the long vowel /ī/ sound and the letter "e" can represent the short vowel /ĭ/ sound, as in the words diet and quiet.

"ie" - "i" represents the long vowel /ē/ sound

In the "ier" and "iest" letter combinations, the letter "i" can represent the long vowel /ē/ sound, as in the words happier and happiest.

Word Box	"ier" represents long vowel /ē/ + /ə/ + /r/ sounds	"iest" represents long vowel /ē/ + /ĕ/ + /s/ + /t/ sounds
early	earlier	earliest
easy	easier	easiest
tiny	tinier	tiniest

"io" represents the /y/ + /ə/ sounds

When the "io" vowel combination is **together** in a word or syllable, it represents the /y/ + /ə/ sounds, as in the word union.

Word Box	communion, companion, dominion, grunion, junior, medallion, million, minion, octillion, onion, opinion, quintillion, rebellion, senior, trillion, union

"iu" represents the long vowel /ē/ + /ə/ sounds

When the "iu" vowel combination is **divided** into two syllables, the letter "i" represents the long vowel /ē/ sound, and the letter "u" represents the schwa vowel /ə/ sound, as in the word sodium.

Word Box	aquarium, consortium, delirium, emporium, medium, millennium, podium, potassium, premium, radium, radius, sodium, stadium, symposium, tedium

Lesson 9.5
Reading Words with the Final Letter "i"

The final letter "i" is pronounced in <u>two</u> different ways.
- It represents the long vowel /ī/ sound, as in the word <u>hi</u>.
- It represents the long vowel /ē/ sound, as in the word <u>taxi</u>.

"i" represents the long vowel /ī/ sound

When the letter "i" is at the end of a word or syllable, it can represent the long vowel /ī/ sound, as in the word <u>hi</u>.

Word Box	*Final letter "i"* alibi, alkali, alumni, anti, cacti, chi, fungi, hi, I, octopi, phi, stimuli, syllabi *Only letter "i" in the first syllable* icon, Idaho, idea, ideal, identical, identify, identity, Iris, Irish, iron, item *Letter "i" is at the end of the first syllable* bias, bicarbonate, biceps, bicycle, bifocal, bilateral, bilingual, binary, bio, biology, bipolar, Chinese, cider, citation, dilate, dilute, dinette, dinosaur, direct, diverge, divert, fiber, final, finalize, giant, liable, library, license, Siberia, silence, silent, sinus, siren, triangle, triceps, tricycle, trifle, vibrate, vibration

"i" represents the long vowel /ē/ sound

When the letter "i" is at the end of a multisyllable word, it can represent the long vowel /ē/ sound, as in the word <u>taxi</u>.

Word Box	bikini, broccoli, chili, confetti, deli, Fiji, graffiti, Haiti, Hindi, Jacuzzi, kiwi, macaroni, maxi, Miami, mini, multi, pepperoni, Pepsi, potpourri, Punjabi, quasi, roti, safari, salami, semi, sushi, Swahili, taxi, teriyaki, yogi, ziti, zucchini

"io" represents the long vowel /ē/ + /ō/ sounds

When the "io" vowel combination is **divided** into two syllables, the letter "i" represents the long vowel /ē/ sound and the letter "o" can represent the long vowel /ō/ sound, as in the words <u>cardio</u> and <u>radio</u>.

"io" represents the long vowel /ē/ + /ŏ/ sounds

When the "io" vowel combination is **divided** into two syllables, the letter "i" represents the long vowel /ē/ sound and the letter "o" can represent the short vowel /ŏ/ sound, as in the words <u>audiology</u> and <u>cardiology</u>.

"io" represents the long vowel /ē/ + /ə/ sounds

When the "io" vowel combination is **divided** into two syllables, the letter "i" represents the long vowel /ē/ sound and the letter "o" can represent the schwa vowel /ə/ sound, as in the word <u>cardiograph</u>.

Lesson 9.6
Reading Letter "i" Words with the Schwa Vowel Sound

"i" represents the schwa vowel /ə/ sound

The vowel "i" can represent the schwa vowel /ə/ sound, as in the word <u>cabinet</u>. The schwa vowel sounds like the /ŭ/ + /h/ sounds.

Schwa it!

Beginning	Within	End
/ə/	/ə/	/ə/
	cabinet	

When the letter "i" is within a word, it can represent the schwa vowel /ə/ sound, as in the word <u>animal</u>.

Word Box	admiral, animal, binocular, capillary, captivate, carnivore, civ<u>i</u>l, condiment, clarinet, crim<u>i</u>nal, crucible, imag<u>i</u>nation, laminate, nominal, nominee, nostril, optimum, orig<u>i</u>nal, pediment, pencil, pestilent, pollinate, sediment, sim<u>i</u>lar, sim<u>i</u>larity, sim<u>i</u>le, spec<u>i</u>fication, stab<u>i</u>lize, stamina, testimony

"ify" - "i" represents the schwa vowel /ə/ sound

In the "ify" letter combination, the letter "i" represents the schwa vowel /ə/ sound, as in the word <u>classify</u>.

Word Box	amplify, beautify, certify, clarify, classify, diversify, exemplify, falsify, fortify, glorify, identify, intensify, justify, modify, mystify, notify, pacify, purify

"ily" - "i" represents the schwa vowel /ə/ sound

In the "ily" letter combination, the letter "i" represents the schwa vowel /ə/ sound, as in the word <u>family</u>.

Word Box	cozily, easily, extraordinarily, happily, heavily, lazily, luckily, monetarily, nosily, primarily, readily, speedily, tastily, temporarily, verily, voluntarily

☞ Exceptions: lily – /ĭ/ sound; daily – silent "i"

Parts of Speech Table

Nouns	Verbs	Adjectives
animals	annihilate	civil
centipede	assimilate	classified
continent	calibrate	continental
decimal	cannibalize	criminal
experiment	captivate	intelligent
pencil	duplicate	pessimistic
president	participate	similar

Lesson 9.7
Reading Words with the "ir" Letter Combination

In the "ir" letter combination, the letter "i" is pronounced in <u>five</u> different ways.
- It represents the short vowel /ĭ/ sound, as in the word <u>mirror</u>.
- It represents the long vowel /ī/ sound, as in the word <u>virus</u>.
- It represents the vowel /û/ sound, as in the word <u>bird</u>.
- It represents the vowel /î/ sound, as in the word <u>nirvana</u>.
- It represents the schwa vowel /ə/ sound, as in the word <u>giraffe</u>.

"ir" represents the short vowel /ĭ/ + /r/ sounds

The "ir" letter combination can represent the short vowel /ĭ/ + /r/ sounds, as in the word <u>mirror</u>.

Word Box	irregular, irreplaceable, irreproachable, irresistible, irrespective, irresponsible, irreverence, irrigate, irrigation, irritate, miracle, mirage, mirror, spiritual

"ir" represents the long vowel /ī/ + /r/ sounds

The "ir" letter combination can represent the long vowel /ī/ + /r/ sounds, as in the word <u>virus</u>.

Word Box	acquire, admire, environment, irate, Ireland, iris, Irish, ironic, irony, irradiate, inspire, mire, pirate, retire, siren, viral, virology, virulent, virus, wire, wiry

"ir" represents the short vowel /ĭ/ + /r/ sounds or long vowel /ī/ + /r/ sounds

The "ir" letter combination can represent the short vowel /ĭ/ + /r/ sounds or the long vowel /ī/ + /r/ sounds, as in the words <u>direct</u> and <u>directory</u>.

"ir" represents the vowel /û/ + /r/ sounds

The "ir" letter combination can represent the vowel /û/ + /r/ sounds, as in the word <u>bird</u>.

Word Box	affirm, bird, birth, chirp, circle, circus, dirt, fir, firm, first, gird, girl, girth, irk, quirk, shirt, sir, skirt, squirm, stir, swirl, third, thirst, thirsty, virtual, virtue

"ir" represents the vowel /î/ + /r/ sounds

The "ir" letter combination can represent the vowel /î/ + /r/ sounds, as in the words <u>conspiracy</u>, <u>souvenir</u> and <u>nirvana</u>.

"ir" represents the schwa vowel /ə/ + /r/ sounds

The "ir" letter combination can represent the schwa vowel /ə/ + /r/ sounds, as in the word <u>giraffe</u>.

Word Box	aspirate, aspiration, aspirator, aspirin, circadian, circuitous, circumference, confirmation, giraffe, inspiration, inspirational, transpiration, virago, Virginia

Lesson 9.8
Reading Letter "i" Words with the Long Vowel /ē/ Sound

The letter "i" can represent the long vowel /ē/ sound, as in the words <u>chic</u> and <u>Belize</u>.

"i" represents the long vowel /ē/ sound

When the letter "i" is at the end of a word, it can represent the long vowel /ē/ sound, as in the word <u>ski</u>.

Word Box	bikini, broccoli, chili, Haiti, hibachi, Hindi, kiwi, macaroni, Malawi, Mali, maxi, Miami, mini, origami, pepperoni, Pepsi, safari, salami, scampi, ski, taxi

"io" represents the long vowel /ē/ + /ō/ sounds

When the "io" vowel combination is **divided** into two syllables, the letter "i" can represent the long vowel /ē/ sound and the letter "o" can represent the long vowel /ō/ sound, as in the word <u>trio</u>.

Word Box	audio, audiobook, barrio, capriccio, cardio, cardiovascular, cheerio, folio, Ontario, patio, pistachio, polio, portfolio, radio, ratio, ravioli, scenario, studio

Grammar Highlight

"i" represents the long vowel /ē/ sound

In the "ier" and "iest" letter combinations, the letter "i" represents the long vowel /ē/ sound, as in the words <u>earlier</u> and <u>earliest</u>.

Word Box	"ier" represents long vowel /ē/ + /ə/ + /r/ sounds comparative adjectives	"iest" represents long vowel /ē/ + /ĕ/ + /s/ + /t/ sounds superlative adjectives
cozy	cozier	coziest
early	earlier	earliest
easy	easier	easiest
merry	merrier	merriest
nosy	nosier	nosiest
tiny	tinier	tiniest

 Reading Check Point
Assignment: Read the sentences.

1. Lisa likes to drive her red car.
2. The trio will sing six new songs.
3. All the kids ate pizza for dinner.
4. My antique radio is on the patio.
5. Irene ate macaroni and shrimp scampi.

Lesson 9.9
Reading Words with a Silent Letter "i"

The vowel "i" can be silent, as in the words business and view.

"ie" has a silent "i" + long vowel /ē/ sound

When the "ie" vowel combination is **together** in a word or syllable, the letter "i" can be silent while the letter "e" represents the long vowel /ē/ sound, as in the word cookies.

Word Box	abilities, achieve, babies, belief, believe, berries, brief, brownie, chief, cities, field, grief, movie, niece, parties, pennies, relief, rotisserie, shield, thief, yield

☞ Exception: friend - /ĕ/ sound

"i" is silent

When the letter "i" is the second vowel in the vowel pair, it can be silent, as in the word grain.

Word Box	aide, afraid, aim, attain, bail, bait, daily, detail, either, heifer, Jamaica, nail, obtain, paid, pain, rail, receipt, sail, stain, straight, suit, trait, vain, wail, waist

Grammar Highlight

"ie" has a silent "i" + long vowel /ē/ sound

In the "ies" and "ied" letter combinations, the letter "i" can be silent, as in the words studies and studied.

Word Box	"ies" has a silent "i" + long vowel /ē/ + /z/ sounds	"ied" has a silent "i" + long vowel /ē/ + /d/ sounds
Present Tense Verbs	**3rd Person Singular Verbs**	**Past Tense Verbs**
carry	carries	carried
copy	copies	copied
hurry	hurries	hurried
marry	marries	married
tarry	tarries	tarried
worry	worries	worried

Silent Letter "i" at a Glance		
Letter	Sound	Anchor Words
"i"	silent "i"	grain
"i"	silent "i"	business

Learn To Read English Textbook

The Reading Challenge
Lesson 9.10
Reading Multisyllable Words

You can read a long word by dividing it into small parts called syllables. Each syllable has <u>one</u> <u>vowel</u> <u>sound</u> and usually one or more consonant sounds.

Three Ways to Divide Words into Syllables

1. A closed syllable ends with a consonant. When a closed syllable has one vowel, it usually has a short vowel.
   Example: finish - fin + ish

   When a closed syllable has two vowels, the first vowel is usually a long vowel while the second vowel is silent.
   Example: allied - al + lied

2. An open syllable ends with a vowel. The vowel at the end of the syllable is usually a long vowel.
   Example: private - pri + vate

3. The "vowel + consonant + e" syllable is at the end of a word. The first vowel in this syllable pattern is usually a long vowel while the final "e" is silent.
   Example: invite - in + vite

Multisyllable Word Lists

2 syllable words	3 syllable words	4 syllable words
illness	icicle	identical
impact	idealize	illegally
impress	influence	illustrator
index	illustrate	impediment
insane	imagine	impossible
inside	important	information
into	industry	intelligent
invade	insurance	intercessor
Irish	intellect	interior
iron	intercept	ironical
island	invited	irregular
issue	inundate	isolated
item	itemize	itinerant

Lesson 9.11
Reading Proper and Common Nouns and Adjectives
Capitalization Rules

Words are written with uppercase and/or lowercase letters. Proper nouns and proper adjectives begin with uppercase letters. Common nouns and common adjectives begin with lowercase letters.

A **proper noun** is a word that names a specific person, place, thing or concept.

A **common noun** is a word that names a general person, place, thing or concept.

	Proper Noun	Common Noun
Person	Inuit	inspector
Place	India	inside
Thing	Internet	igloo
Concept	Islam	innovation

A **proper adjective** is a word that describes a specific person, place, thing or concept.

A **common adjective** is a word that describes a general person, place, thing or concept.

Proper Adjective:	Common Adjective:
Person: Indian citizen Thing: Indonesian food	Person: intelligent student Thing: icy road

Capitalization Rules

Uppercase Letter – "I"

- The first letter of the word that begins a sentence is capitalized.

- The first letter of the word that names a specific person, place, thing or concept is capitalized.

- The first letter of a person's title is capitalized.

- The first letter of each word in a title or subtitle is capitalized.

- As a pronoun, the letter "I" is capitalized.

✐ Note: Lowercase letters are generally used for all other words.

Lowercase Letter – "i"

- The first letter of a word that <u>does</u> <u>not</u> name a specific person, place, thing or concept is written with a lowercase letter.

- The first letter of a word that <u>does</u> <u>not</u> begin a sentence is written with a lowercase letter.

- All letters within and at the end of words are written with lowercase letters.

The Letter "i" at a Glance		
Letter(s)	Sounds	Anchor Words
"i"	/ĭ/	insect
"i"	/ī/	bike
"i"	/ə/	pencil
"i"	/ē/	taxi
"i"	/û/	girl
"i"	/î/	nirvana
"i"	/ă/	meringue
"i"	silent "i"	maid

J/j

Lesson 10.0
Introduction of the Letter J/j

The letter "j" is a consonant. It is the 10th letter in the Roman alphabet of the English language. Letters are written as uppercase and lowercase letters.

	Uppercase Letter	Lowercase Letter
Print	J	j
Cursive	*J*	*j*

Lesson 10.1
Reading Words with the Letter J/j

The letter "j" is pronounced in three ways.
- It represents the /j/ sound, as in the word jet.
- It represents the /h/ sound, as in the word Navajo.
- It represents the /y/ sound, only in the word fjord.

High Frequency, One Syllable Letter "j" Words
jab, jack, jade, jail, jam, jar, jaw, jay, jazz, jeans, jeep, jeer, jest, jet, jib, jig, jive, job, jock, jog, join, joint, joist, joke, jot, joule, jounce, joust, jowl, joy, judge, judged, jug, jugs, juice, juke, jump, June, junk, just

At the beginning and within a word, the letter "j" represents the /j/ sound, as in the words jet and ajar.

Beginning	Within	End
/j/	/j/	/j/
jet	ajar	

Short Vowel Blending Table for the Letter J/j

/ă/ apple	/ĕ/ egg	/ĭ/ insect	/ŏ/ octopus	/ŭ/ up
j a m	j e t	j i g	j o b	j u g
ja m	je t	ji g	jo b	ju g
jam	jet	jig	job	jug

✤ *Reading Words with the Letter J/j*

Long Vowel Blending Table for the Letter J/j

/ā/ ape	/ē/ eagle	/ī/ ice	/ō/ open	/ōō/ glue
j a d e	j e e p	j i v e	j o k e	J u n e
ja de	jee p	ji ve	jo ke	Ju ne
jade	jeep	jive	joke	June

Letter "j" Parts of Speech Table

Nouns	Verbs	Adjectives
jab	jabbed	jade
jacket	jabbing	jagged
jade	jacketed	Jamaican
jail	jailed	Japanese
jalopy	jeopardize	jawed
jam	jingled	jawless
jeep	jingling	jazzy
jelly	jogging	jealous
jersey	joined	jellylike
job	joining	jeweled
jockey	joked	jobless
joint	joking	jocular
journal	jolting	joint
judge	jostle	jolly
juice	jotting	jovial
jumper	judged	joyful
junction	judging	joyous
jury	juggling	jubilant
justice	jumbled	juicy
justification	jumped	jumbo
juxtaposition	justify	jumpy

Unit J Lesson 10.1

Reading Check Point
Assignment: Read the sentences.

1. The jellybeans are in the jar.
2. Jordan's jacket is in the closet.
3. Jim is jumping in the jungle gym.
4. Joyce and Joel like to listen to jazz.
5. Jasmine and Joy ate jam and bread.

Learn To Read English Textbook

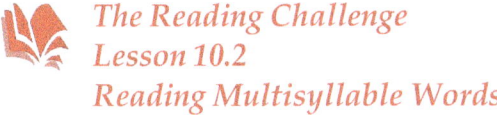

The Reading Challenge
Lesson 10.2
Reading Multisyllable Words

You can read a long word by dividing it into small parts called syllables. Each syllable has <u>one</u> <u>vowel</u> <u>sound</u> and usually one or more consonant sounds.

Three Ways to Divide Words into Syllables

1. A closed syllable ends with a consonant. When a closed syllable has one vowel, it usually has a short vowel.
   Example: jester - jes + ter

   When a closed syllable has two vowels, the first vowel is usually a long vowel while the second vowel is silent.
   Example: jailbird – jail + bird

2. An open syllable ends with a vowel. The vowel at the end of the syllable is usually a long vowel.
   Example: joey - jo + ey

3. The "vowel + consonant + e" syllable is at the end of a word. The first vowel in this syllable pattern is usually a long vowel while the final "e" is silent.
   Example: juxtapose - jux + ta + pose

Multisyllable Word Lists

2 syllable words	3 syllable words	4 syllable words
jacket	jackhammer	jacaranda
jargon	Jamaica	jalapeno
jaybird	jamboree	jambalaya
jealous	janitor	January
jelly	Japanese	jeremiad
jewel	jawbreaker	Jeremiah
journey	jealousy	jocundity
joyful	jellyfish	Johannesburg
juggle	jeopardize	journalistic
juicy	jewelry	jubilantly
July	joyfully	jubilation
jumbo	jubilant	juridical
jumper	juvenile	jurisdiction
jumping	Jupiter	jurisprudence
jungle	justify	juxtaposing

Lesson 10.3
Reading Proper and Common Nouns and Adjectives
Capitalization Rules

Words are written with uppercase and/or lowercase letters. Proper nouns and proper adjectives begin with uppercase letters. Common nouns and common adjectives begin with lowercase letters.

A **proper noun** is a word that names a specific person, place, thing or concept.

A **common noun** is a word that names a general person, place, thing or concept.

	Proper Noun	Common Noun
Person	Jimmy	janitor
Place	Jamaica	junior high school
Thing	January	jello
Concept	Judaism	joy

A **proper adjective** is a word that describes a specific person, place, thing or concept.

A **common adjective** is a word that describes a general person, place, thing or concept.

Proper Adjective:	Common Adjective:
Person: Japanese citizen	Person: jolly clown
Thing: Jeffersonian Era	Thing: junk food

Capitalization Rules

Uppercase Letter – "J"

- The first letter of a word that begins a sentence is capitalized.

- The first letter of a word that names a specific person, place, thing or concept is capitalized.

- The first letter of a person's title is capitalized.

- The first letter of each word in a title or subtitle is capitalized.

- As a pronoun, the letter "I" is capitalized.

? Note: Lowercase letters are generally used for all other words.

Lowercase Letter – "j"

- The first letter of a word that <u>does</u> <u>not</u> name a specific person, place, thing or concept is written with a lowercase letter.

- The first letter of a word that <u>does</u> <u>not</u> begin a sentence is written with a lowercase letter.

- All letters within and at the end of words are written with lowercase letters.

The Letter "j" at a Glance

Letter	Sound	Anchor Word
"j"	/j/	jet
"j"	silent "j"	

Unit K

K/k

Lesson 11.0
Introduction of the Letter K/k

The letter "k" is a consonant. It is the 11th letter in the Roman alphabet of the English language. Letters are written as uppercase and lowercase letters.

	Uppercase Letter	Lowercase Letter
Print	K	k
Cursive	𝒦	𝓀

Lesson 11.1
Reading Words with the Letter K/k

The letter "k" is pronounced in <u>one</u> way.
- It represents the /k/ sound, as in the word <u>king</u>.
- At times it is silent, as in the word <u>knee</u>.

High Frequency, One Syllable Letter "k" Words
kale, karts, keel, keen, keep, keg, kelp, ken, kept, ketch, key, keys, kick, kicks, kid, kids, kind, king, kiss, kit, knack, knew, knife, knight, knit, knits, knob, knobs, knock, knoll, knot, knots, know, known

At the beginning, within and end of a word, the letter "k" represents the /k/ sound, as in the words <u>kit</u>, <u>rocket</u> and <u>back</u>.

Beginning	Within	End
/k/	/k/	/k/
kale	baskets	back
keep	cracker	bookmark
ketchup	leakage	chipmunk
keyboard	pumpkin	gimmick
kidneys	spoken	midweek
knockout	sticker	nonstick
koalas	walking	unlock

❖ Reading Words with the Letter K/k

Short Vowel Blending Table for the Letter K/k

/ă/ apple	/ĕ/ egg	/ĭ/ insect	/ŏ/ octopus	/ŭ/ up
k a pp a	K e n	k i t	ko m chu b a	k u ng fu
ka pp a	Ke n	ki t	kom chu ba	ku ng fu
kappa	Ken	kit	komchuba	kung fu

Long Vowel Blending Table for the Letter K/k

/ā/ ape	/ē/ eagle	/ī/ ice	/ō/ open	/o͞o/ glue
K a t e	k ee n	k i te	k o sh er	K u w ai t
Ka te	kee n	ki te	kosh er	Ku wait
Kate	keen	kite	kosher	Kuwait

Letter "k" Parts of Speech Table

Nouns	Verbs	Adjectives
kale	keening	kaleidoscopic
kava	keep	kapok
kazoo	keeping	keen
keeper	keeps	kempt
kernel	kept	Kenyan
kerosene	keyed	kept
ketchup	kicked	khaki
keyboard	kicking	kinesthetic
keynote	kissed	kind
kickoff	kneeling	kinetic
kidney	knitting	kinky
kilometer	knocked	Korean
kingdom	knotted	kosher
kitchen	knows	knitted

Reading Check Point
Assignment: Read the sentences.

1. The king's knights are brave.
2. The kids are flying their kites.
3. Keanna enjoys singing karaoke.
4. Kathy and Kim are from Kuwait.
5. Kristen read a book about Helen Keller.

Lesson 11.2
Reading Words with the Letter "k" and "ck" Letter Combination

"k" represents the /k/ sound

The letter "k" represents the /k/ sound, as in the word <u>cake</u>.

Long Vowel Blending Table for the Letter "k"

/ā/ ape	/ē/ eagle	/ī/ ice	/ō/ open	/yōo/ cube
t a k e	d e ke	b i k e	sp o k e	p u k e
ta ke	de ke	bi ke	spo ke	pu ke
take	deke	bike	spoke	puke

"ck" has a silent "c" + /k/ sound

The "ck" letter combination represents the /k/ sound, as in the word <u>luck</u>.

Short Vowel Blending Table for the "ck" Letter Combination

/ă/ apple	/ĕ/ egg	/ĭ/ insect	/ŏ/ octopus	/ŭ/ up
b a ck	ch e ck	ch i ck	cl o ck	ch u ck
ba ck	che ck	chi ck	clo ck	chu ck
back	check	chick	clock	chuck

Word Box	acknowledge, back, black, block, bucket, chick, chicken, deck, dock, duck, jacket, kick, lack, lick, lock, luck, neck, nickel, pack, pick, pickle, sick, sock

Long Vowel Cards for the Letter "k"

"ake"	"eke"	"ike"	"oke"	"uke"
bake cake fake	deke eke peke	bike hike strike	awoke broke smoke	duke fluke juke

Short Vowel Cards for the Letter "ck"

"ack"	"eck"	"ick"	"ock"	"uck"
black pack track	check neck speck	brick click pick	block clock lock	chuck duck stuck

Lesson 11.3
Reading Words with the "kle" Letter Combination

"kle" represents the /k/ + /l/ + /ĕ/ sounds

When the "kle" letter combination is at the beginning of a word, it can represent the /k/ + /l/ + /ĕ/ sounds, as in the words <u>kleptomania</u> and <u>kleptomaniac</u>.

"kle" represents the /k/ + /l/ + /ĭ/ sounds

When the "kle" letter combination is within a word, it can represent the /k/ + /l/ + /ĭ/ sounds, as in the word <u>booklet</u>.

Word Box	anklet, booklet, feckless, fecklessly, fecklessness, reckless, recklessly, recklessness, thankless, thanklessness

"kle" represents the /k/ + /l/ + /ē/ sounds

When the "kle" letter combination is at the beginning of a word, it can represent the /k/ + /l/ + /ē/ sounds, as in the word <u>Kleenex</u>.

"kler" represents the /k/ + /l/ + /ə/ + /r/ sounds

When the "kler" letter combination is at the end of a word, it represents the /k/ + /l/ + /ə/ + /r/ sounds, as in the word <u>sprinkler</u>.

Word Box	buckler, sparkler, sprinkler, stickler, swashbuckler, tackler

"kle" represents the /k/ + /ə/ + /l/ sounds + silent "e"

When the "kle" letter combination is at the end of a syllable or word, it represents the /k/ + /ə/ + /l/ sounds + silent "e," as in the word <u>freckle</u>.

Word Box	ankle, buckle, chuckle, crackle, fickle, huckleberry, knuckle, periwinkle, pickle, shackle, sickle, sparkle, sprinkle, suckle, tackle, tickle, twinkle, winkle, wrinkle

"kle" represents /k/ + /ə/ + /l/ sounds + silent "e"	"kles" represents /k/ + /ə/ + /l/ + /s/ sounds	"kled" represents /k/ + /ə/ + /l/ + /d/ sounds
Present Tense Verbs	Third-Person Present Tense Verbs	Past Tense Verbs
buckle	buckles	buckled
crackle	crackles	crackled
shackle	shackles	shackled
wrinkle	wrinkles	wrinkled

Lesson 11.4
Reading Words with a Silent Letter "k"

"kn" has a silent "k" + /n/ sound

In the "kn" letter combination, the letter "k" is silent while the letter "n" represents the /n/ sound, as in the word <u>knock</u>.

Word Box	knack, knap, knave, knead, knee, kneed, kneel, knell, knew, knife, knight, knit, knives, knob, knock, knot, knots, know, knowledge, known, knuckle, knurl

☞ Exception: knish /k/ + /n/ sounds

Short Vowel Blending Table for the "kn" Letter Combination

/ă/ apple	/ĕ/ egg	/ĭ/ insect	/ŏ/ octopus	/ŭ/ up
kn a c k	kn e l t	kn i t	kn o t	kn uc kle
kna ck	kne lt	kni t	kno t	knu ckle
knack	knelt	knit	knot	knuckle

Long Vowel Blending Table for the "kn" Letter Combination

/ā/ ape	/ē/ eagle	/ī/ ice	/ō/ open	/yo͞o/ cube
k n a ve	k n ee l	k n i ght	k n o w	k n ew
kna ve	knee l	kni ght	kn ow	kn ew
knave	kneel	knight	know	knew

 Reading Check Point
Assignment: Read the sentences.

1. Karen and Kim know how to tie a square knot.
2. Kennedy's book is entitled, "Knowledge is Power."
3. The star football player has a serious knee injury.
4. In Kingston, Jamaica many girls know how to knit.
5. The stainless steel knives are in the wooden cabinet.

*The Reading Challenge
Lesson 11.5
Reading Multisyllable Words*

You can read a long word by dividing it into small parts called syllables. Each syllable has <u>one</u> <u>vowel</u> <u>sound</u> and usually one or more consonant sounds.

Three Ways to Divide Words into Syllables

1. A closed syllable ends with a consonant. When a closed syllable has one vowel, it usually has a short vowel.

   Example: kidnap - kid + nap

   When a closed syllable has two vowels, the first vowel is usually a long vowel while the second vowel is silent.

   Example: keeper - keep + er

2. An open syllable ends with a vowel. The vowel at the end of the syllable is usually a long vowel.

   Example: kosher - ko + sher

3. The "vowel + consonant + e" syllable is at the end of a word. The first vowel in this syllable pattern is usually a long vowel while the final "e" is silent.

   Example: keynote - key + note

Multisyllable Word Lists

2 syllable words	3 syllable words	4 syllable words
kazoo	kangaroo	Kalamazoo
keeper	karate	kaleidoscope
ketchup	Kennedy	kamikaze
Kenya	Kentucky	karaoke
keyboard	keratin	karyotype
kidding	ketamine	katakana
kindle	kidnapping	keratinous
kindness	kilogram	kilocycle
kingdom	kilowatt	kiloliter
kissing	kindhearted	kilometer
kitchen	kinetic	kindheartedness
kitten	koala	kindergarten
knitting	Korea	kinesthetic
knockout	knowingly	kirigami
knowledge	knucklehead	knowledgeable

Lesson 11.6
Reading Proper and Common Nouns and Adjectives
Capitalization Rules

Words are written with uppercase and/or lowercase letters. Proper nouns and proper adjectives begin with uppercase letters. Common nouns and common adjectives begin with lowercase letters.

A **proper noun** is a word that names a specific person, place, thing or concept.

A **common noun** is a word that names a general person, place, thing or concept.

	Proper Noun	Common Noun
Person	Mr. Kingsley	king
Place	Kuwait	kitchen
Thing	Kleenex	kiwi
Concept		kindness

A **proper adjective** is a word that describes a specific person, place, thing or concept.

A **common adjective** is a word that describes a general person, place, thing or concept.

Proper Adjective:	Common Adjective:
Person: King Henry VIII	Person: kind man
Thing: Kuwaiti Restaurant	Thing: kinky hair

Capitalization Rules

Uppercase Letter – "K"

- The first letter of a word that begins a sentence is capitalized.

- The first letter of a word that names a specific person, place, thing or concept is capitalized.

- The first letter of a person's title is capitalized.

- The first letter of each word in a title or subtitle is capitalized.

- As a pronoun, the letter "I" is capitalized.

✎ Note: Lowercase letters are generally used for all other words.

Lowercase Letter – "k"

- The first letter of a word that <u>does</u> <u>not</u> name a specific person, place, thing or concept is written with a lowercase letter.

- The first letter of a word that <u>does</u> <u>not</u> begin a sentence is written with a lowercase letter.

- All letters within and at the end of words are written with lowercase letters.

The Letter "k" at a Glance		
Letter	Sounds	Anchor Words
"k"	/k/	king
"k"	silent "k"	knee

L/l

Lesson 12.0
Introduction of the Letter L/l

The letter "l" is a consonant. It is the 12th letter in the Roman alphabet of the English language. Letters are written as uppercase and lowercase letters.

	Uppercase Letter	Lowercase Letter
Print	L	l
Cursive	𝓛	𝓮

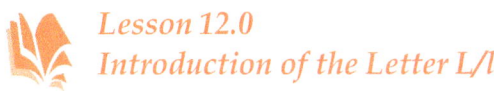

Lesson 12.1
Reading Words with the Letter L/l

The letter "l" is pronounced in <u>two</u> different ways.
- It represents the /l/ sound, as in the word <u>lab</u>.
- It represents the /r/ sound, only in the word <u>colonel</u>.
- At times it is silent, as in the word <u>talk</u>.

High Frequency, One Syllable Letter "l" Words
lab, lace, lack, lake, lamb, land, lane, large, last, late, laugh, law, learn, least, leave, left, leg, lend, less, let, lick, lid, lie, life, lift, light, like, lot, loud, love, low, lump, lunch, lung, lure, lurk, lush, lute

At the beginning, within and end of a word, the letter "l" represents the /l/ sound, as in the words <u>lap</u>, <u>below</u> and <u>bowl</u>.

Beginning	Within	End
/l/	/l/	/l/
lap	below	bowl
let	class	goal
lid	floor	mail
life	false	pool
lift	glass	royal
love	place	school
lunch	select	total
lungs	table	trail

✤ Reading Words with the Letter L/l

Short Vowel Blending Table for the Letter L/l

/ă/ apple	/ĕ/ egg	/ĭ/ insect	/ŏ/ octopus	/ŭ/ up
l a b	l e d	l i p	l o g	l u m p
la b	le d	li p	lo g	lu mp
lab	led	lip	log	lump

Long Vowel Blending Table for the Letter L/l

/ā/ ape	/ē/ eagle	/ī/ ice	/ō/ open	/ōō/ glue
l a ce	l e a d	l i f e	l o g o	l u n ar
la ce	lea d	li fe	lo go	lun ar
lace	lead	life	logo	lunar

Multisyllable Word Lists

2 syllable words	3 syllable words	4 syllable words
label	ladybug	laminator
ladder	lavender	lavatory
lavish	legacy	legendary
leather	lemonade	legislation
legal	liable	legislator
legend	liberty	librarian
letter	library	liberation
limit	lingering	limitation
listen	listening	literacy
little	location	literally
lobster	logical	literature
logic	logistics	litigation
lotion	longitude	locomotion
loyal	luxury	longevity
lyrics	lyrical	lubricating

Reading Check Point
Assignment: Read the sentences.

1. Larry is a lazy lawyer.
2. Lin takes music lessons.
3. Lincoln found a lucky clover.
4. My lovely flowers are lilacs and lilies.
5. At lunchtime, Lucy wrote a long letter.

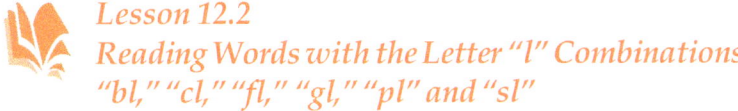

Lesson 12.2
Reading Words with the Letter "l" Combinations
"bl," "cl," "fl," "gl," "pl" and "sl"

Each letter in the letter "l" combination is pronounced quickly. The letters blend together to have distinct consonant sounds.

"bl" represents the /b/ + /l/ sounds

The "bl" letter combination represents the /b/ + /l/ sounds, as in the word black.

Word Box	black, blade, blame, blank, blanket, blaze, bleach, bleed, blend, blew, blind, blink, block, blood, bloom, blouse, blow, blue, bluff, blunder, blurt, blush

"cl" represents the /k/ + /l/ sounds

The "cl" letter combination represents the /k/ + /l/ sounds, as in the word clown.

Word Box	claim, clam, clap, clarify, clash, clasp, class, clay, clean, clear, clerk, clever, click, cliff, climb, clip, clock, close, closet, cloud, clown, club, clue, clutch

"fl" represents the /f/ + /l/ sounds

The "fl" letter combination represents the /f/ + /l/ sounds, as in the word flower.

Word Box	flag, flake, flame, flamingo, flap, flash, flat, flavor, flea, flee, fleet, flew, flexible, flight, flip, flock, float, flood, floor, flop, flora, flow, flower, flu, flute, flies, fly

"gl" represents the /g/ + /l/ sounds

The "gl" letter combination represents the /g/ + /l/ sounds, as in the word glance.

Word Box	glacier, glad, glance, gland, glare, glass, gleam, glee, glide, glimpse, glisten, glitter, gloat, gloomy, glorious, glory, gloss, glossy, glove, glucose, glue

"pl" represents the /p/ + /l/ sounds

The "pl" letter combination represents the /p/ + /l/ sounds, as in the word plenty.

Word Box	place, plain, plan, planet, plant, plastic, plate, play, player, plaza, please, pledge, plentiful, plot, plow, pluck, plugs, plum, plunge, plus, plywood

"sl" represents the /s/ + /l/ sounds

The "sl" letter combination represents the /s/ + /l/ sounds, as in the word sleepy.

Word Box	slack, slang, slant, slate, sled, sleek, sleep, sleeve, slender, slice, slide, slippers, slogan, slope, sloth, slow, slum, slumber, slump, slurp, slush, slushy, sly

Learn To Read English Textbook

Lesson 12.3
Reading Words with a Silent Letter "l"

"l" is silent

The letter "l" can be silent, as in the word calf.

Word Box	almonds, balk, balm, calf, calm, calves, chalk, could, DeKalb, embalm, folk, half, halves, Norfolk, palm, polka, psalm, salmon, salve, stalk, talk, yolk

"l" is silent

The letter "l" can be silent when it is before the following letters: "d," "f," "k," "m" or "v."

"l" letter combinations	"l" is silent	"l" represents the /l/ sound
"ld"	could, should, would	bold, gold, mold, old, world
"lf"	calf, half	fulfill, golf, gulf, self, wolf
"lk"	chalk, folk, stalk, talk, walk, yolk	alkalize, hulky, milk, silky
"lm"	almond, alms, calm, psalm, salmon	almost, film, helmet, realm
"lv"	calves, halves	elves, ourselves, shelves

"ould" - "l" is silent

In the "ould" letter combination, the letter "l" can be silent, as in the word would.

Word Box	could, couldn't, should, shouldn't, would, wouldn't

"ould" - "l" represents the /l/ sound

In the "ould" letter combination, the letter "l" can represent the /l/ sound, as in the words boulder and shoulder.

"ll" represents the /l/ sound + silent "l"

In the "ll" letter combination, the first letter "l" represents the /l/ sound, while the second letter "l" is silent, as in the word tallest.

Word Box	ball, belly, call, chill, collect, dollar, drill, ellipse, enroll, fall, fell, follow, gallon, gill, grill, hall, hallmark, hallow, hello, hill, pillow, valley, wall, wallpaper

Reading Check Point
Assignment: Read the sentences.

1. Linda did not go to Lithuania.
2. Luther is a lawyer at Lincoln Law Office.
3. "The Lion King" is Mr. Lin's favorite musical.
4. Mr. Lindsey teaches English language arts.
5. Lucy learned that the capital of Peru is Lima.

The Reading Challenge
Lesson 12.4
Reading Multisyllable Words

You can read a long word by dividing it into small parts called syllables. Each syllable has one vowel sound and usually one or more consonant sounds.

Three Ways to Divide Words into Syllables

1. A closed syllable ends with a consonant. When a closed syllable has one vowel, it usually has a short vowel.
   Example: limit - lim + it

   When a closed syllable has two vowels, the first vowel is usually a long vowel while the second vowel is silent.
   Example: leaping - leap + ing

2. An open syllable ends with a vowel. The vowel at the end of the syllable is usually a long vowel.
   Example: label - la + bel

3. The "vowel + consonant + e" syllable is at the end of a word. The first vowel in this syllable pattern is usually a long vowel while the final "e" is silent.
   Example: lifetime - life + time

Multisyllable Word Lists

2 syllable words	3 syllable words	4 syllable words
lady	laminate	laminated
laptop	lavender	laterally
lawyer	legally	legendary
legal	lemonade	legionary
legend	leveling	legislation
lemon	liable	legislator
letter	liberty	legitimate
lily	library	liberation
limit	ligament	limitations
linger	limited	linoleum
lipstick	limousine	liquidator
lively	linguistics	literally
London	liquidate	literacy
losing	listening	liquidated
loving	location	locomotion
lucky	lovable	locomotive
lunar	luxury	luxurious

Lesson 12.5
Reading Proper and Common Nouns and Adjectives
Capitalization Rules

Words are written with uppercase and/or lowercase letters. Proper nouns and proper adjectives begin with uppercase letters. Common nouns and common adjectives begin with lowercase letters.

A **proper noun** is a word that names a specific person, place, thing or concept.

A **common noun** is a word that names a general person, place, thing or concept.

	Proper Noun	Common Noun
Person	Lily	librarian
Place	Liberty Square	library
Thing	Labrador	lemon
Concept		liberty

A **proper adjective** is a word that describes a specific person, place, thing or concept.

A **common adjective** is a word that describes a general person, place, thing or concept.

Proper Adjective:	Common Adjective:
Person: Lithuanian dancer Thing: Latin textbook	Person: loving mother Thing: loud music

Capitalization Rules

Uppercase Letter – "L"

- The first letter of a word that begins a sentence is capitalized.

- The first letter of a word that names a specific person, place, thing or concept is capitalized.

- The first letter of a person's title is capitalized.

- The first letter of each word in a title or subtitle is capitalized.

- As a pronoun, the letter "I" is capitalized.

✎ Note: Lowercase letters are generally used for all other words.

Lowercase Letter – "l"

- The first letter of a word that <u>does</u> <u>not</u> name a specific person, place, thing or concept is written with a lowercase letter.

- The first letter of a word that <u>does</u> <u>not</u> begin a sentence is written with a lowercase letter.

- All letters within and at the end of words are written with lowercase letters.

The Letter "l" at a Glance		
Letter	Sounds	Anchor Words
"l"	/l/	lab
"l"	/r/	co<u>l</u>onel
"l"	silent "l"	talk

Unit M

M/m

Lesson 13.0
Introduction of the Letter M/m

The letter "m" is a consonant. It is the 13th letter in the Roman alphabet of the English language. Letters are written as uppercase and lowercase letters.

	Uppercase Letter	Lowercase Letter
Print	M	m
Cursive	*M*	*m*

Lesson 13.1
Reading Words with the Letter M/m

The letter "m" is pronounced in <u>one</u> way.
- It represents the /m/ sound, as in the word <u>mop</u>.
- At times it is silent, as in the word <u>mnemonic</u>.

High Frequency, One Syllable Letter "m" Words
mad, made, maid, mail, make, male, mall, man, map, Mars, me, meal, mean, meat, men, mess, might, mild, milk, mill, mind, mine, miss, mist, mood, moon, mole, more, most, mouse, mouth, move

At the beginning, within and end of a word, the letter "m" represents the /m/ sound, as in the words <u>moon</u>, <u>number</u> and <u>drum</u>.

Beginning	Within	End
/m/	/m/	/m/
math	element	alarm
method	family	bottom
mineral	human	drum
missing	number	esteem
moon	promote	germ
money	remain	redeem
monkey	segment	storm
monthly	symbol	system
musical	thermal	team

Learn To Read English Textbook

✤ Reading Words with the Letter M/m

Short Vowel Blending Table for the Letter M/m

/ă/ apple	/ĕ/ egg	/ĭ/ insect	/ŏ/ octopus	/ŭ/ up
m a d	m e t	m i ss	m o p	m u d
ma d	me t	mi ss	mo p	mu d
mad	met	miss	mop	mud

Long Vowel Blending Table for the Letter M/m

/ā/ ape	/ē/ eagle	/ī/ ice	/ō/ open	/yōō/ cube
m a d e	m e a n	m i n e	m o a t	m u l e
ma de	me an	mi ne	moa t	mu le
made	mean	mine	moat	mule

Letter "m" Parts of Speech Table

Nouns	Verbs	Adjectives
machine	magnetized	magenta
magazine	maintains	magical
magnet	maltreat	magnetic
manners	managed	magnificent
meadow	manipulate	majestic
meeting	mediated	meager
memory	memorizing	meaningful
miracle	metabolized	merciful
mistake	minimized	milky
mission	misinterpret	minimal
mobility	mobilizing	moody
mother	modifying	motionless
movement	motivated	motivated
muffler	multiplied	multicolored
multiplication	murmuring	multicultural

Reading Check Point
Assignment: Read the sentences.

1. Mack made meatballs for dinner.
2. Mary is learning about mammals.
3. My maid is cleaning the mansion.
4. Mom and Dad are listening to music.
5. Meg and Matt are getting married in March.

Lesson 13.2
Reading Words with a Silent Letter "m"

"mn" - "m" is silent

In the "mn" letter combination, the letter "m" can be silent while the letter "n" represents the /n/ sound, as in the word <u>mnemonic</u>.

Word Box	mnemonic, mnemonically, mnemonics, Mnemosyne, Mnemosynes

☞ Exceptions: amnesty, chimney, gymnastics - /m/ + /n/ sounds
            column - /m/ sound + silent "n"

"mm" represents the /m/ sound + silent "m"

In the "mm" letter combination, the first letter "m" represents the /m/ sound while the second letter "m" is silent, as in the word <u>hammer</u>.

Word Box	ammonia, comma, commit, common, community, commute, dilemma, gimmick, grammar, hammer, hummingbird, immediately, immense, immune, mammal, mammoth, Mommy, recommend, summer, summit, symmetry

Reading Multisyllable Words

magnet ⇩ magnetic ⇩ magnetically	magic ⇩ magical ⇩ magically
meaning ⇩ meaningful ⇩ meaningfully	metaphor ⇩ metaphorical ⇩ metaphorically

Reading Check Point

Assignment: Read the sentences.

1. Ms. Mendell is eating a big, juicy mango.
2. My mother is the matriarch of our family.
3. While in Milwaukee, I saw the Milky Way.
4. In the morning, I received a call from Mom.
5. The menu was written by the executive chef.

The Reading Challenge
Lesson 13.3
Reading Multisyllable Words

You can read a long word by dividing it into small parts called syllables. Each syllable has <u>one</u> <u>vowel</u> <u>sound</u> and usually one or more consonant sounds.

Three Ways to Divide Words into Syllables

1. A closed syllable ends with a consonant. When a closed syllable has one vowel, it usually has a short vowel.
   Example: manic - man + ic

   When a closed syllable has two vowels, the first vowel is usually a long vowel while the second vowel is silent.
   Example: meaning - mean + ing

2. An open syllable ends with a vowel. The vowel at the end of the syllable is usually a long vowel.
   Example: media - me + dia

3. The "vowel + consonant + e" syllable is at the end of a word. The first vowel in this syllable pattern is usually a long vowel while the final "e" is silent.
   Example: mandate - man + date

Multisyllable Word Lists

2 syllable words	3 syllable words	4 syllable words
mango	magical	macaroni
master	manicure	Madagascar
matching	mercury	magnesium
measure	medical	magnificent
member	medicine	material
milkshake	melody	maturity
millions	metaphor	medication
minutes	Mexico	mechanical
moment	mineral	millimeter
morning	minister	minority
motion	miracle	miserable
motive	mosquito	moderation
mountain	musical	monopoly
mustard	multiple	motorcycle
music	mystery	mysterious

Lesson 13.4
Reading Proper and Common Nouns and Adjectives
Capitalization Rules

Words are written with uppercase and/or lowercase letters. Proper nouns and proper adjectives begin with uppercase letters. Common nouns and common adjectives begin with lowercase letters.

A proper noun is a word that names a specific person, place, thing or concept.

A common noun is a word that names a general person, place, thing or concept.

	Proper Noun	Common Noun
Person	Mom (when used as a name)	mom (not when used as a name)
Place	Mozambique	museum
Thing	March	money
Concept	Mandaeism	mourn

A proper adjective is a word that describes a specific person, place, thing or concept.

A common adjective is a word that describes a general person, place, thing or concept.

Proper Adjective:	Common Adjective:
Person: Miami Dolphins Thing: Ming Dynasty	Person: magnificent mother Thing: many ducks

Capitalization Rules

Uppercase Letter – "M"

- The first letter of a word that begins a sentence is capitalized.

- The first letter of a word that names a specific person, place, thing or concept is capitalized.

- The first letter of a person's title is capitalized.

- The first letter of each word in a title or subtitle is capitalized.

- As a pronoun, the letter "I" is capitalized.

✎ Note: Lowercase letters are generally used for all other words.

Lowercase Letter – "m"

- The first letter of a word that <u>does</u> <u>not</u> name a specific person, place, thing or concept is written with a lowercase letter.

- The first letter of a word that <u>does</u> <u>not</u> begin a sentence is written with a lowercase letter.

- All letters within and at the end of words are written with lowercase letters.

The Letter "m" at a Glance

Letter	Sound	Anchor Words
"m"	/m/	mop
"m"	silent "m"	<u>m</u>nemonic

N/n

Lesson 14.0
Introduction of the Letter N/n

The letter "n" is a consonant. It is the 14th letter in the Roman alphabet of the English language. Letters are written as uppercase and lowercase letters.

	Uppercase Letter	Lowercase Letter
Print	N	n
Cursive	*N*	*n*

Lesson 14.1
Reading Words with the Letter N/n

The letter "n" is pronounced in <u>two</u> different ways.
- It represents the /n/ sound, as in the word <u>nut</u>.
- It represents the /ng/ sound, as in the word <u>bank</u>.
- At times it is silent, as in the word <u>autumn</u>.

High Frequency, One Syllable Letter "n" Words
nail, name, nap, near, neat, neck, need, nerve, nest, net, new, news, next, nice, night, nine, ninth, nip, no, node, noise, none, noon, nope, nor, nose, not, note, noun, now, numb, nurse, nut

At the beginning, within and end of a word, the letter "n" represents the /n/ sound, as in the words <u>nut</u>, <u>inside</u> and <u>tan</u>.

Beginning	Within	End
/n/	/n/	/n/
name	bend	been
natal	count	born
need	inside	crown
newly	lane	moon
niece	menu	soon
nine	rent	thin
nomad	tend	train
nut	tone	turn

✤ *Reading Words with the Letter N/n*

Short Vowel Blending Table for the Letter N/n

/ă/ apple	/ĕ/ egg	/ĭ/ insect	/ŏ/ octopus	/ŭ/ up
n a p	n e c k	n i p	n o d	n u t
na p	ne ck	ni p	no d	nu t
nap	neck	nip	nod	nut

Long Vowel Blending Table for the Letter N/n

/ā/ ape	/ē/ eagle	/ī/ ice	/ō/ open	/o͞o/ glue
n a me	n e e d	n i n e	n o d e	n u k e
na me	nee d	ni ne	no de	nu ke
name	need	nine	node	nuke

"nk" represents the /ng/ + /k/ sounds

In the "nk" letter combination, the letter "n" represents the /ng/ sound, as in the word <u>bank</u>.

Word Box	ankle, anklet, bank, brink, drink, honk, hunk, ink, junk, link, mink, pink, plank, plink, plunk, rank, sank, shrunk, sink, thank, think, thinking, wink

"n" represents the /ng/ sound

The letter "n" represents the /ng/ sound, as in the word <u>precinct</u>.

Word Box	delinquency, delinquent, pancreas, pancreatitis, precinct, punctual, punctuation, puncture, relinquish, relinquishing, tranquil, tranquilizer

Letter "n" Parts of Speech Table

Nouns	Verbs	Adjectives
nature	nabbed	natural
nectar	nailed	naval
nitrate	neglect	negative
novel	nipped	nervous
number	nodding	normal

Reading Check Point
Assignment: Read the sentences.

1. Nick has a nice necktie.
2. The narrator sounds nasal.
3. My niece, Nicola, is from New Delhi.

Lesson 14.2
Reading Words with the "ng" Letter Combination

The "ng" letter combination is pronounced in four different ways.
- It represents the /ng/ sound, as in the word bang.
- It represents the /n/ + /g/ sounds, as in the word engage.
- It represents the /n/ + /j/ sounds, as in the word ginger.
- It represents the /ng/ + /g/ sounds, as in the word congress.

"ng" represents the /ng/ sound

When the "ng" letter combination is **together** in one syllable, it represents the /ng/ sound, as in the word bang.

Word Box	belong, bring, clung, flung, hang, king, length, long, lung, ring, sang, sing, slang, sling, spring, sting, strength, sung, swing, swung, thing, tongue, wrong, young

"ng" represents the /ng/ sound

When the "ing" letter combination is added to a verb, the letters "n" and "g" represent the /ng/ sound, as in the word coming.

Word Box	acting, aging, being, boring, boxing, camping, caring, coping, crying, eating, fading, filing, lining, loving, lying, paving, rating, riding, running, saving, tying

"ng" represents the /n/ + /g/ sounds

When the "ng" letter combination is **divided** into two syllables, it can represent the /n/ + /g/ sounds, as in the word engage.

Word Box	congratulate, congratulation, downgrade, engage, engaged, engaging, engagement, engrave, engraver, engross, engrossing, engulf, mangrove, ongoing, ungainly, ungovernable, ungracious, ungrateful, unguarded

"ng" represents the /n/ + /j/ sounds

When the "ng" letter combination is **divided** into two syllables, it can represent the /n/ + /j/ sounds, as in the word ginger.

Word Box	angel, arrange, avenger, challenger, change, congest, endanger, engine, engineer, exchange, fringe, lounge, manger, messenger, orange, plunge, plunger, ranger, rearrange, revenge, sponge, strange, stranger, syringe

"ng" represents the /ng/ + /g/ sounds

When the "ng" letter combination is **divided** into two syllables, it can represent the /ng/ + /g/ sounds, as in the word congress.

Word Box	angrily, angry, congregate, congregation, congress, congressional, congruency, congruent, gangrene, hungrily, hungry, mongrel, tangram

Lesson 14.3
Reading Words with a Silent Letter "n"

"nn" represents the /n/ sound + silent "n"

In the "nn" letter combination, the first letter "n" represents the /n/ sound while the second letter "n" is silent, as in the word dinner.

Word Box	banner, bunny, channel, connect, fanny, flannel, funnel, funny, inn, innate, inner, innovation, manner, nanny, penny, questionnaire, sunny, tennis

"mn" represents the /m/ sound + silent "n"

In the "mn" letter combination, the letter "m" represents the /m/ sound while the letter "n" can be silent, as in the word autumn.

Word Box	autumn, column, columns, condemn, damn, hymn, hymns, solemn, solemnly

"mn" represents the /m/ + /n/ sounds

In the "mn" letter combination, the letter "m" represents the /m/ sound while the letter "n" can represent the /n/ sound, as in the word firmness.

Word Box	alumni, amnesia, amnesty, chimney, columnist, gymnast, indemnity, insomnia, omnipotent, omnipresent, omniscient, omnivorous, remnant

 Bonus Lesson
Reading Words with the Letter "n" Blends

"nd" represents the /n/ + /d/ sounds

In the "nd" letter combination, the letter "n" represents the /n/ sound and the letter "d" represents the /d/ sound, as in the word band.

Word Box	and, band, bland, conduct, condiment, find, found, friend, fund, grand, ground, indent, index, intend, mend, pond, round, sound, stand, under

"nt" represents the /n/ + /t/ sounds

In the "nt" letter combination, the letter "n" represents the /n/ sound and the letter "t" represents the /t/ sound, as in the word ant.

Word Box	ant, blunt, cent, control, dent, different, entrance, font, frequent, interact, lament, lint, paint, painting, pant, pint, rant, rent, rented, renting, student

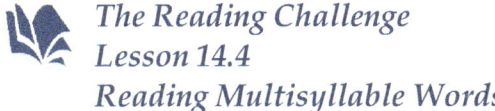

The Reading Challenge
Lesson 14.4
Reading Multisyllable Words

You can read a long word by dividing it into small parts called syllables. Each syllable has <u>one</u> <u>vowel</u> <u>sound</u> and usually one or more consonant sounds.

Three Ways to Divide Words into Syllables

1. A closed syllable ends with a consonant. When a closed syllable has one vowel, it usually has a short vowel.
   Example: napkin - nap + kin

   When a closed syllable has two vowels, the first vowel is usually a long vowel while the second vowel is silent.
   Example: neatly - neat + ly

2. An open syllable ends with a vowel. The vowel at the end of the syllable is usually a long vowel.
   Example: nomad - no + mad

3. The "vowel + consonant + e" syllable is at the end of a word. The first vowel in this syllable pattern is usually a long vowel while the final "e" is silent.
   Example: numerate - nu + mer + ate

Multisyllable Word Lists

2 syllable words	3 syllable words	4 syllable words
napkin	narrator	naturally
nature	national	navigator
needle	natural	necessary
neither	nautical	negatively
nervous	negative	Nigerian
nibble	negligent	nominated
nickel	networking	nonsensical
nightly	nitrogen	nonviolent
nitrate	nobody	noticeable
notice	noticing	notorious
nothing	nocturnal	numeracy
notion	notary	numeration
nourish	November	numerator
nugget	nursery	nutritionist
number	nutrition	nutritiously

Learn To Read English Textbook

Lesson 14.5
Reading Proper and Common Nouns and Adjectives
Capitalization Rules

Words are written with uppercase and/or lowercase letters. Proper nouns and proper adjectives begin with uppercase letters. Common nouns and common adjectives begin with lowercase letters.

A **proper noun** is a word that names a specific person, place, thing or concept.

A **common noun** is a word that names a general person, place, thing or concept.

	Proper Noun	Common Noun
Person	Nancy	novice
Place	New Zealand	nurse's station
Thing	Nestle Inc.	nut
Concept		nuisance

A **proper adjective** is a word that describes a specific person, place, thing or concept.

A **common adjective** is a word that describes a general person, place, thing or concept.

Proper Adjective:	Common Adjective:
Person: Nigerian citizen Thing: Norwegian Airlines	Person: nosey neighbors Thing: noisy pets

Capitalization Rules

Uppercase Letter – "N"

- The first letter of a word that begins a sentence is capitalized.

- The first letter of a word that names a specific person, place, thing or concept is capitalized.

- The first letter of a person's title is capitalized.

- The first letter of each word in a title or subtitle is capitalized.

- As a pronoun, the letter "I" is capitalized.

? Note: Lowercase letters are generally used for all other words.

Lowercase Letter – "n"

- The first letter of a word that <u>does</u> <u>not</u> name a specific person, place, thing or concept is written with a lowercase letter.

- The first letter of a word that <u>does</u> <u>not</u> begin a sentence is written with a lowercase letter.

- All letters within and at the end of words are written with lowercase letters.

The Letter "n" at a Glance		
Letter	Sounds	Anchor Words
"n"	/n/	nut
"n"	/ng/	bank
"n"	silent "n"	autumn

Unit O

O/o

Lesson 15.0
Introduction of the Letter O/o

The letter "o" is a vowel. It is the 15th letter in the Roman alphabet of the English language. Letters are written as uppercase and lowercase letters.

	Uppercase Letter	Lowercase Letter
Print	O	o
Cursive	𝒪	𝑜

Lesson 15.1
Reading Words with the Letter O/o

The letter "o" is pronounced in <u>thirteen</u> different ways.
- It represents the short vowel /ŏ/ sound, as in the word <u>frog</u>.
- It represents the long vowel /ō/ sound, as in the word <u>go</u>.
- It represents the schwa vowel /ə/ sound, as in the word <u>o'clock</u>.
- It represents the /w/+/ŭ/ sounds, as in the word <u>one</u>.
- It represents the long vowel /o͞o/ sound, as in the word <u>cool</u>.
- It represents the vowel /o͝o/ sound, as in the word <u>book</u>.
- It represents the vowel /ô/ sound, as in the word <u>cloth</u>.
- It represents the vowel /oi/ sound, as in the word <u>oil</u>.
- It represents the vowel /ä/ sound, as in the word <u>memoir</u>.
- It represents the short vowel /ŭ/ sound, as in the word <u>son</u>.
- It represents the short vowel /ĭ/ sound, as in the word <u>women</u>.
- It represents the vowel /û/ sound, as in the word <u>colonel</u>.
- It represents the vowel /ou/ sound, as in the word <u>cow</u>.
- At times it is silent, as in the word <u>people</u>.

High Frequency, One Syllable Letter "o" Words
Short vowel words: block, box, clock, cop, dot, fog, got, hot, job, jog, lock, log, lot, mom, mop, not, on, ox, plot, pot, rot, son, top, won
Long vowel words: bold, broke, choke, close, code, cold, cone, fold, froze, go, hole, joke, nose, poke, rode, role, rose, spoke, stoke, woke

Lesson 15.2
Reading Words with the Short Vowel "o" Sound

"o" represents the short vowel /ŏ/ or /ô/ sound

At the beginning of a word, the letter "o" usually represents the short vowel /ŏ/ or /ô/ sound, as in the word <u>on</u>.

The letter "o" usually represents the short vowel /ŏ/ or /ô/ sound, when it is the only vowel within a word or syllable.

When a consonant comes before and after the letter "o," it usually represents the short vowel /ŏ/ or /ô/ sound, as in the words <u>job</u>, <u>frog</u> and <u>lock</u>.

Beginning	Within	End
/ŏ/	/ŏ/	/ŏ/
on	frog	

✎ Note: At the end of a word, the letter "o" does not represent the short vowel /ŏ/ sound.

✤ **Short Vowel "o" Word Families**

"ob" - "o" represents the short vowel /ŏ/ sound

The vowel "o" in the "ob" word family represents the short vowel /ŏ/ sound, as in the word <u>job</u>.

Word Box	Bob, blob, cob, hob, gob, glob, job, knob, mob, rob, sob, slob, snob, throb

"ock" - "o" represents the short vowel /ŏ/ sound

The vowel "o" in the "ock" word family represents the short vowel /ŏ/ sound, as in the word <u>sock</u>.

Word Box	block, chock, clock, crock, dock, flock, frock, hock, jock, knock, lock, mock, pock, rock, shock, smock, sock, stock

"od" - "o" represents the short vowel /ŏ/ sound

The vowel "o" in the "od" word family represents the short vowel /ŏ/ sound, as in the word <u>sod</u>.

Word Box	cod, clod, mod, nod, pod, plod, prod, rod, shod, sod, trod

"og" - "o" represents the short vowel /ŏ/ sound

The vowel "o" in the "og" word family represents the short vowel /ŏ/ sound, as in the word frog.

Word Box	blog, bog, clog, cog, flog, fog, frog, hog, jog, log, smog

☞ Exception: dog - /ô/ sound

"oss" - "o" represents the short vowel /ŏ/ sound

The vowel "o" in the "oss" word family represents the short vowel /ŏ/ sound, as in the word toss.

Word Box	boss, cross, dross, floss, gloss, moss, Ross, toss

"op" - "o" represents the short vowel /ŏ/ sound

The vowel "o" in the "op" word family represents the short vowel /ŏ/ sound, as in the word mop.

Word Box	bop, chop, cop, drop, flop, fop, hop, mop, plop, pop, prop, sop, shop, stop, top

"ot" - "o" represents the short vowel /ŏ/ sound

The vowel "o" in the "ot" word family represents the short vowel /ŏ/ sound, as in the word pot.

Word Box	blot, cot, dot, got, hot, jot, knot, lot, plot, pot, not, rot, shot, slot, spot, tot

"ox" - "o" represents the short vowel /ŏ/ sound

The vowel "o" in the "ox" word family represents the short vowel /ŏ/ sound, as in the word fox.

Word Box	box, fox, lox, ox, pox, sox

Reading Check Point
Assignment: Read the sentences.

1. Don locked the toy fox in the box.
2. The oversized rock fell off the dock.
3. Tom drove to the prom at one o'clock.
4. I saw the flock of birds fly over the pond.
5. My mother's pot is on the kitchen counter.

Lesson 15.3
Reading Words with the Long Vowel "o" Sound

"o" represents the long vowel /ō/ sound

The letter "o" can represent the long vowel /ō/ sound, as in the word oats. A long vowel is pronounced by its letter name.

Beginning	Within	End
/ō/	/ō/	/ō/
oats	bone	go

✢ "o" + consonant + silent "e" word families

The long vowel /ō/ sound has four pattern variations: VCe, CVCe, CCVCe and CCCVCe. The VCe pattern is at the end of many long vowel words.

"vowel + consonant + silent e" patterns	Target Words
VCe	ode
CVCe	pole
CCVCe	broke
CCCVCe	stroke

"ode" - "o" represents the long vowel /ō/ sound

When the "o" + consonant + "e" pattern is at the end of a word, the vowel "o" usually represents the long vowel /ō/ sound, the consonant represents its sound while the vowel "e" is silent, as in the word rode.

Word Box	code, lode, mode, node, ode, rode, strode *Multisyllable Words:* episode, explode

"oke" - "o" represents the long vowel /ō/ sound

When the "o" + consonant + "e" pattern is at the end of a word, the vowel "o" usually represents the long vowel /ō/ sound, the consonant represents its sound while the vowel "e" is silent, as in the word broke.

Word Box	broke, choke, joke, poke, smoke, spoke, stoke, stroke, woke, yoke *Multisyllable Words:* awoke, provoke

"ole" - "o" represents the long vowel /ō/ sound

When the "o" + consonant + "e" pattern is at the end of a word, the vowel "o" usually represents the long vowel /ō/ sound, the consonant represents its sound while the vowel "e" is silent, as in the word hole.

Word Box	dole, hole, mole, pole, role, sole, stole, vole, whole

"one" - "o" represents the long vowel /ō/ sound

When the "o" + consonant + "e" pattern is at the end of a word, the vowel "o" usually represents the long vowel /ō/ sound, the consonant represents its sound while the vowel "e" is silent, as in the word zone.

Word Box	bone, clone, cone, drone, lone, phone, pone, prone, scone, shone, stone, throne, tone, zone

☞ Exceptions: one - /w/ + /ŭ/ sounds; none - /ŭ/ sound; gone - /ŏ/ sound or /ô/ sound

"ope" - "o" represents the long vowel /ō/ sound

When the "o" + consonant + "e" pattern is at the end of a word, the vowel "o" usually represents the long vowel /ō/ sound, the consonant represents its sound while the vowel "e" is silent, as in the word hope.

Word Box	cope, grope, hope, lope, mope, nope, pope, rope, scope, slope *Multisyllable Words:* antelope, elope, envelope, horoscope, interlope, microscope, telescope

"ose" - "o" represents the long vowel /ō/ sound

When the "o" + consonant + "e" pattern is at the end of a word, the vowel "o" usually represents the long vowel /ō/ sound, the consonant represents its sound while the vowel "e" is silent, as in the word expose.

Word Box	chose, close, dose, hose, nose, pose, prose, rose, those

"ote" - "o" represents the long vowel /ō/ sound

When the "o" + consonant + "e" pattern is at the end of a word, the vowel "o" usually represents the long vowel /ō/ sound, the consonant represents its sound while the vowel "e" is silent, as in the word devote.

Word Box	cote, dote, mote, note, quote, rote, smote, tote, vote, wrote

Lesson 15.4
Reading Words with Letter "o" Vowel Pairs

When two vowels are **together** in a word or syllable, the first vowel usually represents a long vowel sound while the second vowel is silent.

"oa" represents the long vowel /ō/ sound + silent "a"

When the "oa" vowel combination is **together** in a word or syllable, the letter "o" usually represents the long vowel /ō/ sound while the letter "a" is silent, as in the word boat.

Word Box	coal, float, gloat, goad, goal, goalie, goat, groan, hoax, load, loaf, loam, loan, moan, moat, oak, oat, oath, roach, road, roam, roast, soak, soap, toad, toast

"oe" represents the long vowel /ō/ sound + silent "e"

When the "oe" vowel combination is **together** in a word or syllable, the letter "o" usually represents the long vowel /ō/ sound while the letter "e" is silent, as in the word aloe.

Word Box	banjoes, doe, echoes, foe, goes, heroes, hoe, hoedown, Joe, mistletoes, oboe, pekoe, potatoes, roe, Tahoe, tiptoe, toe, toenail, toes, tomatoes, woeful

☞ Exceptions: does - /ŭ/ sound; canoe, shoe - /o͞o/ sound

"oi" represents the vowel /oi/ sound

When the "oi" vowel combination is **together** in a word or syllable, it represents the vowel /oi/ sound, as in the word oil. It is important to note the two vowels have one new sound.

Word Box	android, appoint, avoid, boil, broil, choice, coil, coin, cloister, exploit, foil, hoist, invoice, join, joint, moist, moisture, noise, oil, poinsettia, point, poise, rejoice, soil, spoil, steroid, toil, turmoil, typhoid, voice, void, voided

☞ Exception: memoir - /ä/ sound or /ô/ sound

"oo" represents the long vowel /o͞o/ sound

When the "oo" vowel combination is **together** in a word or syllable, it can represent the long vowel /o͞o/ sound, as in the word cool.

Word Box	doom, gloom, harpoon, igloo, kazoo, lagoon, loom, loon, loony, loop, loose, mood, moon, pool, proof, roost, rooster, scoop, tool, toot, tooth, troop, zoom

"oo" represents the vowel /o͝o/ sound

When the "oo" vowel combination is **together** in a word or syllable, it can represent the vowel /o͝o/ sound, as in the word cook.

Word Box	book, brook, cook, crook, foot, good, hood, hook, look, nook, poor, shook, stood, took, wood, wooded, wooden, woody, woof, wool, woolen, woolly

❖ *Reading Words with the "ou" letter combination*

The "ou" letter combination is pronounced in <u>seven</u> different ways.
- It represents the vowel /ou/ sound, as in the word <u>out</u>.
- It represents the long vowel /ōō/ sound, as in the word <u>soup</u>.
- It represents the vowel /ô/ sound, as in the word <u>court</u>.
- It represents the long vowel /ō/ sound, as in the word <u>soul</u>.
- It represents the vowel /ŏŏ/ sound, as in the word <u>tour</u>.
- It represents the schwa vowel /ə/ sound, as in the word <u>famous</u>.
- It represents the short vowel /ŭ/ sound, as in the word <u>couple</u>.

"ou" represents the vowel /ou/ sound

The "ou" vowel combination can represent the vowel /ou/ sound, as in the word <u>out</u>.

Word Box	amount, couch, council, count, doubt, drought, ground, hour, house, loud, lousy, mount, mountain, mouse, mouth, noun, pronoun, rebound, sound

"ou" represents the long vowel /ōō/ sound

The "ou" vowel combination can represent the long vowel /ōō/ sound, as in the word <u>soup</u>.

Word Box	bayou, cougar, coup, coupon, group, soup, through, wound, you, youth

"ou" represents the vowel /ô/ sound

The "ou" vowel combination can represent the vowel /ô/ sound, as in the word <u>court</u>.

Word Box	bought, brought, cough, course, court, courtier, fought, four, fourth, mourn, mourning, ought, pour, sought, thought, thoughtful, thoughtless, trough

"ou" represents the long vowel /ō/ sound + silent "u"

The "ou" vowel combination can represent the long vowel /ō/ sound, as in the words <u>soul</u> and <u>thorough</u>.

"ou" represents the vowel /ŏŏ/ sound + silent "u"

The "ou" vowel combination can represent the vowel /ŏŏ/ sound, as in the words <u>could</u> and <u>tour</u>.

"ou" represents the schwa vowel /ə/ sound

The "ou" vowel combination can represent the schwa vowel /ə/ sound, as in the words <u>famous</u> and <u>tremulous</u>.

"ou" has a silent "o" + short vowel /ŭ/ sound

The "ou" vowel combination can represent the short vowel /ŭ/ sound, as in the words <u>cousin</u> and <u>touch</u>.

Unit O
Lesson 15.4

Learn To Read English Textbook

Lesson 15.5
Reading Words with the Final Letter "o"

"o" represents the long vowel /ō/ sound

When the letter "o" is at the end of a word or syllable, it represents the long vowel /ō/ sound, as in the word go.

Word Box	*Letter "o" is at end of the first syllable* chosen, cocoa, coed, focus, grocer, hotel, modem, motel, open, poker, solo, token *Final letter "o"* alamo, avocado, bravo, cargo, combo, flamingo, ghetto, go, ho, hydro, info, largo, manifesto, metro, mosquito, no, photo, pinto, placebo, portfolio, pro, psycho, radio, so, solo, turbo, undergo, veto, video, volcano, yo-yo, zero

Bonus Lesson
Reading Words with the "oll" and "ost" Letter Combinations

"oll" - "o" represents the long vowel /ō/ sound

The vowel "o" in the "oll" letter combination represents the long vowel /ō/ sound, as in the word poll.

Word Box	droll, knoll, poll, roll, scroll, stroll, toll, troll *Multisyllable Words:* bankroll, enroll, enrolling, enrollment, payroll, polling, rolling, stroller, unroll

☞ Exception: doll - /ŏ/ sound

"ost" - "o" represents the long vowel /ō/ sound

The vowel "o" in the "ost" letter combination can represent the long vowel /ō/ sound, as in the word most.

Word Box	ghost, host, most, post *Multisyllable Words:* almost, hosted, hostess, hosting, mostly, postage, postal, poster, posting

☞ Exceptions: hostel - /ŏ/ sound; cost - /ô/ sound; lost – /ŏ/ sound or /ô/ sound

Reading Check Point
Assignment: Read the sentences.

1. I will go to the condo's focus group.
2. The hotel doors will open in a moment.
3. Owen will open the box with the yo-yo.
4. Today, the pro golf team is a coed group.
5. Alejandro plans to go to the hotel for dinner.

Lesson 15.6
Reading Letter "o" Words with the Schwa Vowel Sound

"o" represents the schwa vowel /ə/ sound

The vowel "o" can represent the schwa vowel /ə/ sound, as in the word o'clock.

Beginning	Within	End
/ə/	/ə/	/ə/
of	parrot	

Word Box

First letter "o"

objective, oblige, oblivious, observance, observant, observe, obsess, obstruct, obtain, occasion, occur, o'clock, of, offense, official, officiate, oppose, original

Letter "o" within a word

bishop, canopy, censor, col*o*r, comf*o*rt, customer, develop, doct*o*r, flavor, freedom, gallop, lemon, lesson, mayor, memory, numerator, parlor, person

Bonus Lesson
Reading Words with the "ow" Letter Combination

Three "ow" letter combination sounds:
- It represents the vowel /ou/ sound, as in the word cow.
- It represents the long vowel /ō/ sound, as in the word glow.
- It represents the short vowel /ŏ/ sound, as in the word knowledge.

"ow" represents the vowel /ou/ sound + silent "w"

When the "ow" letter combination is **together** in a word or syllable, it can represent the vowel /ou/ sound, as in the word cow.

Word Box

brown, cow, coward, crowd, crown, down, drowsy, flower, gown, meow, now, plow, powder, power, towel, tower, town, township, vowel, vow, wow

"ow" represents the long vowel /ō/ sound + silent "w"

When the "ow" letter combination is **together** in a word or syllable, it can represent the long vowel /ō/ sound, as in the word glow.

Word Box

arrow, below, blow, crow, flow, flown, glow, grow, know, low, mow, pillow, row, show, shown, snow, throw, thrown, tomorrow, tow, window, yellow

"ow" represents the short vowel /ŏ/ sound + silent "w"

When the "ow" letter combination is **together** in a word or syllable, it can represent the short vowel /ŏ/ sound, as in the word knowledge.

Lesson 15.7
Reading Words with Vowel "o" Sounds: /ŏ/, /ō/ and /o͞o/

Three letter "o" sounds:
- It represents the short vowel /ŏ/ sound, as in the word frog.
- It represents the long vowel /ō/ sound, as in the word go.
- It represents the long vowel /o͞o/ sound, as in the word to.

"o" represents the short vowel /ŏ/ sound

The vowel "o" can represent the short vowel /ŏ/ sound, as in the word frog.

Word Box	cop, block, box, chomp, clock, crop, dot, drop, fog, frost, got, honk, hot, job, jog, lock, log, lot, mom, mop, not, odd, on, ox, plot, pot, rock, rot, shot, spot

"o" represents the long vowel /ō/ sound

The vowel "o" can represent the long vowel /ō/ sound, as in the word go.

Word Box	bold, bone, broke, choke, code, cold, cone, close, fold, go, grow, hole, hope, joke, mode, no, nose, poke, roast, rode, role, rose, soap, spoke, stoke, woke

"o" represents the long vowel /o͞o/ sound

The vowel "o" can represent the long vowel /o͞o/ sound, as in the word to.

Word Box	do, doers, doing, lose, move, moveable, movement, movers, movies, moving, prove, proved, proven, proving, to, too, two, who, whoever, whosoever

Bonus Lesson
Reading Letter "o" Words with the Short Vowel /ŭ/ Sound

"o" represents the short vowel /ŭ/ sound

The letter "o" can represent the short vowel /ŭ/ sound, as in the word dove.

Word Box	above, blood, brother, brotherhood, come, done, dozen, from, front, frontage, frontier, love, money, mother, none, onion, other, shovel, some, somersault, something, sometimes, son, sponge, stomach, ton, tongue, tons, won, wonder

Reading Check Point
Assignment: Read the sentences.

1. My mom gave me two dollars.
2. Do you know the story's plot?
3. Who is going to mop the kitchen floor?
4. The court officer proved his innocence.
5. Tonight, my family will go to the show.

Lesson 15.8
Reading Words with the "or" and "ore" Letter Combinations

"or" represents the vowel /ô/ + /r/ sounds

When the "or" letter combination is at the beginning of a word, it usually represents the vowel /ô/ + /r/ sounds, as in the word orange.

Word Box	or, oral, orate, orator, oratory, orbit, orca, orchid, order, orderly, ordinal, ordinance, organ, organic, organize, origin, ornate, orphan, orthopedics

"or" represents the vowel /ô/ + /r/ sounds

When the "or" letter combination is within a word, it can represent the vowel /ô/ + /r/ sounds, as in the word corn.

Word Box	border, born, cork, corn, dormant, for, forest, forestry, forget, fork, horn, horse, lord, north, pork, port, short, shortage, sorbet, sort, torch, tore, tort, worn

"or" represents the schwa vowel /ə/ + /r/ sounds

When the "or" letter combination is at the beginning of a word, it can represent the schwa vowel /ə/ + /r/ sounds, as in the word oregano.

"or" represents the schwa vowel /ə/ + /r/ sounds

When the "or" letter combination is within a word, it can represent the schwa vowel /ə/ + /r/ sounds, as in the word correct.

Word Box	corolla, corona, corral, correct, correction, correlative, corrode, corrupt, forensic, forget, forgive, forlorn, morale, morality, morass, morel, Morocco

"or" represents the schwa vowel /ə/ + /r/ sounds

When the "or" letter combination is at the end of a word, it represents the schwa vowel /ə/ + /r/ sounds, as in the word doctor.

Word Box	accelerator, chancellor, commentator, conductor, coordinator, distributor, doctor, instructor, investigator, professor, refrigerator, supervisor, translator

"ore" represents the vowel /ô/ + /r/ sounds + silent "e"

When the "ore" letter combination is at the end of a word, the letter "o" represents the vowel /ô/ sound, as in the word chore.

Word Box	bore, chore, core, fore, lore, more, ore, pore, score, shore, sore, snore, spore, store, swore, tore, wore *Multisyllable Words:* adore, albacore, bedsore, before, deplore, encore, explore, eyesore, herbivore, ignore, implore, offshore, omnivore, restore, seashore, sophomore, therefore

Lesson 15.9
Reading Words with a Silent Letter "o"

"o" is silent

The vowel "o" can be silent, as in the word colonel.

"eo" - "o" is silent

In the "eo" vowel combination, the vowel "o" can be silent, as in the word people.

Word Box	jeopardize, jeopardized, jeopardizing, jeopardy, Leonard, leopard, people

"oe" - "o" is silent

In the "oe" vowel combination, the vowel "o" can be silent, as in the word subpoenas.

Word Box	amoeba, amoebic, onomatopoeia, onomatopoetic, phoebe, phoenix, subpoena

"ou" - "o" is silent

In the "ou" vowel combination, the vowel "o" can be silent, as in the word young.

Word Box	couple, country, double, doubles, doublet, Douglas, rough, roughly, touch, touching, touchy, tough, toughen, trouble, younger, youngest, youngster

Silent Letter "o" at a Glance		
Letters	Sound	Anchor Words
"o"	silent "o"	colonel
"eo"	silent "o"	people
"oe"	silent "o"	subpoenas
"ou"	silent "o"	young

Reading Check Point
Assignment: Read the sentences.

1. Leonard was served with a subpoena.
2. Douglas said, "Do not touch the iron!"
3. The young couple is going to get married.
4. An amoeba is a single-celled simple organism.
5. A lapidary rough rock is a semi-precious gemstone.

The Reading Challenge
Lesson 15.10
Reading Multisyllable Words

You can read a long word by dividing it into small parts called syllables. Each syllable has <u>one</u> <u>vowel</u> <u>sound</u> and usually one or more consonant sounds.

Three Ways to Divide Words into Syllables

1. A closed syllable ends with a consonant. When a closed syllable has one vowel, it usually has a short vowel.
   Example: complex - com + plex

   When a closed syllable has two vowels, the first vowel is usually a long vowel while the second vowel is silent.
   Example: floating - float + ing

2. An open syllable ends with a vowel. The vowel at the end of the syllable is usually a long vowel.
   Example: provide - pro + vide

   The "vowel + consonant + e" syllable is at the end of a word. The first vowel in this syllable pattern is usually a long vowel while the final "e" is silent.
   Example: devote - de + vote

Multisyllable Word Lists

2 syllable words	3 syllable words	4 syllable words
object	oasis	obesity
oceans	objective	officially
offense	observing	operator
office	odyssey	opposition
often	offering	optimistic
olive	official	organizes
onion	omnivore	organizing
other	opponent	ordinary
orbit	optional	oregano
order	orator	origami
organ	outdated	original
outrage	outrageous	ornamental
outside	oxygen	overrated
oven	overall	overreact
oyster	overcome	overwhelming

Lesson 15.11
Reading Proper and Common Nouns and Adjectives
Capitalization Rules

Words are written with uppercase and/or lowercase letters. Proper nouns and proper adjectives begin with uppercase letters. Common nouns and common adjectives begin with lowercase letters.

A **proper noun** is a word that names a specific person, place, thing or concept.

A **common noun** is a word that names a general person, place, thing or concept.

	Proper Noun	Common Noun
Person	Mr. Owens	operator
Place	Ontario	outside
Thing	Oreo	octopus
Concept		optimism

A **proper adjective** is a word that describes a specific person, place, thing or concept.

A **common adjective** is a word that describes a general person, place, thing or concept.

Proper Adjective:	Common Adjective:
Person: Omani citizen Thing: Omani food	Person: outstanding student Thing: operating room

Capitalization Rules

Uppercase Letter – "O"

- The first letter of the word that begins a sentence is capitalized.

- The first letter of the word that names a specific person, place, thing or concept is capitalized.

- The first letter of a person's title is capitalized.

- The first letter of each word in a title or subtitle is capitalized.

- As a pronoun, the letter "I" is capitalized.

✎ Note: Lowercase letters are generally used for all other words.

Lowercase Letter – "o"

- The first letter of a word that <u>does</u> <u>not</u> name a specific person, place, thing or concept is written with a lowercase letter.

- The first letter of a word that <u>does</u> <u>not</u> begin a sentence is written with a lowercase letter.

- All letters within and at the end of words are written with lowercase letters.

The Letter "o" at a Glance

Letter(s)	Sounds	Anchor Words
"o"	/ŏ/	frog
"o"	/ō/	go
"o"	/ə/	<u>o</u>'clock
"o"	/w/+/ŭ/	one
"oo"	/o͞o/	cool
"oo"	/o͝o/	book
"o"	/ô/	cloth
"oi"	/oi/	oil
"oi"	/ä/	mem<u>oi</u>r
"o"	/ŭ/	son
"o"	/ĭ/	women
"o"	/û/	c<u>o</u>lonel
"ow"	/ou/	cow
"o"	silent "o"	people

Unit P

P/p

Lesson 16.0
Introduction of the Letter P/p

The letter "p" is a consonant. It is the 16th letter in the Roman alphabet of the English language. Letters are written as uppercase and lowercase letters.

	Uppercase Letter	Lowercase Letter
Print	P	p
Cursive	P	p

Lesson 16.1
Reading Words with the Letter P/p

The letter "p" is pronounced in <u>one</u> way.
- It represents the /p/ sound, as in the word <u>pan</u>.
- At times it is silent, as in the word <u>cupboard</u>.

High Frequency, One Syllable Letter "p" Words
pad, page, paid, pail, pain, paint, pair, pan, park, part, pass, past, pat, peace, peach, peck, peek, peel, pet, pick, pie, piece, point, poor, pop, plan, plant, plug, plum, plus, price, pro, pull, push, pushed

At the beginning, within and end of a word, the letter "p" represents the /p/ sound, as in the words <u>pan</u>, <u>capital</u> and <u>cup</u>.

Beginning	Within	End
/p/	/p/	/p/
pan	capital	cup
pause	collapse	develop
pencil	inspired	gossip
pineapple	repeated	handicap
politics	shipping	lollipop
presents	tropical	workshop

Learn To Read English Textbook

✤ Reading Words with the Letter P/p

Short Vowel Blending Table for the Letter P/p

/ă/ apple	/ĕ/ egg	/ĭ/ insect	/ŏ/ octopus	/ŭ/ up
p a d	p e t	p i t	p o t	p u ll
pa d	pe t	pi t	po t	pu ll
pad	pet	pit	pot	pull

Long Vowel Blending Table for the Letter P/p

/ā/ ape	/ē/ eagle	/ī/ ice	/ō/ open	/yōō/ cube
p a c e	p e e k	p i e	p o l e	p u k e
pac e	pee k	p ie	po le	pu ke
pace	peek	pie	pole	puke

Word Box	cap, cheap, chip, chop, clip, crop, cup, deep, dip, flop, group, help, hip, hop, lamp, lip, map, mop, nap, nip, rip, step, stoop, sweep, tip, top, tulip, zap, zip

Letter "p" Parts of Speech Table

Nouns	Verbs	Adjectives
package	pacifies	Pacific
padlock	packing	palatial
pageant	paralyzed	papal
pajamas	peeling	pandemic
pamphlet	persuade	peculiar
Panama	picturing	playful
peacock	pinched	plural
pillow	plotting	poetic
plaintiff	pointing	polished
planet	polished	purebred
potassium	punched	purple
potpourri	puzzled	pushy

  Reading Check Point
Assignment: Read the sentences.

1. I saw parakeets and parrots in the park.
2. Paul and Pam have physics first period.
3. Our parents live on Pennsylvania Avenue.
4. Pat picked up the package at the post office.
5. The pharmacist works at the new pharmacy.

Lesson 16.2
Reading Words with the "ph" Letter Combination

The "ph" letter combination is pronounced in <u>three</u> different ways.
- It represents the /p/ + /h/ sounds, as in the word <u>uphill</u>.
- It represents the /f/ sound, as in the word <u>phone</u>.
- It represents the /p/ sound, as in the word <u>shepherd</u>.

"ph" represents the /p/ + /h/ sounds

When the "ph" letter combination is **divided** into two syllables, the letter "p" represents the /p/ sound and the letter "h" represents the /h/ sound, as in the word <u>uphill</u>. The letter "p" is in one syllable and the letter "h" is in the other syllable.

Word Box	cupholder, haphazard, upheaval, upheave, upheaves, upheld, uphill, uphold, upholder, upholding, upholds, upholster, upholsterer, upholstery

"ph" represents the /f/ sound

When the "ph" letter combination is **together** in one syllable, it can represent the /f/ sound, as in the word <u>phone</u>.

Word Box	alphabet, amphibian, atmosphere, asphalt, autograph, biography, dolphin, elephant, geography, graphic, nephew, orphan, pamphlet, paragraph, phase, phonics, photo, photograph, physicist, sophisticate, telegraphic, triumph

"ph" represents the /p/ sound + silent "h"

In the "ph" letter combination, the letter "p" can represent the /p/ sound while the letter "h" is silent, as in the words <u>shepherd</u> and <u>shepherdess</u>.

Reading Multisyllable Words

alphabet ⇩ alphabetical ⇩ alphabetically

photo ⇩ photograph ⇩ photographic

Reading Check Point
Assignment: Read the sentences.

1. The elephant in the photo is from India.
2. I read the powerful book, "Autobiography of Malcolm X."
3. Philip donated money to the newly constructed orphanage.
4. We were elected to preserve, defend and uphold the Constitution.
5. Phyllis furnished her living room with an upholstered sofa and loveseat.

Lesson 16.3
Reading Words with the "pr" Letter Combination

"pr" represents the /p/ + /r/ sounds

In the "pr" letter combination, the letter "p" represents the /p/ sound and the letter "r" represents the /r/ sound, as in the word prize.

Word Box	express, impress, practice, pray, press, prince, princess, pride, prize, problem, prolong, promise, propel, proper, proud, prude, prudent, spring, surprise

Short Vowel Blending Table for the "pr" Letter Combination

/ă/ apple	/ĕ/ egg	/ĭ/ insect	/ŏ/ octopus	/ŭ/ up
pr a n k	pr e ss	pr i m	pr o d	spr u ng
pra n k	pre ss	pri m	pro d	spru ng
prank	press	prim	prod	sprung

Long Vowel Blending Table for the "pr" Letter Combination

/ā/ ape	/ē/ eagle	/ī/ ice	/ō/ open	/o͞o/ glue
pr a y	pr ea ch	pr i de	pr o b e	pr u n e
pr ay	prea ch	pri de	pro be	pru ne
pray	preach	pride	probe	prune

Letter "pr" Parts of Speech Table

Nouns	Verbs	Adjectives
praise	practiced	practical
presenter	predestined	predictable
president	preferred	preferable
pressure	preserving	pregnant
prevention	presiding	prehistoric
printer	pretending	preliminary
prison	prevailed	preliterate
prisoner	prevented	premarital
probate	printing	premature
procedure	proceeded	premium
prodigy	processing	prenatal
profile	proclaimed	problematic
program	provided	propelling
projector	provoked	prudent

Lesson 16.4
Reading Words with the "pl" and "ple" Letter Combinations

"pl" represents the /p/ + /l/ sounds

In the "pl" letter combination, the letter "p" represents the /p/ sound and the letter "l" represents the /l/ sound, as in the word <u>plan</u>.

Word Box	place, plain, plan, plane, planet, plank, plate, play, please, pleasure, pled, pledge, plenty, plight, plod, plop, plot, plow, plug, plum, plump, plural

Short Vowel Blending Table for the "pl" Letter Combination

/ă/ apple	/ĕ/ egg	/ĭ/ insect	/ŏ/ octopus	/ŭ/ up
p l a n	p l e d	p l i n k	p l o t	p l u g
plan	pled	plink	plot	plug

Long Vowel Blending Table for the "pl" Letter Combination

/ā/ ape	/ē/ eagle	/ī/ ice	/ō/ open	/o͞o/ glue
p l a y	p l e a t	p l i g h t		P l u t o
play	pleat	plight		Pluto

"ple" represents the /p/ + /ə/ + /l/ sounds + silent "e"

When the "ple" letter combination is at the end of a word, it represents the /p/ + /ə/ + /l/ sounds + silent "e," as in the word <u>people</u>. It is important to note that the schwa vowel /ə/ sound is inserted between the /p/ and /l/ sounds.

Word Box	apple, couple, cripple, dimple, example, people, pimple, pineapple, principle, purple, ripple, sample, simple, staple, steeple, trample, triple

"ple" represents the /p/ + /l/ + /ĕ/ sounds

When the "ple" letter combination is at the beginning or within a word, it can represent the /p/ + /l/ + /ĕ/ sounds, as in the word <u>pledge</u>.

Word Box	complex, complexion, duplex, multiplex, pleasant, pleasure, pledge, plenteous, perplex, replenish, splendid, splendidly, splendor, triplex

☞ Exceptions: droplet, helpless - /ĭ/ sound; implement - /ə/ sound

"ple" represents the /p/ + /l/ + /ē/ sounds

When the "ple" letter combination is at the beginning or within a word, it can represent the /p/ + /l/ + /ē/ sounds, as in the word <u>completion</u>.

Word Box	complete, completing, completive, deplete, depletion, plea, plead, pleaded, pleading, please, pleasing, pleat, plebe, plenary, replete, repletion, spleen

Lesson 16.5
Reading Words with a Silent Letter "p"

"p" is silent

The letter "p" can be silent, as in the word corps.

Word Box	corps, coup, cupboard, raspberry, receipt, receipts, sapphire

"pp" represents the /p/ sound + silent "p"

In the "pp" letter combination, the first letter "p" represents the /p/ sound while the second letter "p" is silent, as in the word puppet.

Word Box	approve, clipper, dropping, flipper, floppy, grasshopper, happen, happy, opposite, oppress, pepper, puppet, puppy, slippery, support, upper, zipper

"ps" has a silent "p" + /s/ sound

When the "ps" letter combination is at the beginning of a word, the letter "p" is silent while the letter "s" represents the /s/ sound, as in the word psychology.

Word Box	psalm, pseudo, psych, psychiatry, psychic, psychoactive, psychoanalysis, psychodrama, psychology, psychopath, psychosis, psychosomatic

"ps" represents the /p/ + /s/ sounds

When the "ps" letter combination is within or at the end of a word, the letter "p" represents the /p/ sound and the letter "s" represents the /s/ sound, as in the words capsules and caps.

Word Box	*"ps" within a word* biopsy, calypso, capsized, capsize, cheapskate, knapsack, lapse, pepsin *"ps" at the end of a word* camps, dips, flips, groups, hips, jumps, keeps, laps, maps, raps, stamps

"pn" has a silent "p" + /n/ sound

When the "pn" letter combination is at the beginning of a word, the letter "p" is silent while the letter "n" represents the /n/ sound, as in the word pneumonia.

Word Box	pneumatic, pneumatical, pneumococcus, pneumonia, pneumonic

"pt" has a silent "p" + /t/ sound

In the "pt" letter combination, the letter "p" can be silent while the letter "t" represents the /t/ sound, as in the word receipt.

Word Box	ptarmigan, pterodactyl, pterosaur, Ptolemy, ptomaine, receipt, receipts

The Reading Challenge
Lesson 16.6
Reading Multisyllable Words

You can read a long word by dividing it into small parts called syllables. Each syllable has <u>one</u> <u>vowel</u> <u>sound</u> and usually one or more consonant sounds.

Three Ways to Divide Words into Syllables

1. A closed syllable ends with a consonant. When a closed syllable has one vowel, it usually has a short vowel.
   Example: packing - pack + ing

   When a closed syllable has two vowels, the first vowel is usually a long vowel while the second vowel is silent.
   Example: peeping - peep + ing

2. An open syllable ends with a vowel. The vowel at the end of the syllable is usually a long vowel.
   Example: pilot - pi + lot

3. The "vowel + consonant + e" syllable is at the end of a word. The first vowel in this syllable pattern is usually a long vowel while the final "e" is silent.
   Example: provide - pro + vide

Multisyllable Word Lists

2 syllable words	3 syllable words	4 syllable words
paddle	pacemaker	panacea
parade	Pakistan	panorama
parcel	pajamas	paralegal
pardon	parable	paramedic
party	parliament	pedestrian
pecan	pediment	pediatrics
pepper	penalty	photography
photo	pelican	planetary
picture	pilgrimage	plasticity
pigment	pioneer	plentifully
pilgrim	pocketbook	plurality
pipeline	porcupines	polyvalent
platform	powerhouse	proclamation
pressure	presenter	proclivity

Lesson 16.7
Reading Proper and Common Nouns and Adjectives
Capitalization Rules

Words are written with uppercase and/or lowercase letters. Proper nouns and proper adjectives begin with uppercase letters. Common nouns and common adjectives begin with lowercase letters.

A **proper noun** is a word that names a specific person, place, thing or concept.

A **common noun** is a word that names a general person, place, thing or concept.

	Proper Noun	Common Noun
Person	Peter	principal
Place	Poland	plaza
Thing	Parliament	puppy
Concept		pleasure

A **proper adjective** is a word that describes a specific person, place, thing or concept.

A **common adjective** is a word that describes a general person, place, thing or concept.

Proper Adjective:	Common Adjective:
Person: Principal Carter Thing: Polish language	Person: petite lady Thing: purple hat

Capitalization Rules

Uppercase Letter – "P"

- The first letter of a word that begins a sentence is capitalized.

- The first letter of a word that names a specific person, place, thing or concept is capitalized.

- The first letter of a person's title is capitalized.

- The first letter of each word in a title or subtitle is capitalized.

- As a pronoun, the letter "I" is capitalized.

✎ Note: Lowercase letters are generally used for all other words.

Lowercase Letter – "p"

- The first letter of a word that <u>does</u> <u>not</u> name a specific person, place, thing or concept is written with a lowercase letter.

- The first letter of a word that <u>does</u> <u>not</u> begin a sentence is written with a lowercase letter.

- All letters within and at the end of words are written with lowercase letters.

Reading Check Point
Assignment: Read the sentences.

1. The pharmacist prepared the pills.
2. The parade will end at Poodle Plaza.
3. Panama's capital city is Panama City.
4. Pam attended Palmer Primary School.
5. Pat and Paul are performing in a play.

The Letter "p" at a Glance

Letter	Sounds	Anchor Words
"p"	/p/	pan
"p"	silent "p"	cupboard

Unit Q

Q/q

Lesson 17.0
Introduction of the Letter Q/q

The letter "q" is a consonant. It is the 17th letter in the Roman alphabet of the English language. Letters are written as uppercase and lowercase letters.

	Uppercase Letter	Lowercase Letter
Print	Q	q
Cursive	*Q*	*q*

Lesson 17.1
Reading Words with the Letter Q/q

The letter "q" is pronounced in <u>one</u> way.
- It represents the /k/ sound, as in the word <u>queen</u>.
- It represents the /k/ sound, as in the word <u>Iraq</u>.
- At times it is silent, as in the word <u>racquet</u>.

High Frequency, One Syllable Letter "q" Words
quack, quail, quaint, quark, quart, quartz, queen, quench, quest, quick, quiet, quill, quilt, quip, quirk, quirt, quit, quite, quiz, quote

The letter "q" does not have its own sound. It borrows the /k/ sound from the letter "k."

"q" represents the /k/ sound

At the beginning, within and end of a word, the letter "q" and "qu" letter combination can represent the /k/ sound, as in the words <u>Qatar</u>, <u>antique</u> and <u>Iraq</u>.

Beginning	Within	End
/k/	/k/	/k/
Qatar	antique	Iraq

"qu" represents the /k/ + /w/ sounds

When pronouncing the "qu" letter combination's /k/ + /w/ sounds, the speaker's lips usually form a small circular opening and quickly expand outwardly. It does not vibrate because it is unvoiced.

Learn To Read English Textbook

♣ Reading Words with the Letter Q/q

At the beginning and within a word, the "qu" letter combination can represent the /k/ + /w/ sounds, as in the words <u>question</u> and <u>equator</u>.

Beginning	Within	End
/k/ + /w/	/k/ + /w/	/k/ + /w/
question	equator	

Short Vowel Blending Table for the Letter Q/q

/ă/ apple	/ĕ/ egg	/ĭ/ insect	/ŏ/ octopus	/ŭ/ up
qu a ck	qu e s t	qu i ck	qu o kk a	
qua ck	qu est	qui ck	quo kka	
quack	quest	quick	quokka	

Long Vowel Blending Table for the Letter Q/q

/ā/ ape	/ē/ eagle	/ī/ ice	/ō/ open	/yōō/ cube
qu ake	qu ee n	qu ie t	qu o te	q ueue
qua ke	quee n	quie t	quo te	q ueue
quake	queen	quiet	quote	queue

Letter "qu" Parts of Speech Table

Nouns	Verbs	Adjectives
quality	quacked	quadrennial
quantity	quacking	quadruple
quantum	qualifies	quantitative
queen	quarrel	quarterfinal
quest	quench	quarterly
question	questions	questionable
quota	quilted	quickest
quotation	quivering	quintessential
quote	quoting	quirky

Reading Check Point
Assignment: Read the sentences.

1. Mrs. Quincy bought a quart of milk.
2. My mom cuts the quiche into quarters.
3. Queenie ran quickly across the finish line.
4. Quintin asks a lot of interesting questions.
5. Quadri said, "Quadrilaterals are polygons."

Lesson 17.2
Reading Words with the Letter "q" and "qu" Letter Combination

"qu" represents the /k/ + /w/ sounds

The "qu" letter combination usually represents the /k/ + /w/ sounds, as in the word queen.

Word Box	aquatic, acquire, acquit, conquest, delinquent, equal, equate, equator, equip, equipment, frequency, quack, quail, queer, quest, question, quick, quiet, quilt, quit, quite, quiz, quotation, quote, require, sequence, sequential, tranquilize

"q" represents the /k/ sound

The letter "q" and "qu" letter combination can represent the /k/ sound, as in the word antique.

Word Box	acequia, applique, bouquet, etiquette, Iraq, Iraqi, liquor, mesquite, mosquito, quiche, quinoa, Nasdaq, Qatar, Qatari, quay, statuesque, unique, uniquely

Letter "q" and "qu" sounds

/k/ + /w/ sounds	/k/ sound
conquest	boutique
liquid	conquer
queen	mosque
quench	opaque
question	plaque
quiet	statuesque

"qu" is silent

The "qu" letter combination can be silent, as in the words lacquer and racquet.

"q" represents the /k/ sound

When the letter "q" is not followed by the letter "u," it represents the /k/ sound, as in the word Qatar.

Word Box	Compaq, Iraq, Iraqi, Nasdaq, Qatar, Qatari

Reading Check Point
Assignment: Read the sentences.
1. Quincy enjoyed his trip to Qatar.
2. John Quinn is a quick quarterback.
3. Queeny was born in Queens, New York.
4. Dr. Quail starts work at a quarter to nine.
5. In 1964, Queen Elizabeth visited Quebec City.

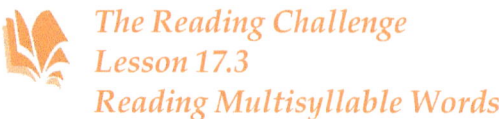

The Reading Challenge
Lesson 17.3
Reading Multisyllable Words

You can read a long word by dividing it into small parts called syllables. Each syllable has <u>one</u> <u>vowel</u> <u>sound</u> and usually one or more consonant sounds.

Three Ways to Divide Words into Syllables

1. When the "qu" letter combination is in a closed syllable, the letter "u" can represent the /w/ sound while the following single vowel usually represents a short vowel.
   Example: qualify - qual + i + fy

   When the "qu" letter combination is in a closed syllable, the letter "u" can represent the /w/ sound while the following vowel team can represent a long vowel sound.
   Example: queenly - queen + ly

2. When the "qu" letter combination is in an open syllable, the letter "u" can represent the /w/ sound while the following single vowel can represent a long vowel sound.
   Example: quota - quo + ta

3. The "vowel + consonant + e" syllable is at the end of a word. The first vowel in this syllable pattern is usually a long vowel while the final "e" is silent.
   Example: quantize - quan + tize

Multisyllable Word Lists

2 syllable words	3 syllable words	4 syllable words
quantum	quandary	quadriplegic
quarter	quadrangle	qualitative
quarters	quadratic	quantization
quartet	quadrillion	quartermaster
quarrel	quarterback	quaternary
quenching	quartering	querulousness
question	questioning	questionable
quickly	questionnaire	questionably
quickness	quickening	quiescently
quiet	quicksilver	quintessential
quilted	quietness	quintuplicate
quitter	quintillion	quintuplicates
quiver	quintuple	quixotical
quota	quivering	quotidian

Lesson 17.4
Reading Proper and Common Nouns and Adjectives
Capitalization Rules

Words are written with uppercase and/or lowercase letters. Proper nouns and proper adjectives begin with uppercase letters. Common nouns and common adjectives begin with lowercase letters.

A proper noun is a word that names a specific person, place, thing or concept.

A common noun is a word that names a general person, place, thing or concept.

	Proper Noun	Common Noun
Person	Queen Elizabeth	queen
Place	Quezon City	quarters
Thing	Queen's English	quotation
Concept		quintessence

A proper adjective is a word that describes a specific person, place, thing or concept.

A common adjective is a word that describes a general person, place, thing or concept.

Proper Adjective:	Common Adjective:
Person: Queen Elizabeth Thing: Qatarian Airlines	Person: qualified applicant Thing: quarterly meeting

Capitalization Rules

Uppercase Letter – "Q"

- The first letter of a word that begins a sentence is capitalized.

- The first letter of a word that names a specific person, place, thing or concept is capitalized.

- The first letter of a person's title is capitalized.

- The first letter of each word in a title or subtitle is capitalized.

- As a pronoun, the letter "I" is capitalized.

✏ Note: Lowercase letters are generally used for all other words.

Lowercase Letter – "q"

- The first letter of a word that <u>does</u> <u>not</u> name a specific person, place, thing or concept is written with a lowercase letter.

- The first letter of a word that <u>does</u> <u>not</u> begin a sentence is written with a lowercase letter.

- All letters within and at the end of words are written with lowercase letters.

The Letter "q" at a Glance		
Letter	Sounds	Anchor Words
"q"	/k/	queen
"qu"	/k/ + /w/	queen
"q"	/k/	Iraq
"q"	silent "q"	racquet

R/r

 Lesson 18.0
Introduction of the Letter R/r

The letter "r" is a consonant. It is the 18th letter in the Roman alphabet of the English language. Letters are written as uppercase and lowercase letters.

	Uppercase Letter	Lowercase Letter
Print	R	r
Cursive	ℛ	ɾ

 Lesson 18.1
Reading Words with the Letter R/r

The letter "r" is pronounced in <u>one</u> way.
- It represents the /r/ sound, as in the word <u>rat</u>.
- At times it is silent, as in the word <u>carrot</u>.

High Frequency, One Syllable Letter "r" Words
race, rain, raise, range, rank, rat, rate, ray, red, rent, rib, rice, rich, ride, ring, rinse, rip, ripe, rise, risk, road, rob, robe, rock, rod, rode, roil, role, roll, room, rope, rose, rot, rote, round, rule, run, runt

At the beginning, within and end of a word, the letter "r" represents the /r/ sound, as in the words <u>ring</u>, <u>break</u> and <u>car</u>.

Beginning	Within	End
/r/	/r/	/r/
rank	break	car
rate	dream	doctor
real	drum	inner
rent	electric	monitor
ring	from	other
ripe	increase	painter
roll	market	speaker
room	network	sponsor
running	surprise	sugar

Reading Words with the Letter R/r

Short Vowel Blending Table for the Letter R/r

/ă/ apple	/ĕ/ egg	/ĭ/ insect	/ŏ/ octopus	/ŭ/ up
r a t	r e d	r i p	r o t	r u t
ra t	re d	ri p	ro t	ru t
rat	red	rip	rot	rut

Long Vowel Blending Table for the Letter R/r

/ā/ ape	/ē/ eagle	/ī/ ice	/ō/ open	/yōō/ cube
r a t e	r e e d	r i g h t	r o p e	r e s c u e
ra te	ree d	righ t	ro pe	res cue
rate	reed	right	rope	rescue

The Controlling Letter "r" Changes the Vowel Sounds

/ă/ → /ä/	/ĕ/ → /û/	/ĭ/ → /û/	/ŏ/ → /ô/	/ŭ/ → /û/
cat → cart	gem → germ	bid → bird	con → corn	bun → burn
par → park	pet → pert	fist → first	spot → sport	bust → burst

Bonus Lesson
Reading Words with a Silent Letter "r"

"r" is silent

The letter "r" can be silent, as in the words <u>drawers</u>, <u>iron</u> and <u>February</u>.

"rr" represents the /r/ sound + silent "r"

When the "rr" letter combination is **together** in one syllable, the first letter "r" represents the /r/ sound while the second letter "r" is silent, as in the word <u>arrow</u>.

Word Box	arrange, berries, carrot, correct, curry, errand, ferret, ferry, garrison, hurray, hurry, marry, merry, narrate, parrot, quarry, sorrel, sorry, terrific, worry

"rr" represents the /r/ + /r/ sounds

When the "rr" letter combination is **divided** into two syllables, the first letter "r" represents the /r/ sound and the second letter "r" also represents the /r/ sound, as in the word <u>override</u>.

Word Box	interracial, interregnum, interrelated, overrate, overreach, overreact, overreaction, overrefine, overregulate, overriding, overrule, overrun

Lesson 18.2
Reading Words with the Letter "r" Combinations "br," "cr," "fr," "gr," "pr" and "tr"

Each letter in the letter "r" combination is pronounced quickly. The letters blend together to make a distinct consonant sound.

"br" represents the /b/ + /r/ sounds

The "br" letter combination represents the /b/ + /r/ sounds, as in the word bride.

Word Box	bracelet, braces, braid, Braille, brain, brake, branch, brave, bread, break, breakfast, breeze, brick, bride, bridge, bright, bring, broke, brother, brush

"cr" represents the /k/ + /r/ sounds

The "cr" letter combination represents the /k/ + /r/ sounds, as in the word crab.

Word Box	crab, crack, cracker, craft, crane, crank, crawl, crayon, crazy, cream, create, creek, crew, cricket, crime, crisis, crisp, crook, crop, cross, crow, crowd, cry

"fr" represents the /f/ + /r/ sounds

The "fr" letter combination represents the /f/ + /r/ sounds, as in the word freeze.

Word Box	fraction, fragile, fragment, frail, frame, frantic, fraud, freckle, free, freeze, frequent, friction, fried, friend, frog, from, front, frost, frown, fruit, fry

"gr" represents the /g/ + /r/ sounds

The "gr" letter combination represents the /g/ + /r/ sounds, as in the word grass.

Word Box	grab, grace, grade, gradual, graduate, grain, grammar, grand, grass, gravy, grease, great, greed, green, greet, grief, grill, ground, group, grow, growth

"pr" represents the /p/ + /r/ sounds

The "pr" letter combination represents the /p/ + /r/ sounds, as in the word practice.

Word Box	practice, praise, precious, predator, predicate, predict, prefer, price, pride, prince, princess, print, prize, probably, problem, product, promise, proud

"tr" represents the /t/ + /r/ sounds

The "tr" letter combination represents the /t/ + /r/ sounds, as in the word train.

Word Box	trace, track, trade, traffic, tragedy, trail, train, translate, trap, trash, travel, tray, treasure, treat, tree, trial, triangle, trick, trim, trip, trouble, truck, try

The Reading Challenge
Lesson 18.3
Reading Multisyllable Words

You can read a long word by dividing it into small parts called syllables. Each syllable has <u>one</u> <u>vowel</u> <u>sound</u> and usually one or more consonant sounds.

Three Ways to Divide Words into Syllables

1. A closed syllable ends with a consonant. When a closed syllable has one vowel, it usually has a short vowel.
   Example: rapid - rap + id

   When a closed syllable has two vowels, the first vowel is usually a long vowel while the second vowel is silent.
   Example: reaping - reap + ing

2. An open syllable ends with a vowel. The vowel at the end of the syllable is usually a long vowel.
   Example: recent - re + cent

3. The "vowel + consonant + e" syllable is at the end of a word. The first vowel in this syllable pattern is usually a long vowel while the final "e" is silent.
   Example: revise - re + vise

Multisyllable Word Lists

2 syllable words	3 syllable words	4 syllable words
racing	radio	radiator
raining	raspberry	rationally
rating	reflection	registration
reaping	register	relaxation
rhyming	resistance	respectively
rolling	restaurant	responsible
running	ridicule	rhinoceros
rushing	robbery	ridiculous

 Reading Check Point
Assignment: Read the sentences.

1. The Spanish royal family is very rich.
2. Romeo and Raphael are Russian residents.
3. The cyclist rode his bike along Rome Road.
4. Fran ran along the edge of the Columbia River.
5. Riley received a postcard from Bucharest, Romania.

Lesson 18.4
Reading Proper and Common Nouns and Adjectives
Capitalization Rules

Words are written with uppercase and/or lowercase letters. Proper nouns and proper adjectives begin with uppercase letters. Common nouns and common adjectives begin with lowercase letters.

A **proper noun** is a word that names a specific person, place, thing or concept.

A **common noun** is a word that names a general person, place, thing or concept.

	Proper Noun	Common Noun
Person	Ricky	relative
Place	Rwanda	room
Thing	Rolex	rattle
Concept	Rastafarianism	righteousness

A **proper adjective** is a word that describes a specific person, place, thing or concept.

A **common adjective** is a word that describes a general person, place, thing or concept.

Proper Adjective:	Common Adjective:
Person: Russian citizen Thing: Renaissance Period	Person: rude resident Thing: red gate

Capitalization Rules

Uppercase Letter – "R"

- The first letter of a word that begins a sentence is capitalized.

- The first letter of a word that names a specific person, place, thing or concept is capitalized.

- The first letter of a person's title is capitalized.

- The first letter of each word in a title or subtitle is capitalized.

- As a pronoun, the letter "I" is capitalized.

✎ Note: Lowercase letters are generally used for all other words.

Lowercase Letter – "r"

- The first letter of a word that <u>does</u> <u>not</u> name a specific person, place, thing or concept is written with a lowercase letter.

- The first letter of a word that <u>does</u> <u>not</u> begin a sentence is written with a lowercase letter.

- All letters within and at the end of words are written with lowercase letters.

The Letter "r" at a Glance		
Letter	**Sound**	**Anchor Words**
"r"	/r/	rat
"r"	silent "r"	carrot

*Unit R
Lesson 18.4*

S/s

 Lesson 19.0
Introduction of the Letter S/s

The letter "s" is a consonant. It is the 19th letter in the Roman alphabet of the English language. Letters are written as uppercase and lowercase letters.

	Uppercase Letter	Lowercase Letter
Print	S	s
Cursive	𝒮	𝓈

 Lesson 19.1
Reading Words with the Letter S/s

The letter "s" is pronounced in <u>four</u> different ways.
- It represents the /s/ sound, as in the word <u>sun</u>.
- It represents the /z/ sound, as in the word <u>his</u>.
- It represents the /sh/ sound, as in the word <u>sugar</u>.
- It represents the /zh/ sound, as in the word <u>vision</u>.
- At times it is silent, as in the word <u>island</u>.

High Frequency, One Syllable Letter "s" Words
said, sail, sale, same, sand, save, saw, say, says, school, sea, search, seat, see, seek, seem, self, sell, send, sense, set, sew, she, show, side, sing, six, size, skip, sleep, slice, small, smart, snow

Letter "s" Word Bank			
2 syllable words		3 syllable words	
second	special	saxophone	signature
seven	standard	secretly	sporadic
silver	sugar	sensation	statistics
sixty	surprise	separate	strawberry
soda	system	several	superman

✤ Reading Words with the Letter S/s

"s" represents the /s/ sound

At the beginning, within and end of a word, the letter "s" represents the /s/ sound, as in the words <u>sun</u>, <u>cost</u> and <u>bus</u>.

Beginning	Within	End
/s/	/s/	/s/
sun	cost	bus

Short Vowel Blending Table for the Letter S/s

/ă/ apple	/ĕ/ egg	/ĭ/ insect	/ŏ/ octopus	/ŭ/ up
s a t	s e t	s i t	s o p	s u p
sa t	se t	si t	so p	su p
sat	set	sit	sop	sup

Long Vowel Blending Table for the Letter S/s

/ā/ ape	/ē/ eagle	/ī/ ice	/ō/ open	/ōō/ glue
s a i l	s e a	s i t e	s o a p	s o u p
sai l	s ea	si te	soa p	sou p
sail	sea	site	soap	soup

Word Box	**"s" at the beginning of a word** sack, scarf, scent, self, sick, silk, ski, sky, sleep, sock, soul, sound, small, smile, snake, snitch, snow, space, spring, star, state, step, stone, suit, sweet, switch **"s" within a word** artist, aside, aspire, basic, best, cast, coast, desk, east, exist, false, horse, house, lastly, most, music, respect, rest, taste, test, these, toast, trust, waste, west **"s" at the end of a word** apps, backs, bus, camps, caps, cats, coughs, cups, hats, lamps, lips, maps, mats, racks, rats, Ruth's, ships, slips, stamps, tacks, times, tops, trips, us

"s" represents the /z/ sound

When the letter "s" is within or at the end of a word, it can represent the /z/ sound, as in the words <u>rose</u>, <u>is</u> and <u>his</u>.

Word Box	allows, asthma, because, bees, boys, bu<u>s</u>iness, busy, daisy, cheese, clothes, cows, design, ease, hose, is, laws, lose, music, noise, nose, ones, peas, pies, please, prose, these, those, rags, raspberry, rise, treason, visit, was, wise

"s" represents the /z/ sound

When the letter "s" is at the end of a word, it can represent the /z/ sound.

	Word List
/ā/ + /z/	airways, always, days, delays, pays, plays, portrays, sprays, trays
/b/ + /z/	bibs, bulbs, cabs, cribs, cubes, cubs, ribs, robes, swabs, tabs, tubes, vibes
/d/ + /z/	adds, cards, fades, foods, friends, kids, lids, minds, pads, trends, words
/ē/ + /z/	activities, babies, berries, cities, donkeys, families, galaxies, reason, keys
/g/ + /z/	bags, begs, brags, defogs, digs, dregs, eggs, frogs, hugs, legs, tags, wigs
/ī/ + /z/	cries, dies, dries, flies, fries, lies, pies, skies, spies, supplies, ties, tries
/l/ + /z/	apples, bells, bulls, canals, couples, fables, feels, girls, hills, puzzles, walls
/m/ + /z/	columns, comes, costumes, farms, hams, homes, rooms, times, welcomes
/n/ + /z/	beans, cans, crowns, fans, hens, lens, pains, pens, sons, stains, turns, wins
/ng/ + /z/	brings, hangs, kings, lungs, rings, savings, sings, songs, things, wings
/ō/ + /z/	bows, crows, flows, glows, knows, nose, pillows, rose, those, toes
/ou/ + /z/	allows, brows, browse, cows, drowsy, endows, plows, vows
/r/ + /z/	alligators, anchors, bakers, cars, colors, fares, grasshoppers, hers, yours
/v/ + /z/	detectives, doves, improves, knives, leaves, loves, nerves, revolves, wives

"es" represents the /ĭ/ + /z/ sounds

At the end of a word, the "es" letter combination can represent the /ĭ/ + /z/ sounds.

	Word List
/ch/ + /ĭ/ + /z/	blotches, branches, inches, patches, riches, roaches, speeches
/j/ + /ĭ/ + /z/	acknowledges, ages, alleges, cages, images, judges, pledges
/s/ + /ĭ/ + /z/	addresses, bosses, buses, discusses, expenses, gases, senses
/sh/ + /ĭ/ + /z/	accomplishes, dishes, flashes, mashes, nourishes, wishes
/z/ + /ĭ/ + /z/	buzzes, closes, dispenses, exercises, impulses, phrases, uses
/zh/ + /ĭ/ + /z/	collages, corsages, garages, loges, massages, sabotages

"s" represents the /sh// sound

When the letter "s" is at the beginning or within a word, it can represent the /sh/ sound, as in the word sugar.

Word Box	assurance, assure, censure, erasure, insurance, insurable, insure, insured, insures, insuring, issue, sugar, sugary, sure, surely, surety, tissue, tissues

"s" represents the /zh/ sound

When the letter "s" is within a word, it can represent the /zh/ sound, as in the word vision.

Word Box	casual, closure, composure, decision, exposure, leisure, mansion, measure, occasion, pleasure, session, television, treasure, usual, version, vision, visual

Learn To Read English Textbook

Lesson 19.2
Reading Words with the "sion," "sial" and "scious" Suffixes

"s" represents the /sh/ sound

The letter "s" represents the /sh/ sound in the following suffixes: "sion," "sial" and "scious."

"sion" letter combination

In the "sion" letter combination, the letter "s" is pronounced in two different ways.
- It represents the /sh/ sound, as in the word pension.
- It represents the /zh/ sound, as in the word vision.

"sion" represents the /sh/ + /ə/ + /n/ sounds

In the "sion" suffix, the letter "s" can represent the /sh/ sound, as in the word pension.

Word Box	comprehension, compression, confession, depression, discussion, expansion, expression, impression, mission, passion, pension, recession, session, tension

"sion" represents the /zh/ + /ə/ + /n/ sounds

In the "sion" suffix, the letter "s" can represent the /zh/ sound, as in the word vision.

Word Box	collision, conclusion, confusion, decision, division, exclusion, explosion, fusion, inclusion, occasion, persuasion, revision, television, version, vision

"sia" and "sian" - "s" represents the /zh/ sound

In the "sia" and "sian" letter combinations, the letter "s" represents the /zh/ sound, as in the words Asia and Asian.

Word Box	amnesia, anesthesia, artesian, Asia, Asian, fantasia, Indonesia, Indonesian, Louisiana, magnesia, magnesian, Malaysia, Persia, Persian, Russia, Russian

☞ Exception: fuchsia - /sh/ sound

"sial" represents the /sh/ + /ə/ + /l/ sounds

In the "sial" letter combination, the letter "s" represents the /sh/ sound, as in the word controversial.

Word Box	ambrosial, controversial, controversialist, controversiality, controversially

"scious" represents the /sh/ + /ə/ + /s/ sounds

In the "scious" suffix, the letter "s" represents the /sh/ sound, as in the word conscious.

Word Box	conscious, luscious, preconscious, semiconscious, subconscious, unconscious, unselfconscious

Lesson 19.3
Reading Words with the "sh" and "sch" Letter Combinations

"sh" represents the /sh/ sound

The "sh" letter combination usually represents the /sh/ sound, as in the word ship. It is important to note that the two letters have a distinct sound.

Beginning	Within	End
/sh/	/sh/	/sh/
ship	ashes	wish

Word Box

"sh" at the beginning of a word
shade, shake, shall, sham, shame, shape, share, shark, she, sheep, sheet, shell, shield, shift, shine, ship, shock, shoe, shop, shore, short, shove, show, shy

"sh" within a word
ashamed, bishop, cashew, cashier, cushion, eggshell, enshrine, fashion, harshly, lavishly, leadership, polished, publisher, pushing, sushi, worship

"sh" at the end of a word
lash, leash, mash, mesh, push, rash, rush, smash, splash, trash, wash, wish

"sh" represents the /s/ + /h/ sounds

The "sh" letter combination can represent the /s/ + /h/ sounds, as in the word mishap.

"sh" represents the /s/ sound + silent "h"

The "sh" letter combination can represent the /s/ sound + silent "h," as in the word dishonest.

"sch" letter combination

The "sch" letter combination is pronounced in two different ways.
- It represents the /s/ + /k/ sounds, as in the word school.
- It represents the /sh/ sound, as in the word schilling.

"sch" represents the /s/ + /k/ sounds

The "sch" letter combination can represent the /s/ + /k/ sounds, as in the word school.

Word Box
schedule, schema, schematic, scheme, scherzo, schizoid, schizophrenia, schizophrenic, scholar, scholarly, scholarship, scholastic, school, schooner

"sch" represents the /sh/ sound

The "sch" letter combination can represent the /sh/ sound, as in the word schilling.

Word Box
Schick test, schilling, schist, schlemiel, schlock, schmear, schmooze, schwa, schmuck, schnook, schnauzer, schrod, schuss

Lesson 19.4
Reading Words with the "scr," "shr," "spl," "spr" and "str" Letter Combinations

Each letter in the letter "s" combination is pronounced quickly. The three letters blend together to make a distinct consonant sound.

"scr" represents the /s/ + /k/ + /r/ sounds

The "scr" letter combination represents the /s/ + /k/ + /r/ sounds, as in the word scroll.

Word Box	inscribed, scram, scramble, scrap, scrapbook, scrape, scratch, scream, screech, screen, screw, screwdriver, scribble, scribe, script, scroll, scrub, scruffy

"shr" represents the /sh/ + /r/ sounds

The "shr" letter combination represents the /sh/ + /r/ sounds, as in the word shrivel.

Word Box	shred, shredder, shrew, shrewd, shrewish, shriek, shrift, shrike, shrill, shrimp, shrine, shrink, shrive, shrivel, shrub, shrug, shrunk, shrunken

"spl" represents the /s/ + /p/ + /l/ sounds

The "spl" letter combination represents the /s/ + /p/ + /l/ sounds, as in the word splendid.

Word Box	splash, splashdown, splashy, splat, splatter, splay, spleen, splendid, splendor, splice, spliced, splint, splinter, split, splitter, splotch, splurge, splutter

"spr" represents the /s/ + /p/ + /r/ sounds

The "spr" letter combination represents the /s/ + /p/ + /r/ sounds, as in the word spreading.

Word Box	offspring, sprain, sprang, sprawl, spray, sprays, spread, spring, sprinkle, sprinkler, sprinkling, sprint, sprout, spruce, sprung, spry, widespread

"str" represents the /s/ + /t/ + /r/ sounds

The "str" letter combination represents the /s/ + /t/ + /r/ sounds, as in the word strain.

Word Box	straight, straighten, strain, strand, strap, strawberry, stray, streak, stream, street, strength, stress, stretch, strip, strive, stroke, stroll, strong, struck

Lesson 19.5
Reading Words with the "sl" and "sle" Letter Combinations

"sl" represents the /s/ + /l/ sounds

In the "sl" letter combination, the letter "s" represents the /s/ sound and the letter "l" represents the /l/ sound, as in the word <u>slam</u>.

Word Box	slab, slack, slag, slam, slain, slander, slang, slant, slap, slash, slat, slate, sled, sleep, sleeve, slide, slight, slogan, slope, slot, slumber, slump, slur, sly

"sle" represents the /s/ + /l/ + /ĕ/ sounds

When the "sle" letter combination is at the beginning or within a word, it can represent the /s/ + /l/ + /ĕ/ sounds, as in the word <u>sled</u>.

Word Box	dogsled, dyslexia, misled, sled, sledded, sledding, sledge, slender, slenderer, slenderest, slenderize, slenderly, slenderness, slept

"sle" represents the /s/ + /l/ + /ē/ sounds

When the "sle" letter combination is at the beginning or within a word, it can represent the /s/ + /l/ + /ē/ sounds, as in the word <u>sleep</u>.

Word Box	asleep, mislead, misleader, misleading, misleads, parsley, sleazy, sleek, sleeked, sleeker, sleekest, sleekness, sleep, sleeper, sleeping, sleet, sleeve

"sle" represents the /s/ + /l/ + /ĭ/ sounds

When the "sle" letter combination is within a word, it can represent the /s/ + /l/ + /ĭ/ sounds, as in the word <u>corslet</u>.

"sle" represents the /s/ + /l/ + /o͞o/ sounds

When the "sle" letter combination is at the beginning of a word, it can represent /s/ + /l/ + /o͞o/ sounds, as in the words <u>sleuth</u> and <u>slew</u>.

"sle" represents the /s/ + /ə/ + /l/ sounds + silent "e"

When the "sle" letter combination is at the end of a word, it represents the /s/ + /ə/ + /l/ sounds + silent "e," as in the words <u>hassle</u> and <u>tussle</u>.

"sle" represents the /z/ + /ə/ + /l/ sounds + silent "e"

When the "sle" letter combination is within a word, it can represent the /z/ + /ə/ + /l/ sounds + silent "e," as in the word <u>measles</u>.

"sle" represents the /z/ + /l/ + /ĕ/ sounds

When the "sle" letter combination is within a word, it can represent the /z/ + /l/ + /ĕ/ sounds, as in the word <u>newsletter</u>.

"sle" has a silent "s" + /l/ sound + silent "e"

When the "sle" letter combination is at the end of a word, it can have a silent "s" + /l/ sound + silent "e," as in the word <u>aisle</u>.

Lesson 19.6
Reading Words with the "sm" Letter Combination

The "sm" letter combination is pronounced in <u>three</u> different ways.
- It represents the /s/ + /m/ sounds, as in the word <u>smell</u>.
- It represents the /z/ + /m/ sounds, as in the word <u>cosmic</u>.
- It represents the /z/ + /ə/ + /m/ sounds, as in the word <u>autism</u>.

"sm" represents the /s/ + /m/ sounds

When the "sm" letter combination is at the beginning or within a word, it usually represents the /s/ + /m/ sounds, as in the word <u>smell</u>.

Word Box	*First letters "sm"* small, smart, smash, smell, smile, smock, smoke, smog, smooth, smoothie *Letters "sm" within a word* businessmen, classmate, dismantle, dismay, dismember, dismiss, dismount, dressmaker, mismanage, mismatch, sportsman, statesman, transmitting

"sm" represents the /z/ + /m/ sounds

When the "sm" letter combination is within a word, it can represent the /z/ + /m/ sounds, as in the word <u>cosmic</u>.

Word Box	bridesmaid, charisma, charismatic, chiasma, cosmetic, cosmetician, cosmetology, cosmic, cosmonaut, cosmopolitan, cosmopolite, cosmos, dismal, Erasmus, mesmerize, newsman, newsmonger, plasma, plasmatic, plasmin

"sm" represents the /z/ + /ə/ + /m/ sounds

When the "sm" letter combination is at the end of a word, it represents the /z/ + /ə/ + /m/ sounds, as in the word <u>autism</u>. It is important to note that the schwa vowel /ə/ sound is inserted between the /z/ and /m/ sounds.

Word Box	activism, behaviorism, bilingualism, capitalism, chasm, chauvinism, cynicism, dualism, embolism, enthusiasm, extremism, globalism, nationalism, prism, racism, realism, schism, skepticism, socialism, tourism, urbanism, vandalism

"sn" represents the /s/ + /n/ sounds

In the "sn" letter combination, the letter "s" represents the /s/ sound and the letter "n" represents the /n/ sound, as in the word <u>snap</u>.

Word Box	misnomer, snack, snake, snail, snap, snapper, snatch, sneak, sneaker, sneer, snicker, sniff, snip, snob, snoop, snorkel, snow, snowy, snub, snuff, snuggle

Lesson 19.7
Reading Words with the "ss" Letter Combination

The "ss" letter combination is pronounced in <u>five</u> different ways.
- It represents the /s/ sound, as in the word <u>mess</u>.
- It represents the /sh/ sound, as in the word <u>tissue</u>.
- It represents the /zh/ sound, as in the word <u>scission</u>.
- It represents the /z/ sound, as in the word <u>dissolve</u>.
- It represents the /s/ + /s/ sounds, as in the word <u>misspelled</u>.

"ss" represents the /s/ sound + silent "s"

When the "ss" letter combination is within or at the end of a word, it can represent the /s/ sound, as in the word <u>mess</u>.

Word Box	*Letters "ss" within a word*
	assembly, assist, assort, blossom, classical, classify, dessert, embarrassment, essential, glossary, impossible, impressive, missing, necessary, necessity, passage, passenger, possible, processor, progressive, rotisserie, successful
	Letters "ss" at the end of a word
	bass, boss, business, chess, class, compress, congress, distress, dress, express, floss, grass, guess, kindness, less, loss, mass, mattress, moss, pass, princess, progress, sickness, success, suppress, tasteless, toss, waitress, worthless

"ss" represents the /sh/ sound

When the "ss" letter combination is **together** in one syllable, it can represent the /sh/ sound, as in the word <u>tissue</u>.

Word Box	aggression, assure, compassion, concession, concussion, discussion, emission, expression, impression, issue, issues, mission, passion, pressure, session

"ss" represents the /zh/ sound

When the "ss" letter combination is **together** in one syllable, it can represent the /zh/ sound, as in the words <u>rescission</u> and <u>scission</u>.

"ss" represents the /z/ sound

When the "ss" letter combination is **together** in one syllable, it can represent the /z/ sound, as in the word <u>dissolve</u>.

Word Box	dissolvable, dissolve, dissolved, Missouri, po<u>ss</u>ession, po<u>ss</u>essive, scissors

✦ Reading Words with the "ss" Letter Combination

"ss" represents the /s/ + /s/ sounds

When the "ss" letter combination is **divided** into two syllables, it represents the /s/ + /s/ sounds, as in the words misspell and misspend.

- A word with a prefix that ends with the letter "s" and a base word that begins with the letter "s" is divided into separate syllables.

Word Box	dissatisfaction, dissatisfy, disservice, misspeak, misspelled, misspelling, misspend, misspoke, misspoken, misstate, misstated, misstating, misstep

"ssh" represents the /s/ + /sh/ sounds

When the "ssh" letter combination is **divided** into two syllables, it can represent the /s/ + /sh/ sounds, as in the words misshape and misshapen.

Bonus Lesson
Reading Words with the "st" and "sw" Letter Combinations

"st" represents the /s/ + /t/ sounds

In the "st" letter combination, the letter "s" represents the /s/ sound and the letter "t" represents the /t/ sound, as in the word stop.

Word Box	best, biggest, constant, district, instill, list, nest, stamp, stand, state, status, stem, step, stick, stigma, string, stomach, stone, story, studio, study, stump

"st" at the beginning of a word represents the /s/ + /t/ sounds		"st" within a word represents the /s/ + /t/ sounds		"st" at the end of a word represents the /s/ + /t/ sounds	
stack	stoke	adjusting	mostly	best	most
staff	stony	custody	postage	blast	past
star	stormy	custom	resting	coast	thirst
status	strain	esteem	system	fast	toast
stigma	stolen	master	testify	just	yeast

"st" represents the /s/ sound + silent "t"

In the "st" letter combination, the letter "s" represents the /s/ sound and the letter "t" can be silent, as in the words listen and castle.

"sw" represents the /s/ + /w/ sounds

In the "sw" letter combination, the letter "s" represents the /s/ sound and the letter "w" represents the /w/ sound, as in the word swim.

Word Box	swam, swan, swank, swap, swatch, sway, swear, sweat, sweep, sweet, swell, swim, swing, swirl, Swiss, switch, swoon, swoop, sword, swum, swung

Lesson 19.8
Reading Words with a Silent Letter "s"

"s" is silent

The letter "s" can be silent, as in the word <u>island</u>.

Word Box	aisle, Arkansas, debris, Illinois, island, islander, isle, islet

"ss" represents the /s/ sound + silent "s"

In the "ss" letter combination, the first letter "s" usually represents the /s/ sound while the second letter "s" is silent, as in the word <u>mess</u>.

Word Box	*Letters "ss" within a word* assert, assist, blossom, cassette, classical, classify, embassy, excessive, fossil, glossary, grasshopper, impressive, passage, passport, possible, processor *Letters "ss" at the end of a word* across, actress, bass, bypass, confess, class, cross, discuss, empress, endless, excess, gross, kiss, less, mess, moss, overpass, pass, process, stress, unless

Reading Multisyllable Words

progress
⇩
progressive
⇩
progressively

recess
⇩
recessive
⇩
recessively

obsess
⇩
obsessive
⇩
obsessively

impress
⇩
impressive
⇩
impressively

pass
⇩
passive
⇩
passively

excess
⇩
excessive
⇩
excessively

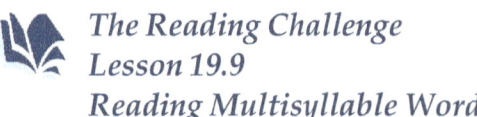

*The Reading Challenge
Lesson 19.9
Reading Multisyllable Words*

You can read a long word by dividing it into small parts called syllables. Each syllable has <u>one</u> <u>vowel</u> <u>sound</u> and usually one or more consonant sounds.

Three Ways to Divide Words into Syllables

1. A closed syllable ends with a consonant. When a closed syllable has one vowel, it usually has a short vowel.
   Example: scandal - scan + dal

   When a closed syllable has two vowels, the first vowel is usually a long vowel while the second vowel is silent.
   Example: sailor - sail + or

2. An open syllable ends with a vowel. The vowel at the end of the syllable is usually a long vowel.
   Example: sofa - so + fa

3. The "vowel + consonant + e" syllable is at the end of a word. The first vowel in this syllable pattern is usually a long vowel while the final "e" is silent.
   Example: salute - sa + lute

Multisyllable Word Lists

2 syllable words	3 syllable words	4 syllable words
safety	saxophone	salutation
sandy	scholarship	stationery
science	September	secondary
season	smothering	separation
sixteen	sophomore	serenity
social	strawberry	simplicity
special	submission	simulation
status	subtraction	stimulation
struggle	suggestion	stipulation
sugar	sycamore	subjugation
summer	sympathy	supermarket
sweater	symphony	supernova
system	symmetry	symposium

Lesson 19.10
Reading Proper and Common Nouns and Adjectives
Capitalization Rules

Words are written with uppercase and/or lowercase letters. Proper nouns and proper adjectives begin with uppercase letters. Common nouns and common adjectives begin with lowercase letters.

A proper noun is a word that names a specific person, place, thing or concept.

A common noun is a word that names a general person, place, thing or concept.

	Proper Noun	Common Noun
Person	Sammy	singer
Place	Singapore	slum
Thing	September	snowman
Concept		sensation

A proper adjective is a word that describes a specific person, place, thing or concept.

A common adjective is a word that describes a general person, place, thing or concept.

Proper Adjective:	Common Adjective:
Person: Senegalese citizen Thing: Spanish food	Person: successful salesperson Thing: six seals

Capitalization Rules
Uppercase Letter – "S"
- The first letter of a word that begins a sentence is capitalized.
- The first letter of a word that names a specific person, place, thing or concept is capitalized.
- The first letter of a person's title is capitalized.
- The first letter of each word in a title or subtitle is capitalized.
- As a pronoun, the letter "I" is capitalized.

✎ Note: Lowercase letters are generally used for all other words.

Lowercase Letter – "s"

- The first letter of a word that <u>does</u> <u>not</u> name a specific person, place, thing or concept is written with a lowercase letter.

- The first letter of a word that <u>does</u> <u>not</u> begin a sentence is written with a lowercase letter.

- All letters within and at the end of words are written with lowercase letters.

The Letter "s" at a Glance		
Letter	**Sounds**	**Anchor Words**
"s"	/s/	sun
"s"	/z/	his
"s"	/sh/	sugar
"s"	/zh/	vision
"s"	silent "s"	island

T/t

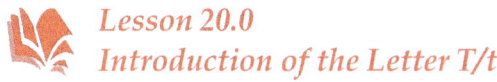

Lesson 20.0
Introduction of the Letter T/t

The letter "t" is a consonant. It is the 20th letter in the Roman alphabet of the English language. Letters are written as uppercase and lowercase letters.

	Uppercase Letter	Lowercase Letter
Print	T	t
Cursive	𝒯	𝓉

Lesson 20.1
Reading Words with the Letter T/t

The letter "t" is pronounced in <u>five</u> different ways.
- It represents the /t/ sound, as in the word <u>ten</u>.
- It represents the soft /th/ sound, as in the word <u>this</u>.
- It represents the hard /th/ sound, as in the word <u>the</u>.
- It represents the /sh/ sound, as in the word <u>education</u>.
- It represents the /ch/ sound, as in the word <u>mutual</u>.
- At times it is silent, as in the word <u>castle</u>.

High Frequency, One Syllable Letter "t" Words
tab, take, talk, tall, tap, tape, teach, team, tear, tease, teeth, tell, text, than, that, the, their, them, theme, then, there, they, thing, think, this, though, time, to, too, tree, trick, trip, true, try, turn, two, type

At the beginning, within and end of a word, the letter "t" represents the /t/ sound, as in the words <u>tent</u>, <u>history</u> and <u>coat</u>.

Beginning	Within	End
/t/	/t/	/t/
taking	ability	coat
temple	capital	crescent
tender	central	elephant
tribal	greater	prohibit
teasing	history	resident
tunnel	meeting	support
turkey	setting	without

✤ Reading Words with the Letter T/t

Short Vowel Blending Table for the Letter T/t

/ă/ apple	/ĕ/ egg	/ĭ/ insect	/ŏ/ octopus	/ŭ/ up
t a p	t e n t	t i p	t o p	t u b
ta p	ten t	ti p	to p	tu b
tap	tent	tip	top	tub

Long Vowel Blending Table for the Letter T/t

/ā/ ape	/ē/ eagle	/ī/ ice	/ō/ open	/ōō/ glue
t a p e	t e a m	t i d e	t o a d	t u b e
ta pe	tea m	ti de	toa d	tu be
tape	team	tide	toad	tube

Letter "t" Parts of Speech Table

Nouns	Verbs	Adjectives
task	tacking	tailored
taxi	tackle	tainted
teacher	tagged	tangible
ticket	taking	tedious
timber	talked	teenage
tissue	tamper	thankful
toilet	taunting	thematic
token	terminate	thermal
tourist	testified	thirsty
tradition	thanking	timeless
tuition	ticking	tiresome
tunnel	timed	tolerant
turban	toasted	traumatic
tycoon	touching	tropical
typhoon	tumbled	typical

Reading Check Point
Assignment: Read the sentences.

1. Mrs. Tripp has three thick textbooks.
2. The tourists are having fun in Thailand.
3. The two teenagers play tennis together.
4. My teacher, Mrs. Tent, traveled to Texas.
5. Troy trembles every time he hears thunder.

Lesson 20.2
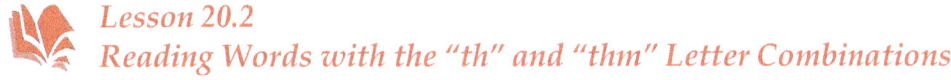
Reading Words with the "th" and "thm" Letter Combinations

The "th" letter combination is pronounced in two different ways.
- It represents the soft /th/ sound, as in the word this.
- It represents the hard /th/ sound, as in the word the.
- At times it is silent, as in the word clothes.

"th" represents the soft /th/ sound

The "th" letter combination can represent the soft /th/ sound, as in the word math. It is important to note that the two letters have one voiceless sound.

Word Box	athlete, bath, birth, booth, bother, broth, cloth, fifth, math, moth, north, path, teeth, thank, theme, third, though, threat, thrift, thrive, throw, thunder

"th" represents the hard /th/ sound

The "th" letter combination can represent the hard /th/ sound, as in the word the. It is important to note that the two letters have one voiced sound.

Word Box	brother, father, gather, mother, rather, smooth, together, than, that, the, their, them, then, there, these, they, this, those, though, thus, weather, whether

"th" is silent

The "th" letter combination can be silent, as in the word clothes.

Word Box	asthma, asthmatic, clothes, clothing, isthmus, northeaster

"thm" represents the soft /th/ + /ə/ + /m/ sounds

When the "thm" letter combination is at the end of a word, it represents the soft /th/ + /ə/ + /m/ sounds, as in the word rhythm.

Word Box	algorithm, antilogarithm, biorhythm, logarithm, rhythm, rhythms

"thm" represents the soft /th/ + /m/ sounds

When the "thm" letter combination is **divided** into two syllables, it represents the soft /th/ + /m/ sounds, as in the words bathmat and birthmark.

"thm" has a silent "th" + /m/ sound

In the "thm" letter combination, the letters "t" and "h" can be silent, as in the word asthma.

Word Box	asthma, asthmatic, asthmatically, isthmian, isthmus

Lesson 20.3
Reading Words with the "tion," "tial" and "tious" Suffixes

"tion" represents the /sh/ + /ə/ + /n/ sounds

In the "tion" suffix, the letter "t" represents the /sh/ sound, as in the word education.

Word Box	addition, action, ambition, caption, celebration, composition, condition, definition, direction, function, operation, nation, revolution, tradition

"tion" represents the /ch/ + /ə/ + /n/ sounds

In the "tion" suffix, the letter "t" represents the /ch/ sound, as in the words question and suggestion.

"tion" represents the /zh/ + /ə/ + /n/ sounds

In the "tion" suffix, the letter "t" represents the /zh/ sound, as in the word equation.

"tial" represents the /sh/ + /ə/ + /l/ sounds

In the "tial" suffix, the letter "t" represents the /sh/ sound, as in the word partial.

Word Box	confidential, credential, deferential, essential, experiential, impartial, initial, martial, partial, potential, quintessential, sequential, substantial

"tious" represents the /sh/ + /ə/ + /s/ sounds

In the "tious" suffix, the letter "t" represents the /sh/ sound, as in the word ambitious.

Word Box	ambitious, bumptious, cautious, conscientious, contentious, facetious, fictitious, flirtatious, infectious, nutritious, pretentious

Bonus Lesson
Reading Words with the "tience" and "tient" Suffixes

"tience" represents the /sh/ + /ə/ + /n/ + /s/ sounds

In the "tience" suffix, the letter "t" can represent the /sh/ sound, as in the word patience.

Word Box	impatience, insentience, patience, sentience

"tient" represents the /sh/ + /ə/ + /n/ + /t/ sounds

In the "tient" suffix, the first letter "t" can represent the /sh/ sound, as in the word patient.

Word Box	impatient, insentient, patient, quotient, sentient

Lesson 20.4
Reading Words with the "tr" Letter Combination

"tr" represents the /t/ + /r/ sounds

In the "tr" letter combination, the letter "t" represents the /t/ sound and the letter "r" represents the /r/ sound, as in the word <u>strawberry</u>.

Word Box	abstract, artistry, astray, betray, central, citrus, contract, control, construct, country, electric, entry, extra, extreme, instrument, metrics, metro, ministry, neutral, obstruct, ostrich, pastry, poetry, restrict, strap, straw, stream, striking, strip, strong, strongly, structure, struggle, subtract, ultra, waitress

Letter "tr" Parts of Speech Table

Nouns	Verbs	Adjectives
track	traced	traditional
tractor	tracking	transferred
trader	trades	transient
traffic	trailed	transitional
train	trailing	transpacific
transit	transcribed	transparent
tread	transform	traumatic
treadmill	transports	treacherous
treason	traveling	treatable
treasure	treasured	tree-lined
triangle	trembles	tremendous
tribunal	tricked	triumphant
tribute	triggered	troublesome
trimester	trimming	troubling
trophy	troubled	trustworthy
trumpet	trying	truthful

Reading Check Point
Assignment: Read the sentences.

1. Preschoolers learn to trace letters.
2. The hairdresser will trim my hair.
3. Tran walks on the treadmill every day.
4. We had an exciting class trip to the zoo.
5. Troy received a trophy for winning the race.

Lesson 20.5
Reading Words with the "tle" Letter Combination

"tle" represents the /t'l/ sounds + silent "e"

When the "tle" letter combination is at the end of a word, it can represent the /t'l/ sounds + silent "e," as in the word bottle.

Word Box	battle, beetle, bottle, brittle, cattle, entitle, kettle, little, rattle, settle, shuttle, skittle, subtitle, subtle, title

"tle" represents the /t/ + /l/ sounds + silent "e"

When the "tle" letter combination is at the end of a word, it can represent the /t/ + /l/ sounds + silent "e," as in the word turtle.

Word Box	disgruntle, dismantle, gentle, hurtle, mantle, myrtle, turtle

"tle" represents the /t/ + /l/ + /ĭ/ sounds

When the "tle" letter combination is within a word, it can represent the /t/ + /l/ + /ĭ/ sounds, as in the word cutlet.

Word Box	countless, cutlet, effortless, frontlet, gantlet, gauntlet, heartless, limitless, meatless, plantlet, rootlet, restless, spiritless, tartlet, thoughtless, wristlet

"tle" represents the /t/ + /l/ + /ĕ/ sounds

When the "tle" letter combination is within a word, it can represent the /t/ + /l/ + /ĕ/ sounds, as in the words bootleg and outlet.

"tle" represents the /t/ + /l/ + /ē/ sounds

When the "tle" letter combination is within a word, it can represent the /t/ + /l/ + /ē/ sounds, as in the words motley and Nutley.

"tler" represents the /t/ + /l/ + /ə/ + /r/ sounds

When the "tler" letter combination is at the end of the word, it can represent the /t/ + /l/ + /ə/ + /r/ sounds, as in the words antler and settler.

"stle" represents the /s/ + silent "t" + /ə/ + /l/ sounds + silent "e"

In the "stle" letter combination, the letter "t" is silent. The letter combination represents the /s/ sound + silent "t" + /ə/ + /l/ sounds + silent "e," as in the word castle.

Word Box	apostle, bristle, bustle, castle, epistle, gristle, hustle, hustler, jostle, mistletoe, nestle, pestle, rustle, thistle, whistle, wrestle, wrestler

Lesson 20.6
Reading Words with the Letter "t" Sounds

In the "tu" letter combination, the letter "t" is pronounced in <u>three</u> different ways.
- It represents the /t/ sound, as in the word <u>tub</u>.
- It represents the /sh/ sound, as in the word <u>position</u>.
- It represents the /ch/ sound, as in the word <u>actual</u>.

"tu" – "t" represents the /t/ sound

In the "tu" letter combination, the letter "t" can represent the /t/ sound, as in the word <u>tub</u>.

Word Box	tub, tube, tuck, tuff, tuft, tulip, tumble, tumid, tumor, tundra, tune, tuner, tunic, turf, turkey, turn, turtle, tusk, tutor, tutu, stub, stuck, study, stump

"tu" – "t" represents the /sh/ sound

In the "tu" letter combination, the letter "t" can represent the /sh/ sound, as in the word <u>position</u>.

Word Box	action, adoption, caption, caution, demotion, edition, emotion, fiction, lotion, mention, motion, nation, portion, option, section, station, suction

"tu" – "t" represents the /ch/ sound

In the "tu" letter combination, the letter "t" can represent the /ch/ sound, as in the word <u>actual</u>.

Word Box	century, congratulate, constituency, constituent, culturally, fortunate, fortune, futuristic, misfortune, natural, naturalist, perpetual, Portugal, Portuguese, statuary, statuesque, statuette, stature, statute, statutory

"tu" letter "t" represents /t/ sound	"tu" letter "t" represents /ch/ sound
tub	cultural
tug	habitual

"tuate" – "t" represents the /ch/ sound

When the "tuate" letter combination is at the end of a word, the first letter "t" represents the /ch/ sound, as in the words <u>fluctuate</u> and <u>punctuate</u>.

"ture" - "t" represents the /ch/ sound

When the "ture" letter combination is at the end of a word, the letter "t" represents the /ch/ sound, as in the word <u>picture</u>.

Word Box	agriculture, aperture, architecture, culture, denture, feature, fixture, fracture, future, immature, legislature, mature, nature, nurture, pasture, rapture

❖ *Reading Words with the Letter "t" Sounds*

"tual" represents the /ch/ + /o͞o/ + /ə/ + /l/ sounds

When the "tual" letter combination is at the end of a word, the letter "t" represents the /ch/ sound, as in the word <u>mutual</u>.

Word Box	accentual, actual, contextual, contractual, effectual, eventual, factual, habitual, intellectual, mutual, perceptual, punctual, ritual, spiritual, textual, virtual

"ctu" represents the /k/ + /ch/ + /o͞o/ sounds

When the "ctu" letter combination is within a word, it represents the /k/ + /ch/ + /o͞o/ sounds, as in the word <u>actual</u>.

Word Box	actual, actually, actuality, actualization, actualize, actualized, actualizes, actualizing, actuarial, actuarially, actuaries, actuary, actuate, actuator

"ct" represents the /k/ + /t/ sounds

In the "ct" letter combination, the letter "c" can represent the /k/ sound while the letter "t" represents the /t/ sound, as in the word <u>octuplet</u>.

Word Box	adjunct, conflict, conjunct, connect, construct, contact, contract, direct, electricity, expect, fact, impact, indicted, pact, product, subject, suspect

"ct" represents the /k't/ sounds

When the "ct" letter combination is within a word, it can represent the /k't/ sounds, as in the word <u>factor</u>.

Word Box	acting, actor, actress, cactus, connective, contractor, director, directory, electric, expectancy, factor, factories, factoring, factory, projector, tactics

"ct" has a silent "c" + /t/ sound

In the "ct" letter combination, the letter "c" can be silent while the letter "t" represents the /t/ sound, as in the word <u>indict</u>.

Word Box	Connecticut, indict, indictable, indicted, indictee, indicting, indictment, indicts, victual, victuals

 Reading Check Point
Assignment: Read the sentences.

1. In actuality, he was fired!
2. Stuart was indicted for securities fraud.
3. The actress is performing in Connecticut.
4. Tracy can differentiate between facts and opinions.
5. The instructor has high expectations for her students.

Lesson 20.7
Reading Words with a Silent Letter "t"

"t" is silent

The letter "t" can be silent, as in the words <u>depot</u> and <u>castle</u>.

Word Box	acts, apostle, ballet, bouquet, buffet, castle, Christmas, clothes, crochet, debut, depot, fasten, glisten, gourmet, kitchen, listen, Margot, merlot, mortgage, often, rapport, ricochet, soften, sorbet, tsunami, whistle

"sten" – "t" is silent

When the "sten" letter combination is at the end of a syllable, the letter "t" can be silent, as in the word <u>listening</u>.

Word Box	chasten, chastener, fasten, fasteners, fastening, fastens, glisten, hasten, listen, listener, listeners, listening, listens, moisten, moistness, unfasten

"stle" – "t" is silent

In the "stle" letter combination, the letter "t" can be silent, as in the word <u>castle</u>.

Word Box	apostle, bristle, bustle, castle, epistle, gristle, hustle, hustler, jostle, mistletoe, nestle, pestle, rustle, thistle, whistle, whistler, wrestle, wrestler

"tt" represents the /t/ sound + silent "t"

In the "tt" letter combination, the first letter "t" represents the /t/ sound while the second letter "t" is silent, as in the word <u>butter</u>.

Word Box	attic, attorney, battery, better, bottle, cotton, cutting, fitted, glitter, hotter, kitten, little, matter, pattern, permitted, pottery, putting, rattle, settle, utterly

"tch" - "t" is silent

In the "tch" letter combination, the letter "t" is silent, as in the word <u>catch</u>.

Word Box	batch, catch, clutch, dispatch, ditch, Dutch, hatch, hitch, itch, kitchen, match, matching, patch, pitch, sketch, snatch, snitch, stretch, swatch, switch, watch

Reading Check Point
Assignment: Read the sentences.

1. Wrestling is a challenging Olympic sport.
2. The antique watches are stored in the attic.
3. The royal family resides in the medieval castle.
4. A cat's litter usually consists of two to five kittens.
5. The 911 dispatcher speaks English and Dutch fluently.

The Reading Challenge
Lesson 20.8
Reading Multisyllable Words

You can read a long word by dividing it into small parts called syllables. Each syllable has one vowel sound and usually one or more consonant sounds.

Three Ways to Divide Words into Syllables

1. A closed syllable ends with a consonant. When a closed syllable has one vowel, it usually has a short vowel.
   Example: timber - tim + ber

   When a closed syllable has two vowels, the first vowel is usually a long vowel while the second vowel is silent.
   Example: teapot - tea + pot

2. An open syllable ends with a vowel. The vowel at the end of the syllable is usually a long vowel.
   Example: tuna - tu + na

3. The "vowel + consonant + e" syllable is at the end of a word. The first vowel in this syllable pattern is usually a long vowel while the final "e" is silent.
   Example: turnstile - turn + stile

Multisyllable Word Lists

2 syllable words	3 syllable words	4 syllable words
tablet	tastefully	Tajikistan
teacher	tapestry	tarantula
thankful	technical	taxonomy
thirteen	teenager	technology
thirty	teenagers	telegraphy
thousand	telephone	television
Thursday	temperate	temporary
tiger	tenderness	tenderizer
timber	terminal	tentatively
today	terminate	terminated
trophy	thanksgiving	terrarium
trumpet	together	thermometer
Tuesday	tolerance	timidity
turtle	tomatoes	totality
twelve	tropical	tropically
twenty	tutoring	tubercular

Lesson 20.9
Reading Proper and Common Nouns and Adjectives
Capitalization Rules

Words are written with uppercase and/or lowercase letters. Proper nouns and proper adjectives begin with uppercase letters. Common nouns and common adjectives begin with lowercase letters.

A **proper noun** is a word that names a specific person, place, thing or concept.

A **common noun** is a word that names a general person, place, thing or concept.

	Proper Noun	Common Noun
Person	Mrs. Tipps	teacher
Place	Tanzania	town
Thing	Twitter	teapot
Concept		tranquil

A **proper adjective** is a word that describes a specific person, place, thing or concept.

A **common adjective** is a word that describes a general person, place, thing or concept.

Proper Adjective:	Common Adjective:
Person: Togolese citizen Thing: Twi language	Person: tall man Thing: tiny beans

Capitalization Rules

Uppercase Letter – "T"

- The first letter of a word that begins a sentence is capitalized.

- The first letter of a word that names a specific person, place, thing or concept is capitalized.

- The first letter of a person's title is capitalized.

- The first letter of each word in a title or subtitle is capitalized.

- As a pronoun, the letter "I" is capitalized.

✐ Note: Lowercase letters are generally used for all other words.

Lowercase Letter – "t"

- The first letter of a word that <u>does</u> <u>not</u> name a specific person, place, thing or concept is written with a lowercase letter.

- The first letter of a word that <u>does</u> <u>not</u> begin a sentence is written with a lowercase letter.

- All letters within and at the end of words are written with lowercase letters.

The Letter "t" at a Glance		
Letter	**Sounds**	**Anchor Words**
"t"	/t/	ten
"th"	soft /th/	this
"th"	hard /th/	the
"t"	/sh/	education
"t"	/ch/	mutual
"t"	silent "t"	castle

U/u

 Lesson 21.0
Introduction of the Letter U/u

The letter "u" is a vowel. It is the 21st letter in the Roman alphabet of the English language. Letters are written as uppercase and lowercase letters.

	Uppercase Letter	Lowercase Letter
Print	U	u
Cursive	𝒰	𝓊

 Lesson 21.1
Reading Words with the Letter U/u

The letter "u" is pronounced in <u>eleven</u> different ways.
- It represents the short vowel /ŭ/ sound, as in the word <u>tub</u>.
- It represents the long vowel /ōō/ sound, as in the word <u>rule</u>.
- It represents the schwa vowel /ə/ sound, as in the word <u>circus</u>.
- It represents the vowel /ŏŏ/ sound, as in the word <u>put</u>.
- It represents the long vowel /yōō/ sound, as in the word <u>cube</u>.
- It represents the /y/ + /ə/ sounds, as in the word <u>occupy</u>.
- It represents the vowel /û/ sound, as in the word <u>burn</u>.
- It represents the vowel /yŏŏ/ sound, as in the word <u>pure</u>.
- It represents the /w/ sound, as in the word <u>queen</u>.
- It represents the short vowel /ĕ/ sound, as in the word <u>bury</u>.
- It represents the short vowel /ĭ/ sound, as in the word <u>busy</u>.
- At times it is silent, as in the word <u>building</u>.

High Frequency, One Syllable Letter "u" Words
Short vowel words: bug, bun, bus, but, club, cup, cut, drum, fun, gum, hug, jug, jump, lump, mud, mug, nut, rug, run, rush, sun
Long vowel words: blue, clue, cube, cute, due, duke, dune, fluke, flute, fuse, huge, juke, mule, mute, prune, puke, rule, tune, use

Lesson 21.2
Reading Words with the Short Vowel "u" Sound

"u" represents the short vowel /ŭ/ sound

At the beginning of a word, the letter "u" usually represents the short vowel /ŭ/ sound, as in the word up.

The letter "u" usually represents the short vowel /ŭ/ sound when it is the only vowel within a word or syllable.

When a consonant comes before and after the letter "u," it usually represents the short vowel /ŭ/ sound, as in the words tub and luck.

Beginning	Within	End
/ŭ/	/ŭ/	/ŭ/
up	tub	

✎ Note: At the end of a word, the letter "u" does not represent the short vowel /ŭ/ sound.

✤ Short Vowel "u" Word Families

"ub" - "u" represents the short vowel /ŭ/ sound

The vowel "u" in the "ub" word family represents the short vowel /ŭ/ sound, as in the word tub.

Word Box	chub, club, cub, dub, grub, hub, pub, rub, sub, scrub, shrub, snub, stub, tub

"uck" - "u" represents the short vowel /ŭ/ sound

The vowel "u" in the "uck" word family represents the short vowel /ŭ/ sound, as in the word luck.

Word Box	buck, chuck, cluck, duck, luck, muck, pluck, puck, struck, stuck, suck, truck, tuck, yuck

"ud" - "u" represents the short vowel /ŭ/ sound

The vowel "u" in the "ud" word family represents the short vowel /ŭ/ sound, as in the word mud.

Word Box	bud, crud, cud, dud, mud, spud, thud

"uff" - "u" represents the short vowel /ŭ/ sound

The vowel "u" in the "uff" word family represents the short vowel /ŭ/ sound, as in the word stuff.

Word Box	bluff, buff, cuff, fluff, gruff, huff, muff, puff, scuff, snuff, stuff

"ug" - "u" represents the short vowel /ŭ/ sound

The vowel "u" in the "ug" word family represents the short vowel /ŭ/ sound, as in the word tug.

Word Box	bug, chug, drug, dug, hug, jug, lug, mug, plug, pug, rug, shrug, smug, snug, thug, tug

"ull" - "u" represents the short vowel /ŭ/ sound

The vowel "u" in the "ull" word family represents the short vowel /ŭ/ sound, as in the word null.

Word Box	dull, lull, mull, null, skull

☞ Exception: pull - /o͝o/ sound

"um" - "u" represents the short vowel /ŭ/ sound

The vowel "u" in the "um" word family represents the short vowel /ŭ/ sound, as in the word gum.

Word Box	bum, chum, drum, glum, gum, hum, plum, rum, sum, swum

"ump" - "u" represents the short vowel /ŭ/ sound

The vowel "u" in the "ump" word family represents the short vowel /ŭ/ sound, as in the word jump.

Word Box	bump, clump, dump, grump, hump, jump, lump, plump, pump, rump, slump, stump, thump

"un" - "u" represents the short vowel /ŭ/ sound

The vowel "u" in the "un" word family represents the short vowel /ŭ/ sound, as in the word sun.

Word Box	bun, fun, nun, pun, run, shun, stun, sun

"unch" - "u" represents the short vowel /ŭ/ sound

The vowel "u" in the "unch" word family represents the short vowel /ŭ/ sound, as in the word <u>bunch</u>.

Word Box	brunch, bunch, crunch, hunch, lunch, munch, punch, scrunch

"ung" - "u" represents the short vowel /ŭ/ sound

The vowel "u" in the "ung" word family represents the short vowel /ŭ/ sound, as in the word <u>sung</u>.

Word Box	clung, dung, flung, hung, lung, rung, slung, sprung, strung, stung, sung, swung, wrung

"unk" - "u" represents the short vowel /ŭ/ sound

The vowel "u" in the "unk" word family represents the short vowel /ŭ/ sound, as in the word <u>junk</u>.

Word Box	bunk, chunk, drunk, dunk, flunk, hunk, junk, plunk, punk, sunk, trunk

"unt" - "u" represents the short vowel /ŭ/ sound

The vowel "u" in the "unt" word family represents the short vowel /ŭ/ sound, as in the word <u>hunt</u>.

Word Box	blunt, bunt, hunt, grunt, punt, runt, stunt

"up" - "u" represents the short vowel /ŭ/ sound

The vowel "u" in the "up" word family represents the short vowel /ŭ/ sound, as in the word <u>pup</u>.

Word Box	cup, pup, sup, up

"ush" - "u" represents the short vowel /ŭ/ sound

The vowel "u" in the "ush" word family represents the short vowel /ŭ/ sound, as in the word <u>rush</u>.

Word Box	blush, brush, crush, Cush, flush, gush, hush, lush, mush, plush, rush, shush, slush, thrush

"ust" - "u" represents the short vowel /ŭ/ sound

The vowel "u" in the "ust" word family represents the short vowel /ŭ/ sound, as in the word <u>must</u>.

Word Box	bust, crust, dust, gust, just, must, rust, thrust, trust

"ut" - "u" represents the short vowel /ŭ/ sound

The vowel "u" in the "ut" word family represents the short vowel /ŭ/ sound, as in the word <u>cut</u>.

Word Box	but, cut, glut, gut, hut, nut, rut, shut, strut

☞ Exception: put - /o͝o/ sound

 Bonus Lesson
Reading Letter "u" Words

"u" represents the short vowel /ĭ/ sound

The vowel "u" can represent the short vowel /ĭ/ sound, as in the words <u>busy</u> and <u>minute</u>.

"u" represents the vowel /o͝o/ sound

The vowel "u" can represent the vowel /o͝o/ sound, as in the words <u>brochure</u> and <u>put</u>.

Word Box	bull, bullet, bulletin, bullies, bullion, bully, bush, bushel, bushes, butcher, cushion, full, fullness, pudding, pull, pullet, pulley, pulpit, push, put, sugar

Reading Multisyllable Words

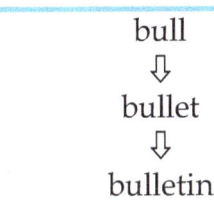
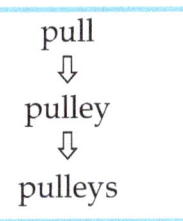

 Reading Check Point
Assignment: Read the sentences.

1. Bruce rubbed mud on the rug.
2. Sue brushed her long, lush hair.
3. At lunch, the students ate cups of fruit.
4. The cubs dug a huge hole in the ground.
5. We jumped up at the sound of the drums.

Lesson 21.3
Reading Words with the Long Vowel "u" Sound

"u" represents the long vowel /yoō/ sound

The letter "u" can represent the long vowel /yoō/ sound, as in the word cube. A long vowel is pronounced by its letter name.

Beginning	Within	End
/yoō/	/yoō/	/yoō/
unit	cube	menu

The letter "u" can represent the long vowel /yoō/ sound, as in the word human.

Word Box	bugle, continue, community, computer, future, humanity, humerus, humid, humiliate, humor, humus, January, menu, museum, music, pupil, unit

The letter "u" can represent the long vowel /oō/ sound, as in the word rule. A long vowel is pronounced by its letter name.

Beginning	Within	End
/oō/	/oō/	/oō/
use	rule	flu

In some words, the letter "u" can be pronounced with the long vowel /yoō/ sound or /oō/ sound, as in the word tube.

Word List /yoō/ sound or /oō/ sound
avenue
due
duty
numeral
reduce
tuna
tune

Reading Check Point
Assignment: Read the sentences.

1. The snow tube glides along the icy slope.
2. At lunchtime, Luke ate a tuna fish sandwich.
3. This January, Sue plans to visit the art museum.
4. Gus' three bedroom apartment is located on Fifth Avenue.
5. The presidential candidate promised to reduce property taxes.

♦ "u" + consonant + silent "e" word families

The long vowel /yo͞o/ sound and /o͞o/ sound have four pattern variations: VCe, CVCe, CCVCe and CCCVCe. The VCe pattern is at the end of many long vowel words.

"vowel + consonant + silent e" patterns	Target Words
VCe	use
CVCe	rule
CCVCe	crude
CCCVCe	spruce

"uce" - "u" represents the long vowel /o͞o/ sound

When the "u" + consonant + "e" pattern is at the end of a word, the vowel "u" usually represents the long vowel /o͞o/ sound, the consonant represents its sound while the vowel "e" is silent, as in the word <u>produce</u>.

Word Box	Bruce, spruce, truce *Multisyllable Words:* induce, introduce, produce, reduce, seduce, traduce

☞ Exception: lettuce - /ə/ sound

"ude" - "u" represents the long vowel /o͞o/ sound

When the "u" + consonant + "e" pattern is at the end of a word, the vowel "u" usually represents the long vowel /o͞o/ sound, the consonant represents its sound while the vowel "e" is silent, as in the word <u>include</u>.

Word Box	crude, dude, lude, nude, prude, rude *Multisyllable Words:* attitude, elude, exclude, include, intrude

"uke" - "u" represents the long vowel /o͞o/ sound

When the "u" + consonant + "e" pattern is at the end of a word, the vowel "u" usually represents the long vowel /o͞o/ sound, the consonant represents its sound while the vowel "e" is silent, as in the word <u>duke</u>.

Word Box	duke, juke, fluke, Luke

☞ Exception: puke - /yo͞o/ sound

"ule" - "u" represents the long vowel /o͞o/ sound

When the "u" + consonant + "e" pattern is at the end of a word, the vowel "u" usually represents the long vowel /o͞o/ sound, the consonant represents its sound while the vowel "e" is silent, as in the word <u>capsule</u>.

Word Box	rule, Yule

☞ Exception: mule - /yo͞o/ sound

"ume" - "u" represents the long vowel /o͞o/ sound

When the "u" + consonant + "e" pattern is at the end of a word, the vowel "u" usually represents the long vowel /o͞o/ sound, the consonant represents its sound while the vowel "e" is silent, as in the word <u>consume</u>.

Word Box	flume, plume *Multisyllable Words:* consume, costume, presume, resume

☞ Exceptions: fume, perfume, volume - /yo͞o/ sound

"une" - "u" represents the long vowel /o͞o/ sound

When the "u" + consonant + "e" pattern is at the end of a word, the vowel "u" usually represents the long vowel /o͞o/ sound, the consonant represents its sound while the vowel "e" is silent, as in the word <u>tune</u>.

Word Box	dune, June, prune, rune, tune

☞ Exceptions: commune, immune - /yo͞o/ sound; fortune - y/ + /ə/ sounds

"use" - "u" represents the long vowel /yo͞o/ sound

When the "u" + consonant + "e" pattern is at the end of a word, the vowel "u" usually represents the long vowel /yo͞o/ sound, the consonant represents its sound while the vowel "e" is silent, as in the word <u>excuse</u>.

Word Box	fuse, muse, use *Multisyllable Words:* abuse, accuse, amuse, confuse, defuse, excuse, refuse

☞ Exception: ruse - /o͞o/ sound

"ute" - "u" represents the long vowel /o͞o/ sound

When the "u" + consonant + "e" pattern is at the end of a word, the vowel "u" can represent the long vowel /o͞o/ sound, the consonant represents its sound while the vowel "e" is silent, as in the word chute.

Word Box	brute, chute, flute, jute, lute
	Multisyllable Words:
	absolute, dilute, pollute, salute

"ute" - "u" represents the long vowel /yo͞o/ sound

When the "u" + consonant + "e" pattern is at the end of a word, the vowel "u" can represent the long vowel /yo͞o/ sound, the consonant represents its sound while the vowel "e" is silent, as in the words cute and mute.

Word Box	commute, dispute, execute, tribute

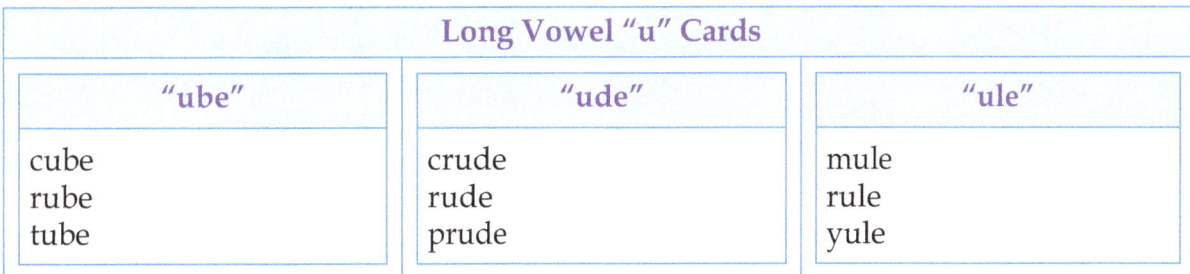

Long Vowel "u" Cards		
"ube"	"ude"	"ule"
cube	crude	mule
rube	rude	rule
tube	prude	yule

 Bonus Lesson
Reading Letter "u" Words

"u" represents the long vowel /yo͞o/ sound

When "u" is the first and only letter in the syllable, it can represent the long vowel /yo͞o/ sound, as in the word unit.

Word Box	Uganda, Ukraine, unicorn, uniform, unify, union, unit, unite, united, universal, university, usual, usurious, usurp, usury, Utah, utensil, utility

"u" represents the vowel /yo͝o/ sound

When "u" is the first and only letter in the syllable, it can represent the vowel /yo͝o/ sound, as in the word Uranus.

Word Box	Ulysses, Uralic, uranium, Uranus, urea, uremia, ureter, urethra, uric, urinal, urinary, urinate, urinated, urination, urine, urology, Uruguay

Lesson 21.4
Reading Words with Letter "u" Vowel Pairs

When two vowels are **together** in a word or syllable, the first vowel usually represents a long vowel sound while the second vowel is silent.

When two vowels are **divided** into two syllables, each vowel represents an individual sound.

"ua" represents the long vowel /o͞o/ + /ə/ sounds

When the "ua" vowel combination is **divided** into two syllables, the letter "u" represents the long vowel /o͞o/ sound and the letter "a" can represent the schwa vowel /ə/ sound, as in the word usual.

Word Box	conceptual, consensual, contractual, effectual, eventual, gradual, habitual, individual, spiritual, spiritually, truancy, truant, usually, virtual, virtually

"ue" represents the long vowel /o͞o/ sound + silent "e"

When the "ue" vowel combination is **together** in a word or syllable, the letter "u" can represent the long vowel /o͞o/ sound while the letter "e" is silent, as in the word glue.

Word Box	blue, clue, glue, rue

"ue" represents the long vowel /o͞o/ + /ĕ/ sounds

When the "ue" vowel combination is **divided** into two syllables, the letter "u" can represent the long vowel /o͞o/ sound while the letter "e" represents the short vowel /ĕ/ sound, as in the words statuette and statuesque.

"ue" represents the long vowel /yo͞o/ sound + silent "e"

When the "ue" vowel combination is **together** in a word or syllable, the letter "u" can represent the long vowel /yo͞o/ sound while the letter "e" is silent, as in the word cue.

Word Box	cue, fuel, hue *Multisyllable Words:* argue, avenue, continue, rescue, value, venue

"ui" represents the long vowel /o͞o/ sound + silent "i"

When the "ui" vowel combination is **together** in a word or syllable, the letter "u" usually represents the long vowel /o͞o/ sound while the letter "i" is silent, as in the word cruise.

Word Box	bruise, bruiser, bruit, cruise, cruiser, cruising, fruitful, fruits, juice, juicer, juicing, juicy, nuisance, pursuit, recruit, suit, suitable, suitably, suitcase, suitor

✤ Reading Words with Letter "u" Vowel Pairs

"ui" has a silent "u" + short vowel /ĭ/ sound

When the "ui" letter combination is **together** in a word or syllable, the letter "u" is silent while the letter "i" represents the short vowel /ĭ/ sound, as in the word built.

Word Box	build, builder, building, builds, built, circuit, circuited, circuiting, circuitry, circuits

"ui" represents the /w/ + /ē/ sound

When the "ui" letter combination is **divided** into two syllables, the letter "u" can represent the /w/ sound and the letter "i" can represent the long vowel /ē/ sound, as in the word acquiesce.

"ui" represents the /w/ + /ĭ/ sounds

When the "ui" letter combination is **divided** into two syllables, the letter "u" can represent the /w/ sound and the letter "i" can represent the short vowel /ĭ/ sound, as in the word quiz.

Word Box	equipment, extinguish, inquisition, inquisitive, prerequisite, quibble, quick, quicken, quintillion, quintuple, quintuplet, quiz, requisite, requisition

"ui" represents the /w/ + /ī/ sounds

When the "ui" letter combination is **divided** into two syllables, the letter "u" can represent the /w/ sound and the letter "i" can represent the long vowel /ī/ sound, as in the word quiet.

Word Box	acquire, acquired, acquiring, inquire, inquiry, quiet, quietly, quietude, quinine, quire, quite, require, required, requirement, requiring, requite, squire

"uou" represents the long vowel /o͞o/ + /ə/ sounds

When the "uou" letter combination is **divided** into two syllables, it can represent the long vowel /o͞o/ sound and the schwa vowel /ə/ sound, as in the word virtuous.

Word Box	arduous, arduously, assiduous, contemptuous, impetuous, presumptuous, sensuous, spirituous, sumptuous, superfluous, tempestuous, tortuous

"uu" represents the long vowel /yo͞o/ sound or /y/ + /ə/ sounds

When the "uu" letter combination is **together** in a word or syllable, it can represent the long vowel /yo͞o/ sound or the /y/ + /ə/ sounds, as in the word vacuum.

"uu" represents the long vowel /yo͞o/ + /ə/ sounds

When the "uu" letter combination is **divided** into two syllables, it can represent the long vowel /yo͞o/ sound and the schwa vowel /ə/ sound, as in the word continuum.

Lesson 21.5
Reading Words with the Final Letter "u"

"u" represents the long vowel /o͞o/ sound

When the letter "u" is at the end of a word, it usually represents the long vowel /o͞o/ sound, as in the word flu.

Word Box	Bantu, ecru, flu, guru, haiku, Hindu, Honolulu, impromptu, jujitsu, kudzu, kuru, lulu, Peru, thru, tofu, tutu, Urdu, zebu, Zulu

"u" represents the long vowel /yo͞o/ sound

When the letter "u" is at the end of a word, it can represent the long vowel /yo͞o/ sound, as in the words emu and menu.

"u" represents the /y/ + /ə/ sounds

When the letter "u" is at the end of a syllable, it can represent the /y/ + /ə/ sounds, as in the word mercury.

Word Box	argument, binocular, calculus, calculate, calculator, cellular, cellulose, circular, circulation, configuration, consecutive, kudos, simulate, stimulate, tutor

The Final Position of the Letter "u"

At the end of the first syllable, letter "u" represents the long vowel /yo͞o/ sound	At the end of the second syllable, letter "u" represents the long vowel /yo͞o/ sound	At the end of a word, letter "u" represents the long vowel /o͞o/ sound
bugle	communicate	flu
cubic	community	guru
future	February	haiku
human	impunity	Peru
humid	inhumane	thru
humor	January	tofu
music	lucubrate	Urdu
tulip	malnutrition	zebu

Reading Check Point
Assignment: Read the sentences.

1. Gustave and June had an intense argument.
2. On Saturday, Sue's attitude was quite crude.
3. Our new menu has Asian-inspired tofu dishes.
4. The prime minister held an impromptu press conference.
5. In June, Joshua and Udella had a fun-filled vacation in Peru.

Lesson 21.6
Reading Letter "u" Words with the Schwa Vowel Sound

"u" represents the schwa vowel /ə/ sound

The letter "u" can represent the schwa vowel /ə/ sound, as in the word <u>circus</u>. The schwa vowel sounds like the short vowel /ŭ/ + /h/ sounds.

Beginning	Within	End
/ə/	/ə/	/ə/
upon	circus	

Word Box	*First letter "u"* until, upon *Letter "u" within a word* album, asparagus, autumn, awful, beautiful, census, circus, difficult, difficulty, faculty, focus, industry, injure, lettuce, litmus, minimum, optimum, pitiful, platinum, playful, radius, stylus, subtract, suggest, surround, voluntary

"u" represents the /y/ + /ə/ sounds

The letter "u" can represent the /y/ + /ə/ sounds, as in the word <u>formula</u>.

Word Box	calculate, failure, figure, insoluble, irregular, irrefutable, jocular, nebula, nebulae, nebulous, occupy, occupancy, opulent, particular, peculate, peninsula, penury, perambulate, perpendicular, populace, popular, vascular

"ful" - "u" represents the schwa vowel /ə/ sound

In the "ful" letter combination, the letter "u" represents the schwa vowel /ə/ sound, as in the word <u>joyful</u>.

Word Box	careful, carefully, colorful, gracefully, grateful, helpful, hopeful, joyful, lawful, painful, peaceful, peacefully, powerful, respectful, resourceful, skillfully, sorrowful, successful, thankful, useful, willfully, wonderful

 Reading Check Point
Assignment: Read the sentences.

1. Doctors and nurses are popular medical occupations.
2. The law requires everyone to complete the national census.
3. The Arabian Peninsula is the largest peninsula in the world.
4. Gus and Lucy ate delicious low-carb lettuce wrap sandwiches.
5. The university faculty members are world-renowned researchers.

Lesson 21.7
Reading Words with the "ur" Letter Combination

In the "ur" letter combination, the letter "u" is pronounced in <u>six</u> different ways.
- It represents the vowel /û/ + /r/ sounds, as in the word <u>burn</u>.
- It represents the schwa vowel /ə/ + /r/ sounds, as in the word <u>surpass</u>.
- It represents the vowel /ŏŏ/ + /r/ sounds, as in the word <u>duress</u>.
- It represents the vowel /yŏŏ/ + /r/ sounds, as in the word <u>fury</u>.
- It represents the short vowel /ĕ/ + /r/ sounds, as in the word <u>bury</u>.
- It represents the /y/ + /ə/ + /r/ sounds, as in the word <u>failure</u>.

"ur" represents the vowel /û/ + /r/ sounds

The "ur" letter combination can represent the vowel /û/ + /r/ sounds, as in the word <u>burn</u>.

Word Box	blur, burger, burst, church, curb, curl, curve, fur, furniture, hurt, lurk, murky, nurse, purple, purse, surf, surname, turkey, turnip, turtle, urge, urgent, urn

"ur" represents the schwa vowel /ə/ + /r/ sounds

The "ur" letter combination can represent the schwa vowel /ə/ + /r/ sounds, as in the word <u>surpass</u>.

Word Box	Burmese, century, curriculum, curtail, purport, pursuance, pursue, surmise, surpassing, surprise, surrender, surround, surveillance, survey, survive

"ur" represents the vowel /ŏŏ/ + /r/ sounds

The "ur" letter combination can represent the vowel /ŏŏ/ + /r/ sounds, as in the word <u>duress</u>.

Word Box	burrito, Burundi, Curacao, curare, durable, durance, duration, duress, during, durum, guru, hurrah, Jurassic, juridical, jury, lurid, Suriname, Ur, Urdu

"ur" represents the vowel /yŏŏ/ + /r/ sounds

The "ur" letter combination can represent the vowel /yŏŏ/ + /r/ sounds, as in the word <u>fury</u>.

Word Box	bureau, bureaucracy, burette, curative, curator, curie, curious, fume, furious, furor, fury, mural, puree, purify, purulent, Uralic, urinary, urine, Uruguay

"ur" represents the short vowel /ĕ/ + /r/ sounds

The "ur" letter combination can represent the short vowel /ĕ/ + /r/ sounds, as in the words <u>burial</u> and <u>bury</u>.

"ur" represents the /y/ + /ə/ + /r/ sounds

The "ur" letter combination can represent the /y/ + /ə/ + /r/ sounds, as in the words <u>configuration</u> and <u>failure</u>.

Lesson 21.7
Reading Words with the "ure" Letter Combination

"ure" represents the vowel /o͝o/ + /r/ sounds + silent "e"

The "ure" letter combination can represent the vowel /o͝o/ + /r/ sounds + silent "e," as in the word <u>sure</u>.

Word Box	assurance, assure, couture, cure, brochure, insurance, insure, insured, literature, lure, miniature, overture, reinsure, temperature, sure, surely

"ure" represents the vowel /yo͝o/ + /r/ sounds + silent "e"

The "ure" letter combination can represent the vowel /yo͝o/ + /r/ sounds + silent "e," as in the word <u>pure</u>.

Word Box	manicure, manure, pedicure, procure, pure, purely, pureness, purer, purest, secure, secured, securely, securest, tenure, urea, uremia, uremic, ureter

"ure" represents the schwa vowel /ə/ + /r/ sounds + silent "e"

The "ure" letter combination can represent the schwa vowel /ə/ + /r/ sounds + silent "e," as in the word <u>nature</u>.

Word Box	adventure, architecture, composure, conjuncture, expenditure, foreclosure, horticulture, manufacture, nurture, pleasure, pressure, puncture, structure

"ure" represents the /y/ + /ə/ + /r/ sounds + silent "e"

The "ure" letter combination can represent the /y/ + /ə/ + /r/ sounds + silent "e," as in the words <u>failure</u> and <u>figure</u>.

Bonus Lesson
Reading Letter "u" Words with the /w/ Sound

"u" represents the /w/ sound

The letter "u" can represent the /w/ sound, as in the word <u>queen</u>.

Word Box	*"gu" represents the /g/ + /w/ sounds* anguish, bilingual, distinguish, extinguish, guacamole, Guadeloupe, Guam, guanine, Guatemala, guava, jaguar, language, languish, linguist, penguin *"qu" represents the /k/ + /w/ sounds* aquatic, consequence, equal, equity, frequent, liquid, quack, quail, queen, quench, question, quick, quiet, quill, quit, quiver, quiz, quota, tranquil *"su" represents the /s/ + /w/ sounds* dissuade, persuade, persuasion, persuasive, persuasively, suave, suede

Lesson 21.8
Reading Words with a Silent Letter "u"

"u" is silent

The vowel "u" can be silent, as in the word build.

Word Box	build, builder, building, built, buoy, buy, dough, doughy, guidance, guide, guidelines, guiding, guild, guile, guilt, guilty, Guinea, guise, guitar, guitarist

"u" is silent

The second vowel in a vowel pair is usually silent, as in the word soul.

Word Box	although, aunt, boulder, cough, coughed, coughing, coughs, gauge, gauged, gauging, laugh, laughed, laughing, laughs, laughter, shoulder, soul, though

"ue" - "u" is silent

In the "ue" letter combination, the letter "u" can be silent, as in the word guess.

Word Box	antique, guerilla, guerillas, guess, guessed, guesser, guesses, guessing, guest, lacquer, Portuguese, statuesque, technique, racquet

"guar" - "u" is silent

In the "guar" letter combination, the letter "u" can be silent, as in the word guard.

Word Box	guarantee, guaranteed, guarantor, guard, guarded, guardedly, guardian, guardianship, guarding, guards, vanguard, vanguardism, vanguardist

"gue" - "ue" is silent

When the "gue" letter combination is at the end of a word, the letter "g" represents the /g/ sound while the vowels "u" and "e" are silent, as in the word vogue.

Word Box	colleague, dialogue, fatigue, league, meringue, monologue, pedagogue, plague, prologue, rogue, synagogue, tongue, vague, vaguely, vogue

Silent Letter "u" at a Glance

Letter	Sounds	Anchor Words
"u"	silent "u"	soul
"u"	silent "u"	built
"u"	silent "u"	guard
"ue"	silent "ue"	vague

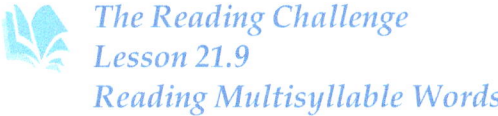

The Reading Challenge
Lesson 21.9
Reading Multisyllable Words

You can read a long word by dividing it into small parts called syllables. Each syllable has <u>one vowel sound</u> and usually one or more consonant sounds.

Three Ways to Divide Words into Syllables

1. A closed syllable ends with a consonant. When a closed syllable has one vowel, it usually has a short vowel.
   Example: tugboat - tug + boat

   When a closed syllable has two vowels, the first vowel is usually a long vowel while the second vowel is silent.
   Example: suitor - suit + or

2. An open syllable ends with a vowel. The vowel at the end of the syllable is usually a long vowel.
   Example: mutant - mu + tant

3. The "vowel + consonant + e" syllable is at the end of a word. The first vowel in this syllable pattern is usually a long vowel while the final "e" is silent.
   Example: tribute - tri + bute

Multisyllable Word Lists

2 syllable words	3 syllable words	4 syllable words
ulcer	Ubangi	ubiquity
ulster	Uganda	Ukrainian
ultra	ulcerate	ulterior
uncle	ultimate	ultimatum
uncles	ultrasound	ultrasonic
union	umbrella	umbilical
unit	unable	unanimous
uproot	unadvised	unbearable
upset	unaware	unfamiliar
upward	unity	universal
urban	universe	unorganized
urgent	usable	unspeakable
usher	username	unsubstantial
usurp	utensil	unwarranted
utmost	utilized	upholstery
utter	utterance	Uzbekistan

Lesson 21.10
Reading Proper and Common Nouns and Adjectives
Capitalization Rules

Words are written with uppercase and/or lowercase letters. Proper nouns and proper adjectives begin with uppercase letters. Common nouns and common adjectives begin with lowercase letters.

A **proper noun** is a word that names a specific person, place, thing or concept.

A **common noun** is a word that names a general person, place, thing or concept.

	Proper Noun	Common Noun
Person	Udell	urologist
Place	Ukraine	university
Thing	United Airlines	umbrella
Concept	Universalism	uncertainty

A **proper adjective** is a word that describes a specific person, place, thing or concept.

A **common adjective** is a word that describes a general person, place, thing or concept.

Proper Adjective:	Common Adjective:
Person: Ugandan citizen Thing: Uruguayan food	Person: unhappy boy Thing: unannounced visit

Capitalization Rules

Uppercase Letter – "U"

- The first letter of the word that begins a sentence is capitalized.
- The first letter of the word that names a specific person, place, thing or concept is capitalized.
- The first letter of a person's title is capitalized.
- The first letter of each word in a title or subtitle is capitalized.
- As a pronoun, the letter "I" is capitalized.

? Note: Lowercase letters are generally used for all other words.

Lowercase Letter – "u"

- The first letter of a word that <u>does</u> <u>not</u> name a specific person, place, thing or concept is written with a lowercase letter.

- The first letter of a word that <u>does</u> <u>not</u> begin a sentence is written with a lowercase letter.

- All letters within and at the end of words are written with lowercase letters.

The Letter "u" at a Glance

Letter	Sounds	Anchor Words
"u"	/ŭ/	tub
"u"	/ōō/	rule
"u"	/ə/	circus
"u"	/ŏŏ/	put
"u"	/yōō/	cube
"u"	/y/ + /ə/	occupy
"u"	/û/	burn
"u"	/yŏŏ/	pure
"u"	/w/	queen
"u"	/ĕ/	bury
"u"	/ĭ/	busy
"u"	silent "u"	building

Unit V

V/v

Lesson 22.0
Introduction of the Letter V/v

The letter "v" is a consonant. It is the 22nd letter in the Roman alphabet of the English language. Letters are written as uppercase and lowercase letters.

	Uppercase Letter	Lowercase Letter
Print	V	v
Cursive	𝒱	𝓋

Lesson 22.1
Reading Words with the Letter V/v

The letter "v" is pronounced in <u>one</u> way.
- It represents the /v/ sound, as in the word <u>van</u>.
- At times it is silent, as in the words <u>divvy</u> and <u>savvy</u>.

High Frequency, One Syllable Letter "v" Words
vague, vain, vale, valve, vamp, van, vane, vas, vase, vat, vault, veal, veep, veer, veil, vein, vent, verb, verge, verse, vest, vet, vex, vibe, vice, view, vile, vim, vine, vogue, voice, void, volt, vote, votes, vow

At the beginning, within and end of a word, the letter "v" represents the /v/ sound, as in the words <u>van</u>, <u>shovel</u> and <u>Bev</u>.

Beginning	Within	End
/v/	/v/	/v/
van	average	Bev
vapor	believe	
vegan	develop	
visit	service	
visor	shovel	
volume	survey	
volute	travel	
vomit	turnover	
voting	weaving	

Reading Words with the Letter V/v

Short Vowel Blending Table for the Letter V/v

/ă/ apple	/ĕ/ egg	/ĭ/ insect	/ŏ/ octopus	/ŭ/ up
v a n	v e s t	v i l l a	v o l l e y	v u l t u r e
va n	ve s t	vill a	voll ey	vul ture
van	vest	villa	volley	vulture

Long Vowel Blending Table for the Letter V/v

/ā/ ape	/ē/ eagle	/ī/ ice	/ō/ open	/yōō/ cube
v a n e	v e t o	v i c e	v o t e	v a l u e
va ne	ve t o	vi ce	vo te	val ue
vane	veto	vice	vote	value

Reading Check Point
Assignment: Read the sentences.

1. The volcanic eruptions are violent.
2. Val will attend Virginia University.
3. Valerie and Vinny have a violet van.
4. Victor gave me a red Valentine's heart.
5. I felt revitalized after taking my vitamins.

Letter "v" Parts of Speech Table

Nouns	Verbs	Adjectives
vaccine	vacate	vacant
vanilla	vacationing	vague
vehicle	vacuumed	valiant
vendor	validating	valuable
verdict	valued	vehement
vessel	vanished	vehicular
vibration	veered	venerable
vignette	ventilated	verbal
vineyard	verify	vibrant
visitor	vibrated	vicious
vitamin	vindicated	Victorian
volcano	visualizes	victorious
voltage	vocalize	vital
vulture	volunteered	vocational

The Reading Challenge
Lesson 22.2
Reading Multisyllable Words

You can read a long word by dividing it into small parts called syllables. Each syllable has one vowel sound and usually one or more consonant sounds.

Three Ways to Divide Words into Syllables

1. A closed syllable ends with a consonant. When a closed syllable has one vowel, it usually has a short vowel.
   Example: victim - vic + tim

   When a closed syllable has two vowels, the first vowel is usually a long vowel while the second vowel is silent.
   Example: vainest – vain + est

2. An open syllable ends with a vowel. The vowel at the end of the syllable is usually a long vowel.
   Example: veto - ve + to

3. The "vowel + consonant + e" syllable is at the end of a word. The first vowel in this syllable pattern is usually a long vowel while the final "e" is silent.
   Example: volume - vol + ume

Multisyllable Word Lists

2 syllable words	3 syllable words	4 syllable words
vacuum	vacancy	vaccination
valley	vanilla	valuable
vapor	various	valuation
vapors	vehicle	vandalism
vegan	verbally	vaporizer
veggie	veteran	velocity
Venice	vibration	vegetable
Venus	Vienna	vegetation
vibrate	vigilance	venerable
village	vinegar	ventilation
villain	vitally	victorious
virus	virtual	violation
vision	visual	visionary
volley	vitamin	visitation
volume	vocalize	vitality
voting	volunteer	vulnerable

Lesson 22.3
Reading Proper and Common Nouns and Adjectives
Capitalization Rules

Words are written with uppercase and/or lowercase letters. Proper nouns and proper adjectives begin with uppercase letters. Common nouns and common adjectives begin with lowercase letters.

A **proper noun** is a word that names a specific person, place, thing or concept.

A **common noun** is a word that names a general person, place, thing or concept.

	Proper Noun	Common Noun
Person	Ms. Valerie	victim
Place	Versailles	vestibule
Thing	Valentine's Day	valentine
Concept	Vedanta	victory

A **proper adjective** is a word that describes a specific person, place, thing or concept.

A **common adjective** is a word that describes a general person, place, thing or concept.

Proper Adjective:	Common Adjective:
Person: Viking warriors Thing: Victorian Era	Person: victorious player Thing: vivid color

Capitalization Rules

Uppercase Letter – "V"

- The first letter of a word that begins a sentence is capitalized.
- The first letter of a word that names a specific person, place, thing or concept is capitalized.
- The first letter of a person's title is capitalized.
- The first letter of each word in a title or subtitle is capitalized.
- As a pronoun, the letter "I" is capitalized.

✎ Note: Lowercase letters are generally used for all other words.

Lowercase Letter – "v"

- The first letter of a word that <u>does</u> <u>not</u> name a specific person, place, thing or concept is written with a lowercase letter.

- The first letter of a word that <u>does</u> <u>not</u> begin a sentence is written with a lowercase letter.

- All letters within and at the end of words are written with lowercase letters.

The Letter "v" at a Glance		
Letter	Sound	
"v"	/v/	van
"v"	silent "v"	savvy

Unit W

W/w

Lesson 23.0
Introduction of the Letter W/w

The letter "w" is a consonant. It is the 23rd letter in the Roman alphabet of the English language. Letters are written as uppercase and lowercase letters.

	Uppercase Letter	Lowercase Letter
Print	W	w
Cursive	*W*	*w*

Lesson 23.1
Reading Words with the Letter W/w

The letter "w" is pronounced in <u>one</u> way.
- It represents the /w/ sound, as in the word <u>wagon</u>.
- At times it is silent, as in the word <u>two</u>.

High Frequency, One Syllable Letter "w" Words
wait, walk, want, warm, wash, wax, way, we, web, well, went, were, west, wet, what, when, where, which, while, whole, why, wife, wig, wild, will, win, wipe, wise, wish, with, word, work

At the beginning and within a word, the letter "w" represents the /w/ sound, as in the words <u>wagon</u> and <u>network</u>. At the end of a word, the letter "w" does not represent the /w/ sound.

Beginning	Within	End
/w/	/w/	/w/
wagon	always	
whale	awake	
wheel	goodwill	
white	hardware	
whole	homework	
windy	network	
wolves	software	

❖ Reading Words with the Letter W/w

Short Vowel Blending Table for the Letter W/w

/ă/ apple	/ĕ/ egg	/ĭ/ insect	/ŏ/ octopus	/ŭ/ up
w a g o n	w e t	w i n d	w o l f	sw u m
wa g on	we t	win d	wo l f	sw um
wagon	wet	wind	wolf	swum

Long Vowel Blending Table for the Letter W/w

/ā/ ape	/ē/ eagle	/ī/ ice	/ō/ open	/o͞o/ glue
w a d e	w e e p	w i d e	w o k e	
wa de	wee p	wi de	wo ke	
wade	weep	wide	woke	

 Reading Check Point
Assignment: Read the sentences.

1. We work at the Waterfront Diner.
2. Mrs. Wilson has a whiz kid in her class.
3. I am invited to Wilma and Will's wedding.
4. The wind blew the wastepaper basket over.
5. The waitress served two warm, fluffy waffles.

Letter "w" Parts of Speech Table

Nouns	Verbs	Adjectives
wagon	walked	warmer
wallet	washed	wasteful
wealth	weaning	watchful
weasel	wearied	weaker
wheat	wearing	weirdest
wheel	welcomed	welcome
whisper	withdraw	western
windmill	witnessed	wholesale
windshield	wondered	wholesome
windstorm	working	widespread
worksheet	wrapped	worthless
workshop	wrote	worthwhile

Lesson 23.2
Reading Words with a Vowel before the Letter "w"

♣ *Reading Words with the "aw" Letter Combination*

"aw" represents the vowel /ô/ sound

When the "aw" letter combination is **together** in a word or syllable, it represents the vowel /ô/ sound, as in the word law.

Word Box	awe, awful, brawny, caw, claw, dawn, draw, flaw, gnaw, jaw, law, lawless, lawn, lawyer, paw, pawl, pawn, raw, saw, slaw, straw, strawberry, thaw

"aw" represents the schwa vowel /ə/ + /w/ sounds

When the "aw" letter combination is **divided** into two syllables, it represents the schwa vowel /ə/ + /w/ sounds, as in the word await.

Word Box	await, awaiting, awake, awaken, awakening, awaking, award, aware, awash, away, aweigh, awhile, awhirl, awoke, awoken, Hawaii, Hawaiian, hawala

♣ *Reading Words with the "ew" Letter Combination*

"ew" represents the long vowel /o͞o/ sound

When the "ew" letter combination is **together** in a word or syllable, it can represent the long vowel /o͞o/ sound, as in the word threw.

Word Box	bestrew, blew, brew, cashew, chew, crew, dew, Dewey, Hebrew, jewel, mews, nephew, new, news, renew, renewable, renewal, screw, shrew, stew, threw

"ew" represents the long vowel /ō/ sound

When the "ew" letter combination is **together** in a word or syllable, it can represent the long vowel /ō/ sound, as in the words sew, sewing and sewn.

"ew" represents the long vowel /yo͞o/ sound

When the "ew" letter combination is **together** in a word or syllable, it can represent the long vowel /yo͞o/ sound, as in the word dew.

Word Box	askew, dew, ewe, ewer, hew, hewed, hewer, hewn, hewing, Hewlyn, pew, pewter, new, newbie, newborn, newly, newlywed, steward, stewardess

"ew" represents the short vowel /ĭ/ + /w/ sounds

When the "ew" letter combination is **divided** into two syllables, it can represent the short vowel /ĭ/ + /w/ sounds, as in the words beware and rewards.

"ew" represents the long vowel /ē/ + /w/ sounds

When the "ew" letter combination is **divided** into two syllables, it can represent the long vowel /ē/ + /w/ sounds, as in the words reword and rewording.

✤ Reading Words with the "ow" Letter Combination

The "ow" letter combination is pronounced in <u>five</u> different ways.
- It represents the vowel /ou/ sound, as in the word <u>cow</u>.
- It represents the long vowel /ō/ sound, as in the word <u>glow</u>.
- It represents the short vowel /ŏ/ sound, as in the word <u>knowledge</u>.
- It represents the schwa vowel /ə/ + /w/ sounds, as in the word <u>toward</u>.
- It represents the long vowel /ō/ + /w/ sounds, as in the word <u>coworker</u>.

"ow" represents the vowel /ou/ sound + silent "w"

When the "ow" letter combination is **together** in a word or syllable, it can represent the vowel /ou/ sound, as in the word <u>gown</u>.

Word Box	allow, bowels, brown, chowder, clown, cow, coward, crowd, crown, down, drowse, drowsy, endow, flowers, however, now, plow, powder, power, prowess, shower, towel, tower, town, township, vowel, vow, wow

"ow" represents the long vowel /ō/ sound + silent "w"

When the "ow" letter combination is **together** in a word or syllable, it can represent the long vowel /ō/ sound, as in the word <u>glow</u>.

Word Box	arrow, below, bestow, blow, blown, borrow, crow, elbow, fellow, flow, flown, follow, grow, grown, grows, know, known, low, meadow, mow, mown, narrow, pillow, rainbow, row, shadow, shallow, show, shown, slow, sown, snow, throw, thrown, tomorrow, tow, widow, window, windows, yellow

"ow" represents the short vowel /ŏ/ sound + silent "w"

When the "ow" letter combination is **together** in a word or syllable, it can represent the short vowel /ŏ/ sound, as in the word <u>knowledge</u>.

"ow" represents the schwa vowel /ə/ + /w/ sounds

When the "ow" letter combination is **divided** into two syllables, it can represent the schwa vowel /ə/ + /w/ sounds, as in the word <u>toward</u>.

Word Box	microwave, toward, towards

"ow" represents the long vowel /ô/ sound + silent "w"

When the "ow" letter combination is **together** in a word or syllable, it can represent the /ô/ sound, as in the word <u>toward</u>.

"ow" represents the long vowel /ō/ + /w/ sounds

When the "ow" letter combination is **divided** into two syllables, it can represent the long vowel /ō/ + /w/ sounds, as in the words <u>coworker</u> and <u>nowhere</u>.

 *Lesson 23.3*
Reading Words with a Silent Letter "w" and "wr" Letter Combination

"w" is silent

The letter "w" can be silent, as in the words <u>answer</u>, <u>sword</u> and <u>two</u>.

"wh" - "w" is silent

In the "wh" letter combination, the letter "w" is silent while the letter "h" represents the /h/ sound, as in the word <u>who</u>. The words in the word box do not have the /hw/ sound.

Word Box	who, whoever, whole, wholehearted, wholesale, wholesome, wholly, whom, whomever, who's, whose, whosoever

"wr" - "w" is silent

In the "wr" letter combination, the letter "w" is silent while the letter "r" represents the /r/ sound, as in the word <u>wrap</u>.

Word Box	awry, playwright, typewriter, wreath, wreck, wrench, wrestling, wriggle, wring, wrinkle, wrist, wristband, write, writers, writing, written, wrong, wrote

"ew" - "w" is silent

In the "ew" letter combination, the letter "w" can be silent, as in the word <u>rewrite</u>.

"ow" - "w" is silent

In the "ow" letter combination, the letter "w" can be silent, as in the word <u>yellow</u>.

Word Box	below, blow, crow, flow, glow, grow, know, low, mow, narrow, owe, own, pillow, row, rows, shadow, show, shown, sorrow, snow, throw, tow, window

 Bonus Lesson
Reading Words with the "wh" Letter Combination

The "wh" letter combination is pronounced in <u>three</u> different ways.
- It represents the /h/ sound, as in the word <u>who</u>.
- It represents the /w/ sound, as in the word <u>whale</u>.
- It represents the /hw/ sound, as in the word <u>whale</u>.

"wh" represents the /w/ sound + silent "h" or /hw/ sound

In the "wh" letter combination, the letter "w" represents the /w/ sound while the letter "h" is silent, as in the word <u>whale</u>. The "wh" letter combination can also represent the /hw/ sound, as in the word <u>whale</u>.

Word Box	whack, whale, wham, wharf, what, wheat, wheel, wheeze, whelm, when, where, whether, which, while, whim, whimper, whimsical, whimsy, whine, whip, whiplash, whirl, whirlpool, whirlwind, whisk, whisker, whisper, whistle, whit, white, whither, whiz, whole, whopper, whopping, why

*The Reading Challenge
Lesson 23.4
Reading Multisyllable Words*

You can read a long word by dividing it into small parts called syllables. Each syllable has <u>one</u> <u>vowel</u> <u>sound</u> and usually one or more consonant sounds.

Three Ways to Divide Words into Syllables

1. A closed syllable ends with a consonant. When a closed syllable has one vowel, it usually has a short vowel.

   Example: within - with + in

   When a closed syllable has two vowels, the first vowel is usually a long vowel while the second vowel is silent.

   Example: weaving – weav + ing

2. An open syllable ends with a vowel. The vowel at the end of the syllable is usually a long vowel.

   Example: woven - wo + ven

3. The "vowel + consonant + e" syllable is at the end of a word. The first vowel in this syllable pattern is usually a long vowel while the final "e" is silent.

   Example: website - web + site

Multisyllable Word Lists

2 syllable words	3 syllable words	4 syllable words
waffle	wallflower	warm-bloodedness
water	wandering	warm-heartedness
wealthy	warrantee	watercolor
weather	watercress	watermelon
wedding	waterproof	waterpower
welcome	weathering	waterproofing
whisper	weatherman	wearisomely
window	whispering	whatsoever
without	wholehearted	weatherizing
woman	wilderness	whippersnapper
women	withdrawal	wholeheartedly
working	withholding	wonderworking
wrestling	workmanship	workaholic

Lesson 23.5
Reading Proper and Common Nouns and Adjectives
Capitalization Rules

Words are written with uppercase and/or lowercase letters. Proper nouns and proper adjectives begin with uppercase letters. Common nouns and common adjectives begin with lowercase letters.

A **proper noun** is a word that names a specific person, place, thing or concept.

A **common noun** is a word that names a general person, place, thing or concept.

	Proper Noun	Common Noun
Person	Mr. Wells	waiter
Place	Wales	waiting room
Thing	Windows	water
Concept		wisdom

A **proper adjective** is a word that describes a specific person, place, thing or concept.

A **common adjective** is a word that describes a general person, place, thing or concept.

Proper Adjective:	Common Adjective:
Person: Welsh resident Thing: Wisconsin glaciation	Person: wealthy man Thing: wholesome food

Capitalization Rules
Uppercase Letter – "W"

- The first letter of a word that begins a sentence is capitalized.

- The first letter of a word that names a specific person, place, thing or concept is capitalized.

- The first letter of a person's title is capitalized.

- The first letter of each word in a title or subtitle is capitalized.

- As a pronoun, the letter "I" is capitalized.

? Note: Lowercase letters are generally used for all other words.

Lowercase Letter – "w"

- The first letter of a word that <u>does</u> <u>not</u> name a specific person, place, thing or concept is written with a lowercase letter.

- The first letter of a word that <u>does</u> <u>not</u> begin a sentence is written with a lowercase letter.

- All letters within and at the end of words are written with lowercase letters.

The Letter "w" at a Glance		
Letter	**Sound**	**Anchor Words**
"w"	/w/	wagon
"w"	silent "w"	two

Unit W
Lesson 23.5

X/x

Lesson 24.0
Introduction of the Letter X/x

The letter "x" is a consonant. It is the 24th letter in the Roman alphabet of the English language. Letters are written as uppercase and lowercase letters.

	Uppercase Letter	Lowercase Letter
Print	X	x
Cursive	𝓧	𝓍

Lesson 24.1
Reading Words with the Letter X/x

The letter "x" does not have its own sound. It borrows sounds from other letters.

The letter "x" is pronounced in <u>seven</u> different ways.
- It represents the /k/+/s/ sounds, as in the word <u>box</u>.
- It represents the /k/ sound, as in the word <u>excel</u>.
- It represents the /z/ sound, as in the word <u>xylophone</u>.
- It represents the /g/ + /z/ sounds, as in the word <u>exist</u>.
- It represents the /g/ + /zh/ sounds, as in the word <u>luxury</u>.
- It represents the /ĕ/ + /k/ + /s/ sounds, as in the word <u>x-ray</u>.
- It represents the /k/ + /'sh/ sounds, as in the word <u>anxious</u>.
- At times it is silent, as in the word <u>Sioux</u>.

Letter "x" Words
First letter "x"
xebec, xenon, xeric, xerography, x-ray, xylem, xylophone, xylophonist
Letter "x" within a word
axe, axis, axle, exercise, exist, expect, explain, express, extra, extreme, oxen
Final letter "x"
apex, ax, box, coax, fax, fix, flax, flex, fox, max, mix, ox, pox, tax, tux, wax

✦ **Reading Words with the Letter X/x**

"x" represents the /k/ + /s/ sounds

Within and at the end of a word, the letter "x" represents the /k/ + /s/ sounds, as in the words text, exercise and box.

Beginning	Within	End
/k/+/s/	/k/+/s/	/k/+/s/
	text	box

Word Box	annex, extra, boxer, climax, complex, detox, excite, fax, fix, fixing, fixture, flex, fox, mix, mixture, next, ox, oxen, paradox, prefix, sixty, suffix, tax, text, waxing

"x" represents the /z/ sound

At the beginning of a word, the letter "x" represents the /z/ sound, as in the word xylophone.

Beginning	Within	End
/z/	/z/	/z/
xylophone		

Word Box	Xanadu, xanthan, xanthene, Xavier, xenon, xenophobe, Xerox, Xerxes, xiphoid, xylan, xylem, xylene, xylitol, xylography, xyloid, xylophone, xylose

"x" represents the /k/ sound

In the "exc" letter combination, the letter "x" represents the /k/ sound and "c" represents the /s/ sound, as in the word excel.

Word Box	*"exce" letter combination* exceed, excellence, excellent, excelsior, except, excepting, exception, excess *"exci" letter combination* excipient, excise, excitable, excitably, excitant, excite, excitement, exciting

The "xc" letter combination represents the /k/ + /s/ sounds.

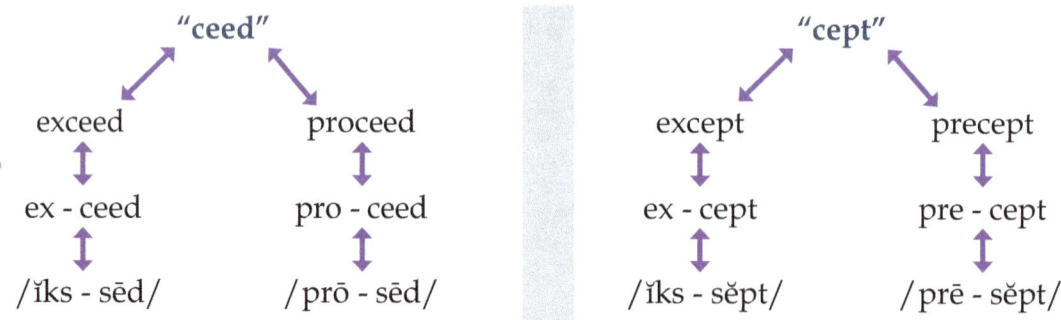

Unit X
Lesson 24.1

"x" represents the /g/ + /z/ sounds

In the "ex" letter combination, the letter "x" can represent the /g/ + /z/ sounds, as in the word examination.

Word Box	exact, exacting, exactitude, exactly, exacts, exaggerate, exasperate, exalt, exam, exams, example, exempt, exert, exhaust, exhibit, exhume, exile, exist, existence

"x" represents the /g/ + /zh/ sounds

The letter "x" can represent the /g/ + /zh/ sounds, as in the word luxury.

Word Box	luxuriance, luxuriant, luxuriantly, luxuriate, luxuriated, luxurious, luxury

"x" represents the /ĕ/ + /k/ + /s/ sounds

When "x" is the only letter in the syllable, it represents the short vowel /ĕ/ + /k/ + /s/ sounds, as in the word x-ray.

Word Box	x-axis, X-linked, x-radiation, x-ray, x-rayed, x-raying, x-rays, Malcolm X

"xious" represents the /k/ + /sh/ + /ə/ + /s/ sounds

In the "xious" suffix, the letter "x" represents the /k/ + /sh/ sounds, as in the words anxious, noxious, and obnoxious.

"xion" represents the /k/ + /sh/ + /ə/ + /n/ sounds

In the "xion" suffix, the letter "x" represents the /k/ + /sh/ sounds, as in the word reflexion.

Word Box	complexion, connexion, deflexion, flexion, fluxion, inflexion, reflexion, suffixion

"xle" represents the /k/ + /s/ + /ə/ + /l/ sounds + silent "e"

When the "xle" letter combination is at the end of a word, it represents the /k/ + /s/ + /ə/ + /l/ sounds + silent "e," as in the words axle and transaxle.

Bonus Lesson
Reading Words with a Silent Letter "x"

The letter "x" can be silent, as in the word Sioux.

Word Box	Bordeaux, faux, faux pas, roux, Sioux

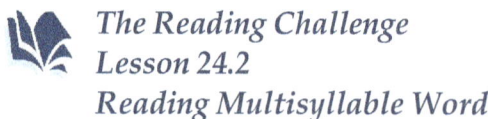

The Reading Challenge
Lesson 24.2
Reading Multisyllable Words

You can read a long word by dividing it into small parts called syllables. Each syllable has <u>one</u> <u>vowel</u> <u>sound</u> and usually one or more consonant sounds.

Three Ways to Divide Words into Syllables

1. A closed syllable ends with a consonant. When a closed syllable has one vowel, it usually has a short vowel.
   Example: xenophobe - xen-o-phobe

2. An open syllable ends with a vowel. The vowel at the end of the syllable is usually a long vowel.
   Example: xenon - xe-non

3. The "vowel + consonant + e" syllable is at the end of a word. The first vowel in this syllable pattern is usually a long vowel while the final "e" is silent.
   Example: xylophone - xy-lo-phone

Multisyllable Word Lists

2 syllable words	3 syllable words	4 syllable words
annex	appendix	approximate
boxing	complexion	exceedingly
climax	examine	excelsior
detox	example	exceptional
exalt	excellent	exclusively
exam	exception	executive
excess	exclusive	exemplify
excite	exercise	exhortation
expels	exhibit	expectation
express	explorer	expenditure
extra	explosion	experienced
fixture	extensive	experiment
index	external	expiration
pixels	extrinsic	exploration
perplex	flexible	exponential
relax	hexagram	exportation
sixteen	luxury	extravagant
taxing	oxygen	oxidation
vertex	paradox	oxidizer

Lesson 24.3
Reading Proper and Common Nouns and Adjectives
Capitalization Rules

Words are written with uppercase and/or lowercase letters. Proper nouns and proper adjectives begin with uppercase letters. Common nouns and common adjectives begin with lowercase letters.

A proper noun is a word that names a specific person, place, thing or concept.

A common noun is a word that names a general person, place, thing or concept.

	Proper Noun	Common Noun
Person	Xavier	xylophonist
Place	Xanthus	x-ray booth
Thing	Xerox	xylophone
Concept		

A proper adjective is a word that describes a specific person, place, thing or concept.

A common adjective is a word that describes a general person, place, thing or concept.

Proper Adjective:	Common Adjective:
Person: Xanthian princess	Person: x-ray tech
Thing: Xerox copy machine	Thing: xerophytic plant

Capitalization Rules

Uppercase Letter – "X"

- The first letter of a word that begins a sentence is capitalized.

- The first letter of a word that names a specific person, place, thing or concept is capitalized.

- The first letter of a person's title is capitalized.

- The first letter of each word in a title or subtitle is capitalized.

- As a pronoun, the letter "I" is capitalized.

✎ Note: Lowercase letters are generally used for all other words.

Lowercase Letter – "x"

- The first letter of a word that <u>does</u> <u>not</u> name a specific person, place, thing or concept is written with a lowercase letter.

- The first letter of a word that <u>does</u> <u>not</u> begin a sentence is written with a lowercase letter.

- All letters within and at the end of words are written with lowercase letters.

Reading Check Point
Assignment: Read the sentences.

1. While in China, I plan to tour Xizang.
2. Malcolm X was a great civil rights leader.
3. Roman numeral XX has a value of twenty.
4. Alex is studying to be a skilled xylophonist.
5. Rex learned that xenon is a colorless element.

The Letter "x" at a Glance

Letter	Sounds	Anchor Words
"x"	/k/ + /s/	box
"x"	/k/	excel
"x"	/z/	xylophone
"x"	/g/ + /z/	exist
"x"	/g/ + /zh/	luxury
"x"	/ĕ/ + /k/ + /s/	x-ray
"x"	/k/ + /sh/	anxious
"x"	silent "x"	Sioux

Y/y

Lesson 25.0
Introduction of the Letter Y/y

The letter "y" is a consonant and a vowel. It is the 25th letter in the Roman alphabet of the English language. Letters are written as uppercase and lowercase letters.

	Uppercase Letter	Lowercase Letter
Print	Y	y
Cursive	𝒴	𝓎

Lesson 25.1
Reading Words with the Letter Y/y

The letter "y" is pronounced in <u>six</u> different ways.
- It represents the /y/ sound, as in the word <u>yes</u>.
- It represents the short vowel /ĭ/ sound, as in the word <u>gym</u>.
- It represents the long vowel /ī/ sound, as in the word <u>by</u>.
- It represents the long vowel /ē/ sound, as in the word <u>baby</u>.
- It represents the schwa vowel /ə/ sound, as in the word <u>syringe</u>.
- It represents the vowel /û/ sound, as in the word <u>myrtle</u>.
- At times it is silent, as in the word <u>day</u>.

High Frequency Letter "y" Words
yacht, yahoo, yak, yam, yammer, yams, yang, yank, Yankee, yanking, yap, yard, yardage, yards, yarn, yaw, yawn, year, yearling, yearly, years, yeast, yeasts, yell, yelled, yelling, yells, yellow, yellowish, yelp, Yemen, yes, yesterday, yet, yield, yielding, yip, yodel, yodeled, yodels, yoga, yogi, yogurt, yoke, yoked, yoking, yolk, yonder, Yoruba, York, you, young, younger, youngest, your, yours, yourself, youth, youthful, youthfully, youthfulness, youths, yo-yo, yucca, yummy, yuppie, yurt

Learn To Read English Textbook

✥ **Reading Words with the Letter Y/y**

Beginning of a word	Beginning of a syllable
/y/	/y/
yellow	lawyer

"y" represents the /y/ sound

At the beginning of a word, the letter "y" represents the /y/ sound, as in the word <u>yellow</u>.

Word Box	yacht, yahoo, yam, yank, yap, yard, yardage, yardstick, year, yeast, yell, yellow, yes, yesterday, yet, yoke, yolk, York, you, young, youngest, yucca

"y" represents the /y/ sound

At the beginning of a syllable, the letter "y" represents the /y/ sound, as in the word <u>lawyer</u>.

Word Box	backyard, banyan, barnyard, beyond, canyon, courtyard, Kenya, Kenyan, lawyer, lawyers, Malayalam, Maya, Mayan, papaya, vineyard, yo-yo

Short Vowel Blending Table for the Letter Y/y

/ă/ apple	/ĕ/ egg	/ĭ/ insect	/ŏ/ octopus	/ŭ/ up
y a n k	y e s	y i p	y o n	y u k
ya nk	ye s	yi p	yo n	yu k
yank	yes	yip	yon	yuk

Long Vowel Blending Table for the Letter Y/y

/ā/ ape	/ē/ eagle	/ī/ ice	/ō/ open	/ōō/ glue
	y i e l d	y i k e s	y o k e	y o u
	yie l d	yi ke s	yo ke	yo u
	yield	yikes	yoke	you

✓ **Reading Check Point**
Assignment: Read the sentences.

1. Why were you yelling at Yardley?
2. Last year, I bought a yellow raincoat.
3. Yousef and his family are from Yemen.
4. Yvette is looking at her senior yearbook.
5. Yolanda said, "Three feet equal one yard."

✤ *Reading Letter "y" Words*

"y" represents the short vowel /ĭ/ sound

When a consonant comes before and after the letter "y," it usually represents the short vowel /ĭ/ sound, as in the words Egypt, gym and cyst.

Word Box	abyss, analysis, analytic, bicycle, calypso, catalyst, crypt, crystal, cynic, cyst, Egypt, gym, hymn, hypnosis, hyssop, hysteria, lyric, mystery, mystify, oxygen, physical, physician, platypus, symbolic, syntax, typical, tyranny

"y" represents the long vowel /ī/ sound

In the "y" + consonant + "e" pattern, the letter "y" usually represents the long vowel /ī/ sound, the consonant represents its sound while the vowel "e" is silent, as in the word style.

Word Box	"yle"	– argyle, freestyle, lifestyle, style
	"yme"	– enzyme, rhyme, thyme
	"ype"	– hype, Skype, stereotype, type
	"yre"	– lyre, pyre, Tyre
	"yte"	– byte, electrolyte, gigabyte, megabyte
	"yze"	– analyze, catalyze, electrolyze, paralyze

"ya" represents the long vowel /ē/ + /ə/ sounds

When the "ya" letter combination is at the end of a word, it can represent the long vowel /ē/ + /ə/ sounds, as in the word Libya.

"ya" represents the /y/ + /ə/ sounds

When the "ya" letter combination is at the end of a word, it can represent the /y/ + /ə/ sounds, as in the words Kenya and papaya.

"ye" represents the long vowel /ī/ sound

When the "ye" letter combination is at the end of a word, it represents the long vowel /ī/ sound, as in the words eye and bye.

"yo" represents the long vowel /ē/ + /ō/ sounds

When the "yo" letter combination is at the end of a word, it can represent the long vowel /ē/ + /ō/ sounds, as in the words embryo and Tokyo.

"yo" represents the long vowel /ē/ + /ŏ/ sounds

When the "yo" letter combination is within a word, it can represent the long vowel /ē/ + /ŏ/ sounds, as in the word embryology.

"yo" represents the silent "y" + /ə/ sound

In the "yo" letter combination, the letter "y" can be silent while the letter "o" represents the schwa vowel /ə/ sound, as in the word mayonnaise.

Lesson 25.2
Reading Words with a Vowel Before the Letter "y"

"ay" represents the long vowel /ā/ sound + silent "y"

When the "ay" letter combination is at the end of a word or syllable, the letter "a" can represent the long vowel /ā/ sound while the letter "y" is silent, as in the word <u>payment</u>.

Word Box	away, bay, clay, decay, delay, display, gray, holiday, jay, layers, may, okay, pay, play, pray, ray, relay, say, stay, stray, subway, sway, today, tray, way

☞ Exceptions: says - /ĕ/ sound; kayak - /ī/ sound

"ey" represents the long vowel /ā/ sound + silent "y"

When the "ey" letter combination is at the end of a word or syllable, it can represent the long vowel /ā/ sound, as in the word <u>they</u>.

Word Box	convey, conveyor, disobey, grey, hey, obey, obeying, prey, survey, they, trey

"ey" represents the long vowel /ē/ sound + silent "y"

When the "ey" letter combination is at the end of a word, the letter "e" can represent the long vowel /ē/ sound while the letter "y" is silent, as in the word <u>key</u>.

Word Box	attorney, barley, chimney, donkey, hockey, honey, jersey, jockey, journey, key, kidney, medley, money, monkey, parley, pricey, turkey, valley, volley

"oy" represents the vowel /oi/ sound

The "oy" letter combination represents the vowel /oi/ sound, as in the word <u>boy</u>. It is important to note that the two vowels have one new sound.

Word Box	*"oy" at the beginning of a word* oyster, oystered, oystering, oysters *"oy" within a word* deployment, employment, enjoyment, joyful, loyal, royal, royalty, voyage *"oy" at the end of a word* annoy, boy, convoy, coy, decoy, deploy, employ, enjoy, joy, ploy, soy, toy

☞ Exception: coyotes - /ī/ sound

"uy" represents the long vowel /ī/ sound

The "uy" letter combination represents the long vowel /ī/ sound, as in the word <u>guy</u>.

Word Box	buy, buyback, buyer, buying, buys, guy, Guyana, Guyanese, guys

☞ Exception: soliloquy - /w/ + /ē/ sounds

Lesson 25.3
Reading Words with the "cy" Letter Combination

The "cy" letter combination is pronounced in three different ways.
- It represents the /s/ + /ĭ/ sounds, as in the word cylinder.
- It represents the /s/ + /ī/ sounds, as in the word cycle.
- It represents the /s/ + /ē/ sounds, as in the word agency.

"cy" represents the /s/ + /ĭ/ sounds

When the "cy" letter combination is at the beginning or within a word, the letter "c" represents the /s/ sound and the letter "y" can represent the short vowel /ĭ/ sound, as in the word cylinder.

Word Box	bicycle, cygnet, Cygnus, cylinder, cylinders, cymbal, cymbalist, cymbals, cynic, cynical, cynically, cynicism, cynics, Cynthia, cyst, cystic, cystoscope, tricycle

"cy" represents the /s/ + /ī/ sounds

When the "cy" letter combination is at the beginning or within a word, the letter "c" represents the /s/ sound and the letter "y" can represent the long vowel /ī/ sound, as in the word cycle.

Word Box	cyan, cyanic, cyanide, cycle, cycled, cycles, cyclical, cycling, cyclist, cyclone, cypress, Cyprus, cytokine, cytologist, cytology, cytoplasm, encyclopedia

"cy" represents the /s/ + /ē/ sounds

When the "cy" letter combination is at the end of a word, the letter "c" represents the /s/ sound and the letter "y" can represent the long vowel /ē/ sound, as in the word agency.

Word Box	bouncy, consistency, contingency, democracy, fancy, fluency, frequency, icy, infancy, juicy, lacy, legacy, mercy, Nancy, pregnancy, pricy, privacy, racy, regency, relevancy, saucy, spicy, sufficiency, tenancy, urgency, vacancy

Singular Nouns	→	Plural Nouns
agency	y ---- ies	agencies
currency	y ---- ies	currencies
policy	y ---- ies	policies
pregnancy	y ---- ies	pregnancies
vacancy	y ---- ies	vacancies

Lesson 25.4
Reading Words with the Final Letter "y"

The final letter "y" is pronounced in two different ways.
- It represents the long vowel /ī/ sound, as in the word dry.
- It represents the long vowel /ē/ sound, as in the word baby.

"y" represents the long vowel /ī/ sound

When the letter "y" is at the end of a one syllable word, it usually represents the long vowel /ī/ sound, as in the word dry.

Word Box	by, cry, dry, fly, fry, my, ply, pry, shy, sky, sly, spy, try, why

"y" represents the long vowel /ī/ sound

When the letter "y" is at the end of a syllable, it can represent the long vowel /ī/ sound, as in the word dynamic.

Word Box	bylaw, bypass, byword, cycle, cyclone, dynamic, hyacinth, hybrid, hydrants, hydrate, hydro, hydrogen, hydrometer, hygiene, hyphen, gynecologist, gyros, myself, nylon, plywood, psychology, pylon, pyrite, python, tycoon, zygote

"y" represents the long vowel /ī/ sound

When the letter "y" is at the end of a multisyllable word, it can represent the long vowel /ī/ sound, as in the word apply.

2 syllable words		3 syllable words		4 syllable words	
apply	deny	classify	modify	dissatisfy	identify
awry	July	dignify	multiply	diversify	intensify
comply	reply	occupy	ratify	electrify	humidify
defy	supply	magnify	testify	exemplify	prequalify

"y" represents the long vowel /ē/ sound

When the letter "y" is at the end of a two syllable word, it can represent the long vowel /ē/ sound, as in the word baby.

Word Box	any, belly, body, bony, candy, city, daddy, duty, easy, happy, icy, jelly, lady, mommy, penny, shiny, sticky, story, sunny, thirsty, tiny, tricky, very, windy

"y" represents the long vowel /ē/ sound

The letter "y" can represent the long vowel /ē/ sound, as in the word embryo.

Word Box	already, community, company, country, difficulty, discovery, elementary, embryo, energy, faculty, healthy, January, melody, society, technology

Lesson 25.5
Reading Words with the "yr" Letter Combination

The "yr" letter combination is pronounced in <u>seven</u> different ways.
- It represents the vowel /û/ + /r/ sounds, as in the word <u>myrtle</u>.
- It represents the short vowel /ĭ/ + /r/ sounds, as in the word <u>pyramid</u>.
- It represents the long vowel /ī/ + /r/ sounds, as in the word <u>gyro</u>.
- It represents the schwa vowel /ə/ + /r/ sounds, as in the word <u>martyr</u>.
- It represents the vowel /î/ + /r/ sounds, as in the word <u>Syria</u>.
- It represents the long vowel /ē/ + /r/ sounds, as in the word <u>copyright</u>.
- It has a silent "y" + /r/ sound, as in the word <u>playroom</u>.

"yr" represents the vowel /û/ + /r/ sounds

The "yr" letter combination can represent the vowel /û/ + /r/ sounds, as in the word <u>myrtle</u>.

Word Box	gyrfalcon, myrrh, myrtle, syrup, syrupy

"yr" represents the short vowel /ĭ/ + /r/ sounds

The "yr" letter combination can represent the short vowel /ĭ/ + /r/ sounds, as in the word <u>pyramid</u>.

Word Box	lyric, lyrical, lyricist, myriad, pyramid, pyramidal, tyrannical, tyrannies, tyrannize, tyrannosaur, tyrannous, tyranny

"yr" represents the long vowel /ī/ + /r/ sounds

The "yr" letter combination can represent the long vowel /ī/ + /r/ sounds, as in the word <u>gyro</u>.

Word Box	Byron, Cyrus, gyrate, gyro, hyrax, lyre, papyrus, pyre, Pyrex, pyrite, pyrites, pyrometer, pyrotechnics, skyrocket, Styrofoam, tyrant, tyro

"yr" represents the schwa vowel /ə/ + /r/ sounds

The "yr" letter combination can represent the schwa vowel /ə/ + /r/ sounds, as in the words <u>martyr</u> and <u>syringe</u>.

"yr" represents the vowel /î/ + /r/ sounds

The "yr" letter combination can represent the vowel /î/ + /r/ sounds, as in the words <u>Syria</u> and <u>Syracuse</u>.

"yr" represents the long vowel /ē/ + /r/ sounds

The "yr" letter combination can represent the long vowel /ē/ + /r/ sounds, as in the word <u>copyright</u>.

"yr" has a silent "y" + /r/ sound

In the "yr" letter combination, the letter "y" can be silent while the letter "r" represents the /r/ sound, as in the words <u>payroll</u> and <u>playroom</u>.

Lesson 25.6
Reading Letter "y" Words with the Schwa Vowel Sound

"y" represents the schwa vowel /ə/ sound

The letter "y" can represent the schwa vowel /ə/ sound, as in the word syringe. The schwa vowel sounds like the short vowel /ŭ/ + /h/ sounds.

Schwa it!

Beginning	Within	End
/ə/	/ə/	/ə/
	syringe	

Word Box	etymological, etymologist, etymology, syringe

"ly" - "y" represents the schwa vowel /ə/ sound

In the "ly" letter combination, the letter "y" can represent the schwa vowel /ə/ sound, as in the word Polynesia.

Word Box	polymer, polymerize, polymerase, Polynesia, Polynesian

"yl" - "y" represents the schwa vowel /ə/ sound

In the "yl" letter combination, the letter "y" can represent the schwa vowel /ə/ sound, as in the word ethyl.

Word Box	beryl, berylline, ethyl, ethylene, methyl, methylated, Pennsylvania, Pennsylvanian

"yl" - "y" represents the long vowel /ī/ sound

In the "yl" letter combination, the letter "y" can represent the long vowel /ī/ sound, as in the word style.

Word Box	argyle, asylum, bylaws, byline, lifestyle, nylon, skylark, skylight, skyline, style, styled, styles, stylish, stylist, stylize, stylus

"yl" - "y" represents the short vowel /ĭ/ sound

In the "yl" letter combination, the letter "y" can represent the short vowel /ĭ/ sound, as in the word cylinder.

Word Box	cylinders, syllabi, syllabic, syllable, syllabus, sylph, sylvan

"yl" - "y" is silent

In the "yl" letter combination, the letter "y" can be silent, as in the words daylight and playlist.

Lesson 25.7
Reading Words with a Silent Letter "y"

"ay" represents the long vowel /ā/ sound + silent "y"

When the "ay" letter combination is at the end of a word, the letter "y" is usually silent, as in the word day.

Word Box	away, bay, birthday, clay, day, display, essay, everyday, gray, hay, holiday, lay, may, pay, play, portray, ray, repay, say, spray, sway, way, yesterday

"ay" represents the long vowel /ā/ sound + silent "y"

When the "ay" letter combination is at the end of a syllable, the letter "y" is usually silent, as in the word playing.

Word Box	crayons, daycare, daylight, delayed, layer, maybe, mayflower, mayonnaise, paycheck, paying, payment, player, playful, playground, playing, taxpayer

"ey" represents the long vowel /ē/ sound + silent "y"

When the "ey" letter combination is at the end of a word or syllable, the letter "y" is usually silent, as in the word valley.

Word Box	alleyway, attorney, chimney, donkey, key, honey, honeycomb, journey, keyboard, keypad, medley, money, monkey, pricey, pulley, trolley, volleyball

"ey" represents the long vowel /ā/ sound + silent "y"

When the "ey" letter combination is at the end of a word or syllable, the letter "y" is usually silent, as in the word conveyor.

Word Box	convey, conveyance, conveying, disobey, disobeying, grey, greyhound, hey, heyday, obey, prey, purvey, survey, surveying, surveyor, they, trey, whey

 Reading Check Point
Assignment: Read the sentences.

1. Young people enjoy sailing on yachts.
2. My friend, Yousef, was born in Yemen.
3. Yul said, "New York is my favorite city."
4. I learned Yiddish at Yeshiva University.
5. Yesterday, I ate four cups of yummy yogurt.

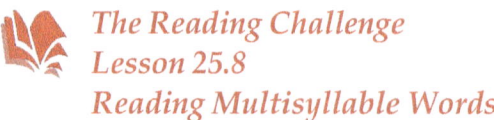

*The Reading Challenge
Lesson 25.8
Reading Multisyllable Words*

You can read a long word by dividing it into small parts called syllables. Each syllable has <u>one</u> <u>vowel</u> <u>sound</u> and usually one or more consonant sounds.

Three Ways to Divide Words into Syllables

1. A closed syllable ends with a consonant. When a closed syllable has one vowel, it usually has a short vowel.
   Example: yesterday - yes + ter + day

   When a closed syllable has two vowels, the first vowel is usually a long vowel while the second vowel is silent.
   Example: yeasty – yeast + y

2. An open syllable ends with a vowel. The vowel at the end of the syllable is usually a long vowel.
   Example: yogurt - yo + gurt

3. The "vowel + consonant + e" syllable is at the end of a word. The first vowel in this syllable pattern is usually a long vowel while the final "e" is silent.
   Example: Yuletide - Yule + tide

Multisyllable Word Lists

2 syllable words	3 syllable words	4 syllable words
birthday	agency	absolutely
country	blackberry	consequently
crystal	currency	contingency
friendly	cylinder	delinquency
healthy	elderly	dependency
journey	energy	discrepancy
keyword	family	effectively
largely	imagery	especially
lawyer	industry	hysterical
monkey	nursery	mysterious
monthly	secondly	polytechnic
systems	scholarly	presidency
yachting	yesterday	proficiency
yardage	yodeling	respectively
yearbook	Yoruba	technology
youngest	symphony	ultimately

Lesson 25.9
Reading Proper and Common Nouns and Adjectives
Capitalization Rules

Words are written with uppercase and/or lowercase letters. Proper nouns and proper adjectives begin with uppercase letters. Common nouns and common adjectives begin with lowercase letters.

A proper noun is a word that names a specific person, place, thing or concept.

A common noun is a word that names a general person, place, thing or concept.

	Proper Noun	Common Noun
Person	Mrs. Yearwood	youngster
Place	Yemen	yard
Thing	Youtube	yeast
Concept		youth

A proper adjective is a word that describes a specific person, place, thing or concept.

A common adjective is a word that describes a general person, place, thing or concept.

Proper Adjective:	Common Adjective:
Person: Yoruba Thing: Yiddish language	Person: young student Thing: yummy dish

Capitalization Rules
Uppercase Letter – "Y"

- The first letter of a word that begins a sentence is capitalized.

- The first letter of a word that names a specific person, place, thing or concept is capitalized.

- The first letter of a person's title is capitalized.

- The first letter of each word in a title or subtitle is capitalized.

- As a pronoun, the letter "I" is capitalized.

✎ Note: Lowercase letters are generally used for all other words.

Lowercase Letter – "y"

- The first letter of a word that <u>does</u> <u>not</u> name a specific person, place, thing or concept is written with a lowercase letter.

- The first letter of a word that <u>does</u> <u>not</u> begin a sentence is written with a lowercase letter.

- All letters within and at the end of words are written with lowercase letters.

The Letter "y" at a Glance		
Letter	Sounds	Anchor Words
"y"	/y/	yes
"y"	/ĭ/	gym
"y"	/ī/	by
"y"	/ē/	baby
"y"	/ə/	syringe
"y"	/û/	myrtle
"y"	silent "y"	day

Unit Y
Lesson 25.9

Z/z

Lesson 26.0
Introduction of the Letter Z/z

The letter "z" is a consonant. It is the 26th letter in the Roman alphabet of the English language. Letters are written as uppercase and lowercase letters.

	Uppercase Letter	Lowercase Letter
Print	Z	z
Cursive	𝒵	𝓏

Lesson 26.1
Reading Words with the Letter Z/z

The letter "z" is pronounced in <u>four</u> different ways.
- It represents the /z/ sound, as in the word <u>zip</u>.
- It represents the /s/ sound, as in the word <u>pretzel</u>.
- It represents the /zh/ sound, as in the word <u>azure</u>.
- It represents the /t/ + /s/ sounds, as in the word <u>pizza</u>.
- At times it is silent, as in the word <u>puzzle</u>.

One Syllable Letter "z" Words
zags, zap, zaps, zeal, zest, zinc, zip, zoo, zoom, zone

At the beginning, within and end of a word, the letter "z" represents the /z/ sound, as in the words <u>zero</u>, <u>frozen</u> and <u>topaz</u>.

Beginning	Within	End
/z/	/z/	/z/
zealous	citizen	blitz
zenith	frozen	buzz
zero	horizon	hertz
zillion	gazelle	pizzazz
zipper	itemize	quartz
zucchini	puzzle	topaz
zygote	tweezer	waltz

❖ **Reading Words with the Letter Z/z**

Short Vowel Blending Table for the Letter Z/z

/ă/ apple	/ĕ/ egg	/ĭ/ insect	/ŏ/ octopus	/ŭ/ up
z a p	z e s t	z i p	z o n k	
za p	zes t	zi p	zo nk	
zap	zest	zip	zonk	

Long Vowel Blending Table for the Letter Z/z

/ā/ ape	/ē/ eagle	/ī/ ice	/ō/ open	/ōō/ glue
z a n y	z e b r a	Z i o n	z o n e	Z u l u
za ny	zeb ra	Zi on	zo ne	Zu lu
zany	zebra	Zion	zone	Zulu

"z" represents the /z/ sound

The letter "z" usually represents the /z/ sound, as in the word <u>amazing</u>.

Word Box	agonize, blaze, Brazil, bronze, Byzantine, cadenza, capitalize, centralize, citizen, colonize, computerize, craze, crazy, criticize, daze, doze, economize, emphasize, energize, fuze, hazard, haze, hazel, influenza, lazy, lizard, magnetize, normalize, quiz, squeeze, verbalize, whiz, zillion, zip, zone, zoo

"z" represents the /s/ sound

The letter "z" can represent the /s/ sound, as in the word <u>pretzel</u>.

Word Box	bar mitzvah, Biarritz, blitz, chutzpah, ersatz, futz, intermezzo, klutz, Lutz, matzo, mezzo-soprano, pretzel, quartz, quetzal, Ritz, waltz

"z" represents the /zh/ sound

The letter "z" can represent the /zh/ sound, as in the word <u>azure</u>.

Word Box	azure, azurite, brazier, seizure

"zle" represents the /z/ + /ə/ + /l/ sounds + silent "e"

When the "zle" letter combination is at the end of a word, it represents the /z/ + /ə/ + /l/ sounds + silent "e," as in the word <u>puzzle</u>. It is important to note that the schwa vowel /ə/ sound is inserted between the /z/ and /l/ sounds.

Word Box	dazzle, drizzle, embezzle, fizzle, frazzle, frizzle, grizzle, guzzle, muzzle, nozzle, nuzzle, puzzle, sizzle, swizzle

Lesson 26.2
Reading Words with a Silent Letter "z"

"zz" represents the /z/ sound + silent "z"

In the "zz" letter combination, one letter "z" represents the /z/ sound while the other letter "z" is silent, as in the word puzzle.

| Word Box | blizzard, buzz, buzzard, buzzer, dazzle, dazzled, dizzy, drizzle, drizzling, embezzle, fizz, fizzle, fizzy, fuzz, fuzzy, gizzard, grizzly, guzzle, Jacuzzi, jazz, mezzanine, muzzle, nozzle, nuzzle, nuzzling, piazza, pizzazz, puzzling, quizzical, sizzle, sizzled, sizzling, swizzle, whizzing |

Bonus Lesson
Exploring an Exception to the "zz" Letter Combination

The "zz" letter combination can represent the /t/ + /s/ sounds, only in the words pizza, pizzeria and mozzarella.

Reading Check Point
Assignment: Read the sentences.

1. In Zimbabwe, Zoe's hotel room had a Jacuzzi.
2. Yesterday, Zelma and Zoey completed the puzzle.
3. Buzzards are typically seen soaring in wide circles.
4. In New Zealand, bridges are closed during blinding blizzards.
5. The British commanders were puzzled by the zeal of the Zulu warriors.

The Position of the Letter "z"

At the beginning of a word, the letter "z" represents the /z/ sound	Within a word, the letter "z" represents the /z/ sound	At the end of a word, the letter "z" represents the /s/ or /z/ sound
Zaire	customize	blintz
zealot	energize	blitz
zealous	freezing	glitz
zebra	garbanzo	hertz
zenith	generalize	jazz
zestful	influenza	quartz
zinger	magazine	quiz
zipline	organized	topaz
zoology	tweezers	waltz
zucchini	vitalize	whiz

The Reading Challenge
Lesson 26.3
Reading Multisyllable Words

You can read a long word by dividing it into small parts called syllables. Each syllable has <u>one</u> <u>vowel</u> <u>sound</u> and usually one or more consonant sounds.

Three Ways to Divide Words into Syllables

1. A closed syllable ends with a consonant. When a closed syllable has one vowel, it usually has a short vowel.

   Example: zinger - zing + er

2. An open syllable ends with a vowel. The vowel at the end of the syllable is usually a long vowel.

   Example: zero - ze + ro

3. The "vowel + consonant + e" syllable is at the end of a word. The first vowel in this syllable pattern is usually a long vowel while the final "e" is silent.

   Example: zygote - zy + gote

Multisyllable Word Lists

2 syllable words	3 syllable words	4 syllable words
amaze	amazing	accessorize
bizarre	antifreeze	capitalize
blizzard	citizen	categorize
buzzard	civilized	citizenship
calzone	customize	computerize
dozen	crystallized	disorganized
emblaze	emphasize	externalize
enzyme	fertilize	generalized
freezing	horizon	hospitalize
frenzy	magazine	internalized
frozen	mobilize	personalized
gazelle	organize	pizzeria
gazette	recognize	metabolize
plaza	socialize	mobilizing
pretzel	stabilize	mozzarella
puzzle	standardize	nationalize
seizure	summarize	stabilizer
tweezers	sympathize	tranquilizer
wheezing	synchronize	uncivilized
zealous	tranquilize	unorganized

Lesson 26.4
Proper and Common Nouns and Adjectives
Capitalization Rules

Words are written with uppercase and/or lowercase letters. Proper nouns and proper adjectives begin with uppercase letters. Common nouns and common adjectives begin with lowercase letters.

A proper noun is a word that names a specific person, place, thing or concept.

A common noun is a word that names a general person, place, thing or concept.

	Proper Noun	Common Noun
Person	Mrs. Zelman	zoologist
Place	Zimbabwe	zoo
Thing	Zoom Inc.	zebra
Concept	Zodiac	zealous

A proper adjective is a word that describes a specific person, place, thing or concept.

A common adjective is a word that describes a general person, place, thing or concept.

Proper Adjective:	Common Adjective:
Person: Zambian citizen Thing: Zimbabwean food	Person: zealous citizen Thing: zesty sauce

Capitalization Rules

Uppercase Letter – "Z"

- The first letter of a word that begins a sentence is capitalized.

- The first letter of a word that names a specific person, place, thing or concept is capitalized.

- The first letter of a person's title is capitalized.

- The first letter of each word in a title or subtitle is capitalized.

- As a pronoun, the letter "I" is capitalized.

✎ Note: Lowercase letters are generally used for all other words.

Lowercase Letter – "z"

- The first letter of a word that <u>does</u> <u>not</u> name a specific person, place, thing or concept is written with a lowercase letter.

- The first letter of a word that <u>does</u> <u>not</u> begin a sentence is written with a lowercase letter.

- All letters within and at the end of words are written with lowercase letters.

The Letter "z" at a Glance		
Letter	**Sounds**	**Anchor Words**
"z"	/z/	zip
"z"	/s/	pretzel
"z"	/zh/	azure
"zz"	/t/ + /s/	pizza
"zz"	/z/ + silent "z"	puzzle

Unit Z
Lesson 26.4

Your Next Step
Learn To Read English Vowels Textbook

www.ingramcontent.com/pod-product-compliance
Lightning Source LLC
Chambersburg PA
CBHW080801300426
44114CB00020B/2788